Charles Eliot Norton

Apostle of Culture in a Democracy

Charles Eliot Norton in 1908

Charles Eliot Norton

Apostle of Culture in a Democracy

By

Kermit Vanderbilt

THE BELKNAP PRESS

of HARVARD UNIVERSITY PRESS

Cambridge, Massachusetts

1959

Distributed in Great Britain by
Oxford University Press, London

Library of Congress Catalog Card Number: 59–10321
Printed in the United States of America

J. a.

FOR OZZIE AND KAREN

Preface

I first became interested in Charles Eliot Norton some years ago while reading the New England histories of Mr. Van Wyck Brooks. Studying Norton further, I began to feel that Mr. Brooks, despite his extensive and valuable labors in bringing to life the period of Norton and his circle, had missed what is vital and unique in Norton's own life and work. Norton pops in and out of Mr. Brooks's pages in no consistent guise, though one receives the frequent impression that Norton was an invalid scholar and a carping, overly gloomy critic of his country. The result is not merely a confusing and partial portrait but, in places, a badly distorted caricature. Norton was, in fact, a first-rate example of Emerson's scholar as a man of *action*. And his consistently failing health suggests, more than anything else, the courage which was necessary to achieve what he did in a long and fruitful life of public service. Above all, Norton was a significant critic of his age — and of ours. Living, as he did, into the dawn of the twentieth century, he foresaw a number of the maladies of American society today. His opinions on such topics as American education, urban life, popular reading tastes, and political campaigns strike a surprisingly welcome and modern note.

This book is the first full-length study of Norton to be published. The excellent *Letters of Charles Eliot Norton,* edited by Norton's daughter Sara Norton and Mark A. DeWolfe Howe (Boston, 1913, 2 volumes), provides biographical commentary between letters Norton wrote to his many eminent friends in America and Europe. Norton appears in these volumes as a gracious letter-writer and valued friend. To a degree, his quality of mind shows through in these letters, although the emphasis on the English friendships leads to a conclusion that Norton was some sort of literary courier or aide-de-camp to Ruskin, Morris, Carlyle, Clough, Dickens, Arnold, and others. The *Letters,* valuable as a chronicle of Norton's personal affairs and friendships, leaves one main task to be done before we can have a proper understanding of his career and significance. The purpose of the present volume is to give a full-length treatment of Norton's ideas in relation to his work, and also to try to describe his influence on his time and on our own.

I have not made any painstaking inquiry into the sources of Norton's thought, for such an investigation is not, in Norton's case, actually necessary. He freely quoted or echoed Tocqueville, Emerson, Lowell, Howells, Ruskin, Mill, Arnold, and disseminated congenial ideas from writers classical and romantic. Norton is interesting not as an original thinker, but as an independent and skeptical mind. His restless intellectual waverings as the country grew and changed, together with his highly varied experience with men and movements, reflect in miniature a complex epoch in American history. Because these changing opinions often profit from his gift of forceful and pungent expression, I have quoted Norton quite frequently, that the reader will become familiar with an important voice which up to now has been neglected.

A comment on my chapter organization. Norton's growth in the early phase (Chapters I through IV) demands a chronological treatment. His opinions on art and life in America develop in these years to foreshadow his more important later work. In his mature period, one finds alternations in his outlook but not, strictly speaking, any development. I have therefore departed from a close year-to-year story for the period from 1874 to 1898 (Chapters V, VI, and VII) in order to bring into clearer focus Norton's major contributions as a teacher, scholar, and citizen.

I am grateful for permission to quote from material held under copyright by the following: Houghton Mifflin Company for *The Education of Henry Adams* and *Letters of Charles Eliot Norton*, and George Allen & Unwin Ltd. for John Ruskin, *Praeterita*. Also, it is a pleasure to acknowledge my debt to a number of scholars, none of whom, however, should be implicated in the shortcomings of this book. Professor Leo Marx of Amherst College gave me valuable suggestions and encouragement at the outset of this study and again during various stages of the writing. Mr. Robert B. Shaffer and Professors Theodore Hornberger of the University of Minnesota and Benjamin Rowland of Harvard University read a large portion of the manuscript. I profited from their criticisms. I am indebted, also, to Professor Ove Preus for the ideas that grew out of our conversations about Norton. Last of all, my thanks to Mr. William A. Jackson and his fine staff for their cooperation in making accessible to me the Norton collection at the Houghton Library, Harvard University.

K.V.

Seattle, Washington
April 1959

Contents

List of Illustrations

We are raising in the level of civilization in America the classes which have heretofore been depressed. The natural result of that work is that the higher levels — that the peaks of civilization — sink, and the mass — the average level — is raised to unexampled elevations. Now the point we have to consider is whether this process can go on without risking the very existence of the most precious fruits of civilization and culture.

(Charles Eliot Norton, speaking at the Tercentenary Celebration at Emmanuel College, Cambridge, England, 1884.)

INTRODUCTION:
DEMOCRACY AND CULTURE

CHARLES ELIOT NORTON'S life as a businessman, humanitarian, magazine editor, teacher, scholar, and citizen was dominated by a single concern. He tried to reconcile the antagonistic claims of "democracy" and "culture" in American society. It was a conflict which had taken on special significance since the Industrial Revolution and the political and social revolutions of the late eighteenth century. Formerly, "culture" had been associated with the training and refinement of the tastes, ideas, and manners of a privileged and dominant aristocracy. But the strongholds of this elite were being threatened in the eighteenth century by the rise to economic and political power of the middle classes of society, as well as the great masses of the population — that segment which Alexander Hamilton had summarily dismissed as a "great beast." This upsurge of "democracy" seemed to threaten the very survival of "culture," not only in Europe but also in America, where many of the older European traditions in thought, tastes, customs, and institutions had been preserved in the midst of a new and revolutionary concept of man in a "free" society. How could one reconcile the old aristocratic concept of "culture" with the new idea of "democracy" in sprawling, heterogeneous, materialistic, and (theoretically) egalitarian America?

Norton shared this dilemma with other social critics of the century. Alexis de Tocqueville, visiting America in the 1830's, had admired the political liberties of the individual in America, and the safeguards against the kind of tyranny present in European political systems. Yet in the very rule of the majority, Tocqueville predicted the eventual tyranny of majority opinion — a leveling or lowering of standards, especially in the choice of political leaders. In the absence of an aristocracy, he also foresaw the eventual loss of tradition and discipline, factors necessary for a rich intellectual and aesthetic life. The growth of literature and the other arts was hopeless under such conditions, and would probably continue to be so in America.

Walt Whitman developed Tocqueville's theme later in the century. Two words, Whitman wrote in *Democratic Vistas* (1871), embodied the central conflict of American life. These words were "Democracy" and "Culture." Whitman as a poet had previously expressed his brotherly feeling for man in the mass, and had celebrated the unbridled individualism of American manhood. But sizing up America more soberly after the Civil War, he called New World democracy "an almost complete failure in its social aspects, and in really grand religious, moral, literary, and esthetic results." Tocqueville would have registered no surprise had he lived to read this commentary on American life. Whitman's analysis of causes, however, was quite different from Tocqueville's. Whitman did not blame these dismal conditions on the tyranny of mass opinion and the absence of an influential elite. Rather, he leveled his charges against those writers who were perpetuating in a young, vigorous country an effete gentility borrowed from the Old World. He warned America, as Emerson had earlier, that worship of "the best" that had been thought and expressed in the past had inhibited the native genius. Summoning the spirits of Dante, Shakespeare, Michelangelo, Kant, and Hegel, Whitman wrote:

> Ye powerful and resplendent ones! Ye were, in your atmospheres, grown not for America, but rather for her foes, the feudal and the old — while our genius is democratic and modern.[1]

The difference between Whitman and Norton's friend Matthew Arnold is clear. Writing in *Literature and Dogma* (1876), Arnold gave his celebrated definition of culture as "the acquainting ourselves with the best that has been known and said in the world." On his visit to America in 1883, Arnold deplored, with Whitman, the artificiality and coarseness of the American mentality — "a false smartness, a false audacity, a want of soul and delicacy." But unlike Whitman, Arnold sided with Plato, who had placed his hope in the men of refinement and intellect — the "remnant" in Athenian society — for which Whitman had such a distaste. Members of this distinguished elite, Arnold wrote in *Culture and Anarchy,* would perpetuate in modern England the spirit of humanistic learning. And through a sort of trickling-down process of popular enlightenment, they would also carry that spirit "outside the clique of the cultivated and learned" and thereby diffuse "sweetness and light. . . from one end of society to the other."

Tocqueville, Whitman, Arnold, and others tried to discover whether a healthy "culture" (meaning an intellectual, aesthetic, and moral life which aims at some degree of excellence and yet can be shared by all) — whether such a "culture" can develop in an "equal society" or "democracy" ruled in large measure by the will of the majority. So did Charles Eliot Norton, and his efforts provide the dominant theme of his career. During his life, Norton struggled to resolve the contraries between, on the one hand, his descent from a leading Puritan family, the celebration of mind, and worship of values and traditions of the past; and on the other, his response to an age of enterprise and reform, to the new egalitarian spirit, and a vigorous civilization springing up in the West. Many of his close associations in England — with Arnold, Ruskin, Carlyle, and Leslie Stephen — strengthened the one, while the teachings of Emerson, the poetry of Whitman, the character of men like John Brown and Abraham Lincoln reinforced the other. Indeed, the story of Norton's life provides us with one of the links in American intellectual history between the world of Emerson and the world of T. S. Eliot.

PART ONE
YEARS OF GROWTH AND CHANGE
(1827–1873)

I

NEW ENGLAND HERITAGE

[Christianity] is to be received on the same ground as we receive all other truths, of which we have not ourselves mastered the evidences . . . Our belief in those truths . . . is founded in a greater or less degree on the testimony of others who have examined their evidence, and whom we regard as intelligent and trustworthy.

(Andrews Norton, " A Discourse on the Latest Form of Infidelity," 1839, in reply to Emerson's Divinity School Address)

THE PURITAN STRAIN

Charles Eliot Norton at the age of ten lay on a sickbed, gravely worried about a personal obligation to his family and his debt to posterity. He said, according to a family tradition, "I wish I could live, so that I could edit Father's works." [1] His father was, of course, Andrews Norton. The place was the Norton home ("Shady Hill") in Cambridge, some one thousand yards northeast of Harvard Yard. And the time the late 1830's, when Andrews Norton, "the hard-headed Unitarian Pope," was engaged in bitter conflict with those New England "infidels," the Transcendentalists. Outside this immediate world, the boy's precocious words carry the ring of generations — or centuries — of family tradition. They could serve as a warning to the Age of Andrew Jackson that, as John Jay Chapman later would put it, "the strong aristocratic feeling of those old Puritan first-families, who felt that they must be leaders in Israel," was still alive in New England.[2]

The early colonial period lived in Charles Eliot Norton's historical imagination, as in Hawthorne's, and deepened his sense of strong clerical roots. The moral and scholarly cast of mind which distinguished Andrews Norton and his son had been an inheritance from the Reverend John Norton. For in a family which had lived for nearly two centuries on New England soil, the ancestral footsteps could still be heard. Traces of temperament and character in the Puritan reappeared in his Unitarian descendants despite a gentler view of the human soul in the later religion.

A portrait of the family's first Puritan appears in the third book of Cotton Mather's *Magnalia Christi Americana.* John Norton was born at Starford in Hertfordshire on May 6, 1606. He showed the marks of a brilliant mind at an early age, and excelled in Latin composition as a boy. In his youth, John Norton became addicted to the vice of card-playing; but after severe pangs of conscience and a searching of the Scriptures, he abandoned this pernicious habit and gravitated toward his calling in the church. Mather describes his peculiar fitness for the life of a divine, and his early reputation as a maker of sermons "with such *ornaments* of *laconic* and well-contrived expression as made him worthy to be called 'the master of sentences.' " Though he was a choleric man by disposition, his behavior was "most affable, courteous, and complaisant." Regarding his scholarship, Mather writes: "Vast was the treasure of learning in this reverend man." [3]

In 1634, Norton could no longer comply with the "rites" of the church in England, and he boarded a ship sailing to America. But a shipwreck outside England deferred these plans and he returned to England. In the following year, he again prepared to sail to America, and in October of 1635 (after a near-shipwreck close to the New England coast) he reached his destination. The arrival is recorded in Bradford's history *Of Plymouth Plantation* and also in Winthrop's *History.*

Massachusetts soon proved fertile for the kind of seed

which John Norton had come to sow. For in spite of the urgencies of frontier life, the colonists in New England shared with the clergy a deep regard for the life of the mind. The settlers respected the erudition of their minister, and did not shrink from the challenge of his highly intellectual sermon. Those who could write brought along inkhorn and paper on Sunday morning, and returned to their homes with matter enough to provide them with days of religious discussion and debate.

That schoolboys and college students were compelled to attend these sermons and to take notes for future recitations gives further evidence of the vital link between the intellectual and the spiritual life in John Norton's New England. The higher education was widely encouraged. Ministers and magistrates who made up the dominant class in the colony perpetuated their rule through the education of a select group of future leaders, while the early settlers donated wheat, wampum, or pine-tree shillings "for the mayntenance of poore schollars at the Colledg at Cambridg." But Puritan leaders also considered a program of *public* education necessary in order to resist the strategies of the "old deluder." A period of grammar-school training was therefore required by local law in the early years of the settlement. There were sharp limits, however, to the extent of such popular schooling. A certain amount of education would afford the people the religious enlightenment necessary to understand the purpose of their Bible commonwealth. To go beyond this minimum training might invite the claims of reason to conflict with established religious authority, and pave the way for the spreaders of dissent and anarchy — the "Antinomians, democratical spirits, and Levellers." For in the Puritan state, the common welfare was identified with the will of God, as understood by the leaders of the commonwealth, the "elect," since they alone were capable of interpreting God's will to unregenerate man. In their view, society was not an aggre-

gation of independent men working out their separate des-
tinies, but rather an organism wherein each person played
his own part, always remembering his station in life and holding a due respect for the leadership of the holy and regenerate.
Tensions developed within this concept of society, but they
did not disrupt the pattern of government in the Puritan
oligarchy, for the majority of settlers read their catechism and
accepted a theocracy from the beginning. Theirs was the
most homogenous of all the colonies, and under the strict
control of magistrates and clergy, their settlement could live
on without fear of internal disturbances.

John Norton's ministry in Massachusetts, first at Ipswich
and later as John Cotton's successor at the First Church of
Boston, brought him high distinction as a leader of the
church and a counselor in affairs of state. His lasting contributions included three works which he wrote at the request of the ministers and General Court of the colony. All
three were unified by a single theme: to justify and consoli-
date the Puritan form of government in the colony. The first
of these was an essay on the church-government in Massachusetts, which he completed in 1645, and was believed by Cotton Mather to be the first American book written in classical
Latin. The two other works were aimed at stamping out
various forms of heresy in the colony. He replied in 1653 to
an *"erroneous treatise"* on God's wrath and Christ's suffering,
The Meritorious Price of Man's Redemption, written by a
Massachusetts gentleman, William Pynchon. And before his
death in 1663, Norton made one last effort to curb the invasion of certain odious sects into the colony, by writing *A
Brief Tractate Concerning the Doctrine of the Quakers.*

Thus the Reverend John Norton came to the wilderness
in America (one of the New England "Johannes in eremo,"
Mather calls him) to become a power in the church and state
and one of America's first scholars. "This was our Norton!"
Mather writes in the concluding words of his invaluable

sketch, ". . . and though he left no *children*, yet he has a *better name than that of sons and daughters.*"

There was, however, a nephew, also named John Norton, who perpetuated the Norton line of ministers. His mother was a niece of Governor John Winthrop. He accepted the pastoral duties at the Hingham Church in 1678. Like his more famous uncle, the younger Norton bore the stamp of disciplined intellectual training common among the finest members of the clergy in this later period also. His descendent, Charles Eliot Norton, described him as a man of strong literary interests (he wrote a funeral elegy on the death of Mrs. Anne Bradstreet), the possessor of a vigorous mind which had been nourished and toughened in religious controversy, and, in short, a minister who "could hardly fail to quicken [the people's] intellectual life." [4]

John Norton (the younger) preached to a later generation of Puritans, one which had grown less submissive to the rule of a church-government, however capable its leaders might be. The late seventeenth century in New England was a period of transition, when "the beginnings of civil democracy were weakening the hold of a dominant class." [5] Ideals implicit in the compact theory of government — the voluntary agreement of free men, the appeal to human reason, the spirit of free inquiry — had for some time been fermenting in the colony despite effective efforts to command civil and religious obedience. The new charter (1692) cut sharply the political power of the theocracy. In religion, the revelation of the "inner light" of Quakerism had become more and more a menace to Puritan doctrine and authority, while on the frontier, men were beginning to demand a religion which would gladden their hearts rather than oppress their minds. Contemporaries of John Norton sensed the danger and painted hell in colors more fearful than ever before. In his *Diary*, on January 13, 1796, Samuel Sewall described the effect on his daughter after hearing one of John Norton's sermons:

> A little after diner [sic] she burst out into an amazing cry, which caus'd all the family to cry too; Her Mother ask'd the reason; she gave none; at last said she was afraid she should goe to Hell, her Sins were not pardon'd. She was first wounded by my reading a Sermon of Mr. Norton's, about the 5th of Jan.[6]

Clergymen of the old guard expressed their growing alarm over the leveling influences in colonial society by preaching that man was created to live in a stratified society, with inequalities of station and privilege. The desperate plight of the established church in New England has been described by two modern historians of the Puritan mind:

> By the beginning of the eighteenth century the task of buttressing the classified society, maintaining the rule of the well-trained and the culturally superior both in church and society seems to have become the predominant concern of the clergy. Sermon after sermon reveals that in their eyes the cause of learning and the cause of a hierarchical, differentiated social order were one and the same.[7]

ANDREWS NORTON AND THE RISE OF UNITARIANISM

The fall of the Puritan clergy from authority in New England was completed in the eighteenth century. Historians have recited some of the major causes. A rising merchant class had gained political and social power. The findings of Newtonian physics were altering man's concept of the deity —Calvin's God of Wrath had become the Deist's impersonal and expert Watchmaker. In the backwoods settlements, men formerly oppressed by the dogma of a ruling oligarchy were discovering under the expansive frontier skies a new truth about individual freedom and personal salvation.

A further reason for the movement away from the asperities of the Puritan creed and the dominant rule of a minority can be found in a certain laxity within the Puritan government itself. Since conformity to the Calvinistic system of belief was generally taken for granted from the beginning, the patriarchs admitted the early settlers to the church without requiring assent to a given creed. Thus the colonists felt at liberty to speak openly on religious topics without the cramping fear of violating any oath of allegiance they might have given to a body of doctrine. Among some of the livelier minds, Calvinism had begun to dissolve slowly, even within the first generations of the settlement. One of the earliest works to indicate the weakening hold of the traditional faith came in 1650 from John Norton's enemy, William Pynchon, in his *The Meritorious Price of Our Redemption,* already mentioned. Pynchon's views on the atonement were considered so heretical that the General Court in Boston ordered all copies burned in the marketplace. The Court also requested John Norton (the elder) to publish a reply to Pynchon's blasphemy. Norton's book appeared in 1653, bearing the title, *A Discussion of that Great Point in Divinity the Sufferings of Christ. . .* Pynchon returned to England, where he found other dissenters who were willing to endorse his tract against the Puritan doctrine of redemption. In England, Pynchon expanded his original text to three times its former size and published the work as an answer to Norton.

Pynchon's disturbing views did not seriously challenge the Puritan regime in the mid-seventeenth century, although their publication indicated that colonial thought was moving away from the prevailing Calvinism. Not long after Pynchon's work came political and social changes, and also the liberating influence of English writers like Milton, Tillotson, Locke, and others. By the early eighteenth century, the Calvinists clearly were losing ground throughout New England. The new Brattle Street Church threatened New England orthodoxy, while the writings of John Wise dealt a further blow to church authority. The Mathers fought the innovators with ink, oratory, and prayer. But the decline of the church-state could be traced in the changed attitude of the orthodox clergy itself. Ministers like John Norton (the younger) could still bring the hardened sinner to his knees, but Norton was one of the last of the old hell-fire Puritan divines. After his death in October, 1716, the situation grew steadily worse, and in 1722, Cotton Mather decried the growing laxity of the church and the apathy of its clergy. When the Great Awakening came in the 1730's, it seemed momentarily that Edwards' neo-Calvinism might help to revive the ruling dogma of the previous century. But the emotions and bigotries released by the Great Awakening only encouraged many ministers to adopt a creed more reasonable and gentle in spirit. Young men like Charles Chauncy and Jonathan Mayhew, as well as older ministers, were beginning to withdraw from the traditional doctrines of the Trinity, total depravity, and salvation of the elect — cornerstones of the old Calvinism.

One among this latter group was the Reverend Ebenezer Gay (1696–1787), who succeeded John Norton at Hingham. A learned scholar like his predecessor, Gay reflected in his outlook the new change in colonial religious thought. He considered the Great Awakening a deplorable instance of religious enthusiasm in a civilized society. By 1740, he had expressed his reservations about the Trinity, and was well on the way to becoming the father of American Unitarianism. Ebenezer Gay's contemporaries did not call him a rebel or a heretic, however. The change from the older religious mood and dogma to the new was almost imperceptible. A modern authority on Unitarian history has noted the quiet transition at Hingham from the older faith to the new spirit in religion which was to call itself Unitarianism:

[Gay's] active service covers almost the whole period of the transition from the strict Calvinism of the first settlers to the emancipated Christianity of the last decade of the century, yet it is impossible to say just when the Hingham church crossed the dividing line. When he died his congregation had for two generations heard from his pulpit none of the doctrines of old Calvinism, and they had long since abandoned these without being aware when or how, as was also the case with most of the congregations which silently became liberal without controversy or division.[8]

In 1786, the year before Ebenezer Gay's death, the father of Charles Eliot Norton was born in Hingham, Massachusetts. As a boy, Andrews Norton followed the pattern of the earlier Norton line. He was quiet and studious, and found in theology the proper materials to exercise his precocious mind. He entered Harvard College in 1800, when open rivalry was breaking out between the old faction and the new. In 1803, the Hollis Professorship in Divinity was left vacant after the death of Professor David Tappan. The liberal candidate was Norton's pastor at Hingham — Gay's successor, the Reverend Henry Ware. His rival in the orthodox camp was the Reverend Jesse Appleton. Ware was a known Arian, although he denied that he was a Unitarian. The appointment was held up for more than a year until on February 5, 1805, Ware was finally elected to the Hollis Chair. Ware's election brought no revolutionary changes at Harvard, for the climate had been congenial to such an appointment for some time. His victory did, however, symbolize the final conquest of the new theology over the dynasty of Calvinists who had ruled New England and Harvard College for more than a century and a half. The ideas held by Ware became the official creed of the Divinity School, and their impact soon influenced the young men at Harvard. Among them was Andrews Norton.

His first contribution to the new movement was in journalism. Andrews Norton was barely in his twenties when he began to write for the *Monthly Anthology* (subtitle: *Magazine of Polite Literature*) and the *Literary Miscellany*. In their cordial reception of foreign literature, these magazines encouraged a taste in America for the best writers on the Continent. Unwittingly they also introduced to the American readers the European proponents of philosophic idealism, whose influence would soon bring Unitarians to so much grief.

Andrews Norton was twenty-five when, in 1812, he founded

The General Repository and Review (January 12, 1812 to October 13, 1813). The short-lived *Repository* gave Unitarians an opportunity to argue their own tastes in current literature, and to present to their readers the religious issues of the day. The opening article of the first number carried the heading "A Defense of Liberal Christianity," and was written by Norton. It was followed in later issues by essays on "The Deity of Christ" and continuing debates over the meaning of such theological terms as "Son of God." The two remaining sections of the *Repository* — the "Literary Department" and "Review" — helped to justify the magazine's claim of representing an urbane outlook in America. By 1812, however, Norton showed signs that he had become wary of certain writers from across the seas. The authors discussed in the literary sections were predominantly English rather than Continental — writers like Moore, Byron, Scott, and Southey, whose works would be free of the post-Kantian heresy. In its time, Norton's *General Repository* was the first magazine in America to express the philosophical basis and the literary tastes of Unitarianism. In the history of American journalism, it may have been a "connecting link" between the earlier *Monthly Anthology* and the *North American Review,* established three years later.[9]

Andrews Norton was involved in the religious controversies during the early nineteenth century, not only as a journalist, but also as a teacher of New England's new generation of ministers. Appointed a tutor at Harvard in 1811, he received the Dexter Lectureship in Biblical Criticism two years later. He held this chair from 1813 to 1819, and in 1819 was elected Dexter Professor of Sacred Literature. In 1830, Norton resigned his Professorship in order to complete his chief work, *The Evidences of the Genuineness of the Gospels* (3 volumes, 1837–1844).

Students who came under the powerful instruction of Andrews Norton at Harvard included Ralph Waldo Emerson, George Ripley, James Freeman Clarke, Horace Hedge, and William Henry Furness — young men who would presently take up arms against him as Transcendentalists. For at the Harvard Divinity School in those days, the student was receiving a double education. In Norton's classroom, Ripley, Emerson, Clarke, and the others heard the gospel according to Locke and Berkeley on the evidence of Christian revelation. But in their dormitory rooms, they were being indoctrinated in an exciting and different education in the writings of Coleridge, Carlyle, and other literary spokesmen for Kant and German idealism.

During Andrews Norton's professorship, the faculty had not yet awakened to the threat of Transcendentalism, nor had they fully gauged the influence of Kant on the divinity students. In 1819, when William Ellery Channing delivered his address at the ordination of Jared Sparks, the enemy of the Unitarians was still John Calvin. Repeating essentially the same objections Norton had raised in his "Defense of Liberal Christianity," Channing assailed the old doctrines of human depravity, predestination, and the tyrannical God of Wrath, and declared them repugnant to the understanding of rational men. To the Unitarian, God was a benevolent Father and Jesus a man who had been sent to dwell among other men and teach them to live a virtuous life. In liberating men from a concept of innate depravity, the Unitarian theologians did not extol man's innate goodness nor his inner capacity to discover God's revelation to man. Their psychology was rooted in Lockean rationalism. Revelation must come from rational experience — from the clear evidence of divine intervention in history. The human mind was merely a product of the sense impressions which it had received since birth, and contained no innate faculty capable of perceiving spiritual truth, or of distinguishing the damned from the elect.

By the 1830's Norton and his colleagues discovered that

while they were attacking the weakened forces of Calvinism, Unitarians were being confronted with a new and more powerful enemy called Transcendentalism. Emerson and other young men now spoke out against Norton's empirical approach to revelation through miracles properly validated by a specialist in scriptural history. To the Transcendentalist, the denial of intuitive knowledge and the personal revelation of God in man was as severe a blow to human dignity as the Calvinist's doctrine of human depravity. The Transcendentalist found the divine wherever he looked in the natural world. All nature was miraculous: the secret of the universe could be discovered in a flower or a grain of sand.

The conflict between Unitarian and Transcendentalist grew sharper and more bitter as the decade advanced. The man temperamentally equipped to lead the Unitarians into battle was not William Ellery Channing, however, but Andrews Norton. As co-editor of *The Select Journal of Foreign Periodical Literature* (January, 1833, to October, 1834), he lashed out at his enemies and attacked both Goethe and Carlyle. He also contributed articles to the Unitarian *Christian Register,* acted for a time as co-editor of the *Christian Examiner,* and when his personal fight with the Transcendentalists became too heated even for the Unitarian journals, he vented his anger in signed letters to local newspapers. On some occasions, he attacked the enemy head-on. At other times, he denounced them by implication, ridiculing their taste for " 'that hasher up of German metaphysics,' the Frenchman, Cousin; and, of late, that hyper-Germanized Englishman Carlyle, [who] has been the great object of admiration and model of style." [10]

By condemning European literature, Andrews Norton angered a man who was to become one of his most irascible critics — the brilliant and erratic Orestes Brownson. With Brownson, the Transcendentalist strategy took a new turn. Both the theology and the literary taste of Unitarians, Brownson declared, were un-American and "aristocratic." Reviewing George Ripley's *Specimens of Foreign Standard Literature,* Brownson acclaimed modern French and German writers while disparaging the favorite literature of the Unitarians. The literature of England (said Brownson) "bristles from beginning to end with Dukes and Duchesses, Lords and Ladies, and overflows with servility to the great, and with contempt, or what is worse, condescension for the little." [11]

Brownson repeated the same theme — the Unitarian's quiet contempt of the masses — after the publication in 1838 of Andrews Norton's *Evidences of the Genuineness of the Four Gospels.* Brownson's review appeared in the Boston Quarterly Review, his own publication which he had established in that year to furnish an outlet for his superabundance of ideas. " 'The democrat,' " he wrote, believes in "the 'inner light,' " granted to all men for the revelation of truth. But, according to Brownson, men like Norton had no faith in the common sense of the people:

> The disciple of Locke may compassionate the people, but he cannot trust them; he may patronize the masses, but he must scout universal suffrage, and labor to concentrate all power in the hands of those he looks upon as the enlightened and respectable few.[12]

Andrews Norton's retaliation came not in a reply to Brownson's review, but in his celebrated answer to Emerson's address delivered to the Harvard Divinity School on July 15, 1838. Norton read "A Discourse on the Latest Form of Infidelity" to the alumni of the Divinity School at their meeting on July 19, 1839. In spite of Brownson and his allies, Norton had not retreated from his view of man. Locke had described the problem of knowledge accurately. Man could not apprehend truth through the unformed impressions of childhood, nor from the intuition, nor the incommunicable gleanings of pantheism. Religious belief required miraculous proof established by reason and investigation, and such evidence necessarily rested in the findings of the specialist, as did truth in all other fields of knowledge. The masses of men should defer to the judgment of religious authorities, for an accurate interpretation of Christian revelation lay "beyond the capacity or the opportunities of a great majority of men." [13]

Andrews Norton's historic "Discourse" was promptly published as a pamphlet, and the expected recriminations followed. The Unitarians (their enemies alleged) were out of touch with democratic society, they scorned the human heart and preached not the glad tidings which the Gospel spoke to all men, but the logical evidences which a learned elite alone were capable of verifying. Norton's former student George Ripley reminded him that Christ did not reveal the divine plan to men of " 'extensive learning' "; the Disciples were humble, ignorant men. These and other answers to Norton's attack (it was his last major thrust at the Transcendentalists) did not disturb the incrusted old Unitarian. Norton returned to his private studies, and before long, tempers on all sides had begun to cool. Ripley was soon engaged in his social experiment at Brook Farm; Brownson was converted to the Roman Catholic Church; and in the next decade, when Theodore Parker looked back on these years of heated controversy (in *Theodore Parker's Experience as a Minister,* 1859), he paid a generous tribute to Andrews Norton's rare scholarship. Parker remembered, without bitterness, Norton's insistence that "the mass of men must accept the doctrines of religion solely on the authority of the learned, as they do the doctrines of mathematical astronomy." And George Ripley, in the *Memorial History of Boston* (1880), described Andrews Norton's influence on the literary taste of this earlier period:

> His thorough scholarship served to give form and substance to the literary enthusiasm which at that time prevailed in Cambridge. His refined and exquisite taste cast an air of purity and elegance around the spirit of the place. . . His love of literature was a passion.[14]

THE CHILDHOOD OF CHARLES ELIOT NORTON

Charles Eliot Norton grew up in the midst of his father's warfare with the Transcendentalists. In his boyhood, he could not help absorbing some of the spirit of battle. In 1837 he was ready, at the age of ten, to help the cause by editing his father's writings. Some of his letters describe the evenings when the most vigorous minds of New England gathered at the Norton home to discuss current problems. But the earliest letters tell of childhood days spent in a home which was warm with the love and sympathy of parents and children.

In 1821, Andrews Norton had married Catherine Eliot, the daughter of the wealthy Boston merchant Samuel Eliot. The union of two prominent families was characteristic of Boston. For Andrews Norton, the marriage opened a world of social engagements and permitted him to live in far greater affluence than was customary for a Harvard Divinity School professor. In a few months, they had settled at "Shady Hill," a white colonial-style mansion on fifty acres situated within one mile of Harvard Yard. The home was a part of the bride's dowry. The Nortons also owned a handsome carriage which Thomas Wentworth Higginson remembered as being the only carriage in Cambridge at one time. It bore the initials "A. & C.N." This indication of joint ownership, rare in those days, suggests that the carriage, too, was probably a gift of the bride's father. At Shady Hill on November 16, 1827, the third of the Norton's six children, Charles Eliot, was born. Before his first birthday, Charles Norton traveled with his parents on a six-month journey through England and Scotland, and made his first acquaintance with English men of letters. He sat on Wordsworth's knee, and "met" such notable figures of the period as Joanna Baillie, George Crabbe, Mrs. Hemans, and Southey. It was a symbolic journey for a very young American who in later years would become a close friend of the greatest English writers of the century.

Norton's childhood in Cambridge did not fall into the usual pattern of a boy's life. Family papers leave no record that he ever tumbled out of trees, roamed away from home, or brought stray animals into the house. In a very real sense, he appears never to have been a child at all. He had an early acquaintance with death. In 1833, his three-year-old brother, William, died. The following year a sister died shortly after birth. At the age of seven, Charles Norton was already keeping a diary of his day-to-day experiences and impressions, and had begun to perfect his skill in the art of letter-writing. These letters are full of precocious opinions about sermons and public lectures he had recently attended. They contain charming descriptions of flowers growing outside his window, a carefully worded apology for creating some misunderstanding in a previous letter, or a rebuke of his careless penmanship and tendency to ramble.

He was trained from childhood to adopt the values of polite New England society. One can trace the results of such training in his concern for graceful penmanship and proper expression, and occasionally in comments about people and places he had been observing. After visiting the summer home of his Aunt Wigglesworth, Norton wrote to his parents: "The persons who keep the house are very neat, obliging, and have much more refinement than is common among country people." [15] Thomas Wentworth Higginson remembered another part of this social training in his treks up to Shady Hill to attend a dancing-school which met in the Norton home. On the first of those afternoons, however, the attempt to cultivate polite manners and social graces among the younger set of refined Cambridge society turned into a dismal failure. For Higginson produced a pair of scissors, cornered "Pope Charles" (as his playmates called him) and snipped off Norton's front hair.

His formal schooling followed the New England pattern of education which had begun in Puritan times. Tutored until the age of seven, Norton was then enrolled in the Cambridge Classical School, directed by E. B. Whitman. There he received the traditional grounding in the ancient classical writers. A school report still extant contains high marks which indicate that Norton was prepared to continue the family tradition of distinguished scholars.

In 1840, Norton's letters are addressed from Brookline, Massachusetts, where he was attending a secondary school run by a Mr. Ingraham. His curriculum was rigorous by any standards. Writing to his father (May 16, 1840), Norton described the daily schedule: in the morning, two hours of translation in Latin or Greek, and two hours of composition in either language; in the afternoon, one hour of English composition and one hour of arithmetic. Some days past, he had translated 350 lines of the *Aeneid*, Book XII, within two hours. With understandable pride, he wrote to Andrews Norton: "Wasn't that a good deal Father? I just exactly did it and I learnt them pretty well too."

The letters of this time also reveal a beginning of one of Norton's abiding passions in later life — the love of rare books and art objects. At twelve, he had become the official buyer for the family library. He informed Andrews Norton (May 9, 1840) that Leone's *Arabian Nights,* regularly nine dollars a volume, could be obtained at four dollars in a local bookstore. Some weeks later, he attended an auction of Governor Winthrop's library of three or four thousand volumes, but he wrote to his father afterward in disappointment, "I did not see many valuable books among them" (May 29, 1840). One book had caught his fancy, however — Aikin's *Life of Queen Elizabeth* — and in the genuine spirit of Yankee horse-trading, he out-bargained another collector for the volume. He had also acquired a Latin version of the Psalms published in Germany in the fifteenth century ("some of the illuminated capitals are most beautifully finished") and was anxious to receive Andrews Norton's opinion of it. Still later, he proudly announced that he had obtained a "most beautiful" French painting, though he was forced to pay twenty-five dollars for it.

Another youthful interest appeared in the following year. On May 9, 1841, the first number of "The Cent Magazine" ("Conducted by a body of Gentlemen") made its appearance. With youthful wittiness, Norton and his co-editor, cousin William Eliot, announced the purpose of the magazine in the first issue:

> We intend to publish it weekly, combining the useful and instructive with the amusing. It will be printed on the best paper at Pen, Tuk and Company's establishment, which has long sustained a high reputation in our community . . .
>
> After all have read it who wish to, it will be sold without reserve to the highest bidder.

The magazine was "printed" in Norton's own careful longhand. The fourteen pages, four-by-six inches in size, included a serialized novel, *Rome*; a "Children's Department"; a Brother Jonathan letter in the "Correspondence"; and a final page devoted to current news.

After two issues, "The Cent Magazine" had a large enough circulation (twenty-five subscribers) to change its format and increase the price to two cents. It was now called "The Cousin's Magazine." Norton solicited articles from his Dwight, Eliot, Ticknor, and Wigglesworth cousins, and from his sisters Louisa and Jane. The contents provided an excellent example of the quality of education which children then received in America. Contributions included original literary efforts as well as translations of foreign literature. One number, dated October 4, 1841, even has a certain historical interest, for it carried a droll verse sent to the editors in reply to a subscriber's challenge to rhyme the word *assafaetida*:

A pretty lass *I met to day*
Perfumed with assafaetida;
     Quoth I, "Fair maiden mine,
How shall I *pass so wet a day?*"
She answered, *"Ah Sir set a day,*
And then I will be thine."

The lines were written by a close friend of the family and
signed "H. W. L." Several months later, "The Cousin's Magazine" ceased publication under circumstances which remain
unknown.

Norton's boyhood years, then, were marked by the continuity of family tradition in scholarship and manners. He
was weaned on the verses of the Latin and Greek poets. He
showed an early confidence in judging rare books and paintings. His remarkably keen social sense came to him naturally
from the family relationships in Boston and Cambridge "society." The letters and "magazine" contributions he wrote
in these earliest years revealed Charles Norton as a boy with
rare perceptiveness and tact, as well as a young writer consciously groping for the power of graceful expression. Equally
important was Norton's early family life. With his parents
and three sisters — Louisa, Jane, and Grace — he enjoyed a
rich childhood in a home filled with harmony and love. He
had a child's fondness for saving various small objects and
scraps of paper whose value only a child can understand.
Among these treasures which he put away and guarded with
jealous care were the affectionate notes his mother used to
pin to his night jacket. And on the day before his father's
death, Norton wrote (in a letter to Arthur Hugh Clough)
of the gentle and constant regard with which Andrews Norton looked after the happiness of his son:

You, much as you saw of us, my dear Clough, can hardly estimate
and understand the happiness of the home that we have had, and the
unbroken union of affection that there has been among us as long as
I can remember. My earliest recollections are of my Father's interest
in all that concerned me, of his telling me stories, of his walking with

me, of his waiting for me to come home from school to take me with him to drive, — and ever since he has been not only the best of counsellors but the most loving of friends.[16]

STUDENT AT HARVARD

At fourteen, Charles Eliot Norton entered Harvard College. The President of Harvard at that time was the great early champion of academic freedom and one-time reform mayor of Boston, Josiah Quincy. Despite his high-minded ideals, Quincy succeeded in making himself odious to students and faculty alike, particularly for maintaining the recitation system and administering the "Scale of Merit." The recitation method gave to many a classroom the fearsome atmosphere of a police station. Teachers were not expected to inspire the student, but to cross-examine him on his prepared lessons. Fortunately, some of the members of Quincy's brilliant faculty rebelled. Jared Sparks, the McLean Professor of Ancient and Modern History, refused to teach by set recitations, as did Longfellow, who had succeeded George Ticknor as Professor of Modern Languages. Teachers who were overworked and shackled by the recitation system during Norton's years at Harvard included Asa Gray (Botany), Edward T. Channing (English), Cornelius Felton (Greek), and Benjamin Peirce (mathematics and "natural philosophy"). The personal genius of such men in the comparatively small classes, however, fired students like Norton, Francis Child, and George Martin Lane with a love of learning despite the undesirable effects of the "system."

The "Scale of Merit" was geared to the recitation method. It granted a daily eight points toward graduation honors to the student who had recited his lessons properly. But deductions for unprepared lessons or for slips in discipline could wipe out several days of merit points. Sixteen credits were subtracted for skipping Sunday chapel, and thirty-two for failure to prepare a theme or declamation. A public admonishment brought a penalty of sixty-four points. Quincy himself insisted on totaling each teacher's reports, and thereby insured the frequently hostile relations between teacher and student.

President Quincy deserves credit, however, for breaking the ground for Charles W. Eliot's later elective system. (Credit also belongs to George Ticknor, who, earlier, had returned from study in Germany to urge that American students, like German, have a certain freedom of choice in their courses.) Latin, Greek, and mathematics were now required only in the freshman year. In the following years, the student could select from a small variety of courses which the college and faculty were able to offer with the limited funds on hand. The electives, though, allowed only one-half as many merit credits as the prescribed studies in the fixed curriculum.

Norton's freshman year was interrupted by an eye infection which became so serious that in January of 1843 he was sent to an oculist in New York. His absence brought him a severe disappointment; it prevented his winning the coveted "Detur," a book inscribed with the college seal and awarded to the student who had shown distinguished scholarship in his freshman year. The blow was softened, however, when Quincy called Norton into the president's office and presented him with a volume of Campbell's *Poems,* inscribed with Norton's name and a few words of approval.

The next year, Norton moved to Holworthy Hall in the Yard and roomed with his cousin, Charles Eliot Guild. The record of the next three years is not so full as we could wish. Norton seems to have written few letters at Harvard. His family and friends were at Cambridge where he could meet them regularly and visit with them personally. At the end of his sophomore year, he did record a horseback trip through northern New England with his cousin, William Eliot. During the following summer, he also recorded some rigorous weeks of mountain-climbing in New Hampshire. And in February of 1846, he spent a vacation by traveling south as far as Washington, where he wrote home describing the tension of the Oregon debate which he had heard in the halls of Congress. The experience increased an interest in politics which had already been awakened in his classes at Harvard. The other letters extant during the Harvard years make very few references to the college life or his classes with Felton, Channing, Sparks, and others. But they abound with descriptions of the talk at Shady Hill during the evenings and week ends. The Norton home appears to have provided him with as vital a part of his education as the classroom at Harvard. Names of the visitors comprised a roll call of intellectual Cambridge: Parkman, Quincy, Belknap, Ticknor, Longfellow, Felton, Bancroft, Bowen. The conversation ranged from the contents of the latest *North American Review* to the politics or the literature of England ("Most of the evening was taken up in discussing Miss Austen's novels, and the requisites of a good novel in general").[17] On other evenings when these visitors from the community or the college were not calling, the Norton family preserved an old custom by reading literature aloud. It was the literature of England, however, and not of America.

Norton's earlier passion for collecting continued to grow during his college years. His letters contain glowing descriptions of paintings, engravings, and books which he had acquired. A five-volume set of Xenophon, "beautifully printed and beautifully bound," found its way to the Norton library, along with other classical works which Charles Norton judged necessary in filling out his father's collection. The library also contained the family's subscriptions to leading English periodicals — *Blackwood's Magazine, The Classical Museum, Edinburgh Review,* and *Quarterly Review.* But the more vital questions about Norton's reading cannot be positively

answered. One can safely assume that he read his Longfellow, Whittier, and Lowell, and perhaps Irving and Hawthorne. Did he also read Cooper and Poe? Was he imbibing
Emerson and the German idealists along with the official
curriculum at Harvard? It is certain, in any case, that he
fulfilled in some measure the promise of his earlier years as
a youthful scholar. He graduated Phi Beta Kappa in the class
of 1846 (sixty-six members), with distinction in Greek, Latin,
and political economy. After the long-drawn-out graduation
exercises typical of those days, when class orators grew hoarse
and ladies fainted, the Reverend John Pierce reported in his
diary of August 26, 1846, the following item: "A dissertation 'Sante Croce,' by Charles Eliot Norton, son of Professor
Norton, was among the best exercises both for composition
and elocution." [18]

II

FROM BUSINESS TO SCHOLARSHIP

> It is not, then, to the people that we are to look for wisdom and intelligence . . . They could not, if they would, rescue themselves from evil; and they have no help for others. But their progress must be stimulated and guided by the few who have been blessed with the opportunities, and the rare genius, fitting them to lead.
>
> (Norton in *Considerations on Some Recent Social Theories*, 1853)

> Cathedrals were essentially expressions of the popular will and the popular faith. They were the work neither of ecclesiastics nor of feudal barons. They represent, in a measure, the decline of feudalism, and the prevalence of the democratic element in society.
>
> (Norton's essay on the Duomo at Orvieto, March, 1856)

THE COUNTINGHOUSE — A MEANS TO AN END

AFTER his graduation from Harvard, Norton set out to learn the ways of the business world. The clerical background of the Norton family had influenced his character and training, but he did not hear a calling to the ministry. A business life may have been an unwelcome alternative, but Norton chose it and he endured it with a hereditary Yankee toughness and Puritan devotion to work. In later life, he recalled these years and wrote:

The day after I spoke my Commencement part I entered a countingroom on a wharf in Boston, and for a couple of years used to freeze in winter and to roast in summer overseeing the warehousing of thousands of bales of Calcutta hides; I had to run errands, to do work that even a

Freshman would not expect to do. It was against the grain, but it had to be done, and I stuck it out, and am not sorry now that I did so.[1]

The countinghouse belonged to the East India merchants Bullard and Lee, and during the next nine years became the proving ground for Norton's career as a businessman. The work was frequently tedious and irksome. It required close attention to a thousand details involved in the smooth functioning of a commercial house. In addition to supervising the work out on the dock, Norton handled business correspondence, invoices, insurance policies, the records of prices current, and kept any number of additional account books up to date.

These practical concerns, however, did not monopolize Norton's mind and energies. Late in 1846, he prevailed on the city of Cambridge to let him use a school on Garden Street twice a week during the winter. There he began evening classes for men and boys who had been forced to go to work in order to support their families, and were unable to complete their regular schooling. The school's enrollment and curriculum are not known. The faculty was small but impressive. Besides Norton, the teachers included John Holmes (brother of the poet), Sidney Coolidge, and Francis Child. Norton believed this to be the first night school in Cambridge and the state of Massachusetts. Whether or not it had an influence on later evening schools in America has not been established, but Norton did discover from time to time that the school had achieved results. One pupil, Pat McCarty, a son of Irish immigrants, tended cows by day and came to Norton's school at night. He later studied law and became the mayor of Providence, Rhode Island. In a letter to a Providence newspaper after his election, he called Norton's night school one of the major influences of his life and gave it credit for providing him with a start in life.

Norton studied closely the conditions of the poor, both in America and England, and probably engaged his father in evening discussions of local poverty and crime, concerns which both men shared. A recent Harvard student of political economy, he could not ignore the imminent social and political revolutions in England and on the Continent. His outlook at this time is significant. He found that his sympathies lay on the side of the Chartists in England. In French politics of the late 1840's, he was an outspoken admirer of Lamartine. When news of the 1848 Revolution reached the street corners in America, Norton bought a copy of the newspaper and rushed to the house of George Ticknor to share the excitement with his cosmopolitan uncle. His interest in American politics was no less keen. He visited Washington for the second time within three years to attend President Taylor's inauguration.

During these early years in the countinghouse, Norton was also making his first contributions as a scholar. The *North American Review* carried his article on William Tyndale and another on archeological remains in America. These two widely contrasting articles revealed separate themes which would recur later; an admiration for personal suffering and martyrdom; and a fascination with the civilization of the American West. This second article may have been related to his friendship with Francis Parkman, then writing *The Oregon Trail* for serial publication in *Knickerbocker Magazine*. In 1848, Parkman asked Norton to help in revising these numbers for publication in a complete volume. Norton later recalled these nights when he and Parkman, both in their early twenties, met on the Boston wharf to work on Parkman's epic of the American West. "Many an evening," he wrote, "when there was not other work to be done, was spent by me and him in the solitary counting-room in going over his work." [2] Norton made still another contribution to scholarship in 1848 by serving as treasurer of a committee of the Boston Athenaeum which raised $3750.00 to buy a large part of the library of George Washington for the Athenaeum.

PASSAGE TO INDIA

A fateful opportunity came to Norton in the following year when Bullard and Lee offered him the post of supercargo in the firm's ship *Milton*. The destination was India. On May 21, 1849, Norton left America for some twenty months of travel on a trip which was to have a powerful, liberating influence on his outlook and career. "Up to my leaving home for India in 1849," he wrote afterwards, "I had led a narrow life, in a sense, of domestic seclusion in Cambridge, — pleasant, good for a foundation, — but the circumstances were fortunate which finally took me out of it and enlarged my vision of the world." [3]

During the ocean crossing of one hundred and two days, Norton read widely and critically in writers ancient and modern. To prepare himself for his duties in India, he read James Mill's *History of India*, Colman's *Hindu Mythology*, and Milburn's *Oriental Commerce*. Some of his other reading was a small liberal education in itself: Milman's *Life of Horace*, John Stuart Mill's *Political Economy*, much of Shakespeare, three-fourths of Gibbon, and the whole of Milton's poetry. But with filial devotion, he wrote to Andrews Norton: "The books which I have read, my dear Father, with much the most interest and much the most pleasure have been your Statement of 'Reasons' [for not believing the current doctrine of the Trinity] and your translations from the New Testament." [4]

The *Milton* arrived in Madras on September 1, 1849. Within two weeks, Norton wrote to his firm describing the commercial prospect in Madras. Though densely populated, Madras was far from realizing her capacity, either in production or consumption. Norton fixed the blame on the English colonial policy in India, and expressed an American's revulsion for the British caste system for both social and economic reasons. His analysis of business possibilities in India clearly was leading Norton into large problems of Indian society:

> The English, with a short-sighted policy, seem to regard the natives only as they can make them useful for present immediate objects. There is but little exertion made to develop their wants and resources. Of course for this there are many excuses, but an American sees much in the treatment of the natives which offends both his prejudices and his principles.[5]

Writing several weeks later from Calcutta, Norton gave signs that his humanitarian sympathies were growing stronger. He deplored the capricious manner in which the British treated native servants. And he was struck by the vast inequalities of wealth between the natives and their English rulers:

> The greatest wealth, the most miserable poverty, stand side by side like the palace and the hut which they occupy. The beauty of Calcutta is extremely diminished by the manner in which the low mud hovels of the natives are crowded into the vacant spaces between the large and often handsome houses of the English.[6]

As he analyzed more carefully the economic conditions in India, and the organization of society under the British, Norton softened his picture of English tyranny, and even modified his earlier feelings toward the natives. He learned that the British were, in fact, building schools and hospitals, and trying to increase economic self-sufficiency in India. They had encouraged the construction of canals to irrigate the soil. And they were building railroads to stimulate the investment of capital, develop natural resources, and provide jobs for native labor. Furthermore, Norton had been in closer contact with the Indian people and had found the experience somewhat disagreeable. They seemed to him shiftless, easily bribed, and endowed with a very limited understanding of truth and virtue.

He continued his travels northward in India, but the trip, which he described later in an article for *Putnam's,* was interrupted by a detour to Bombay, where he received news of his father's illness. He sailed from India early in 1850 to have time enough for further travel before summer, when his father's health was usually worse, and also to be closer to America for a short voyage home. Norton left India with contradictory impressions about the Indian society he had been observing during the past few months. He was disturbed by what he had seen and, sailing westward, he remembered the people with mingled feelings of pity and disappointment. On principle, he still had a strong distaste for the oppressive caste system of the British, but he could not wholeheartedly embrace the depraved and superstitious masses of Indian people. His attitudes were unresolved, although one thing is certain. He had received an uncomfortably close view of degradation and misery in a society governed by a privileged minority, and his social consciousness had been awakened. In the years to come, Norton's experiences in India were to provide the basis for a more searching look at the social order, both in America and Europe.

ART AND SOCIETY IN EUROPE

Norton's route west sent him through the Suez, with successive stops at Alexandria, Smyrna, and Trieste. He stayed several weeks in northern Italy, where, among other interests, he discovered his liking for the Palladian architecture at Vicenza. In late spring, he arrived in Paris. Supplied with letters of introduction from Edward Everett and from his uncle George Ticknor, Norton now made his first acquaintance with the international world of art and letters in the salons of Madame de Circourt and Mrs. Lee-Childe (sister of the South's Robert E. Lee). During these few crowded weeks in Paris society, he met minor figures like the painter Ary Scheffer, and major ones including Alexis de Tocqueville, Alfred de Vigny, and his hero of the French Revolution of 1848, Lamartine. He had lost none of his earlier enthusiasm for French politics and visited the Assembly to hear Victor

Hugo. But the meeting with Lamartine was disillusioning. Norton described an evening in the home of this colossal egoist, who kept in three rooms alone, twenty-two (by Norton's count) portraits of himself. Strangely, the most important friendship for Norton during his brief visit in Paris was formed with another American, George Curtis, whose concern about political graft Norton was to share during the later years of the century. Also in Paris, the twenty-two-year-old Norton was smitten by the actress Rachel, and delayed his departure to see her once more in a presentation of *Phèdre*. He left Paris remembering the thrill of almost touching her hand in the crowd after one of her performances.

On June 6, 1850, Norton crossed the English channel to be nearer America if his father's health should decline seriously in the summer. He soon met and was the guest of John Kenyon, Crabb Robinson, Joanna Baillie (long a friend of Andrews Norton), Mrs. Gaskell, and several others — all minor figures, but helpful in acquainting him with the atmosphere of literary life in London. He saw Ruskin at a party, but did not meet him. During the summer months, another new world began to open for Norton. He first toured the famous art galleries (and found that he liked the Van Dykes in Windsor Castle). More important, this summer in England marked the beginning of his excitement over the architecture of the medieval church. After trips to Ely, York, and Durham, he had intimations of an entire field of history which lay fallow, and announced a desire to read widely in the age of the great cathedrals. In September he wrote:

> I know so little about what I see compared to what is to be known, there are such treasures of history, and of romance, such studies of art and of life which I have never even approached, and which I long to unfold. I know enough to awaken my enthusiasm and my admiration, but I feel as if it were a waste of opportunity to see so much and not to know more.[7]

Norton returned to the Continent in the fall of 1850, drawn

by this awakened curiosity for the "studies of art and of life."
By November, he had arrived in Florence, where he met
Horatio Greenough and (through John Kenyon) Elizabeth
and Robert Browning. Though he was barely twenty-three,
Norton was cordially welcomed by the Brownings, and he
visited with them regularly during the next several weeks.
Browning guided Norton's unformed taste in art by accompanying him in the shops and advising against the purchase
of inferior paintings. Conversations together led them into
discussions of the decline of art in modern Italy, the low
character of the clergy, and the politics of Mazzini (Browning
lent Norton a copy of *Foi et Avenir*). But family and business
responsibilities forced Norton to cut short these visits and
return to America. On January 18, 1851, he sailed into New
York harbor and returned, after an absence of twenty months,
to his account books at the Central Wharf in Boston.

BROADENED HORIZONS — HUMANITARIANISM

The disturbing effects of the previous months of travel
appeared in Norton's writing and work after his return to
America. In the *North American Review* of July, 1851, he
wrote the first of a number of articles based on his experience
in India. "Sir Jamsetzee Jeejeebhoy" described the first Indian
to be knighted by the British, a businessman "possessing
those qualities most desirable in a merchant, integrity, judgment and enterprise. . ." Norton's main theme, however,
was not enterprise and trade, but rather the businessman as
humanitarian. (Since his return, Norton had become an independent merchant in the East India trade.) Sir Jamsetzee
was a benevolent merchant living in a rapidly changing society who used his wealth to build hospitals, hostelries, and
other charitable works in India. The lesson for America was
clear, but Norton spelled it out for his readers. The prosperous classes in America could profitably direct their atten-

tion to the plight of the poor, not merely because it was the moral duty of the rich to do so, but also because a sense of enlightened self-interest dictated their easing the lives of the poor in America. For private property was now endangered everywhere by the stirrings of class discontent: "While the laws which regulate the acquisition and the possession of property are so ill understood as they at present are all the world over, benevolence is not simply a duty, it is a necessity." With a Yankee businessman's eye for the pecuniary benefits of any proposal, Norton also reminded the taxpayer:

> Benevolence is dictated by the most refined selfishness, as well as by virtue. We have learnt that expensive schools are the cheapest institution of the state; we have yet to learn that the prevention of pauperism, at any cost, is cheaper than the care of it when it exists . . .

Speaking with all the fervor of a Brownson or a Garrison, Norton urged that

> every one in his own way devote a portion of his possessions, it matters not whether it be his labor, his money, or his thought, to the good of others. Whatever he does for their happiness will return in tenfold happiness to himself, for benevolence is the most divine of virtues.[8]

In the months to come, Norton himself practiced "the most divine of virtues." He continued to work closely with the Evening School after his return from Europe in 1851. A notebook in which he kept a record of "Accounts of Expenses for Evening School" shows a total of $60.27 during 1851–52, although the accounts do not indicate whether Norton himself assumed the burden of this expense. He also carried the campaign for popular education into the pages of the *North American Review*. In the April, 1852, issue of the *Review*, he wrote an article, "Dwellings and Schools for the Poor," urging Americans to establish evening schools in their cities, and to operate them at public expense. Norton presented his cause in the name of Christian charity, but he explained that education of the poor, and especially the train-

ing of children, would prevent moral and economic dangers
which could affect all members of society in the future:

> It is in the earliest years that the mind is most easily moulded, and
> it is then that the bitter experiences of want, sickness, and unkindness
> are, for the most part, the lot of young children of the poorest classes.
> The example of vice is often their daily lesson, and they grow up
> ignorant of their duties as well as of the necessary consequences of their
> conduct. They are children, but with little of the innocence, still less of
> the happiness, of childhood.[9]

In the same article, Norton launched a campaign to improve the living conditions of the poor in Boston. This interest in housing came from several sources. Andrews Norton
had expressed alarm over the wretched living quarters on the
Cambridge side of Beacon Hill and the crime which flourished
in such slum areas. And Charles Norton's own recent experiences in Europe and India had led him to further reading on the laboring classes in Europe. He now argued in the
North American Review that "there is no one of us who is
without ability to do something for those beneath him in the
world." Better dwellings for the poor would, in fact, bring
practical benefits to the landlord class: the owners would
find that property values would rise through such improvements. Furthermore, a failure to ameliorate squalid living
conditions would create, ultimately, a danger to the very
tenure of private property in America, for many of the
tenants in these slums were immigrants who were only too
well acquainted with the revolutionary doctrines current in
Europe. Norton pointed out (with clear echoes from Thomas
Jefferson) that social antagonism, vice, and crime sprang up
in cities where the lower classes were forced to live in squalid
housing areas, for "the character of the population depends
upon the nature of its habitations." Norton called for aid
from the municipal government in the inspection and condemnation of dwellings which failed to meet proper standards
of health, especially with regard to polluted water, bad drain-

age, and inadequate ventilation. Finally, he tried to encourage new construction of housing units by including in the article pictures of model lodginghouses in England, together with a sample floor plan.[10]

Norton's concern for better homes for the laboring classes continued to grow as the months passed. After a trip to New York, he contrasted the "reckless wastefulness" of the lavish new St. Nicholas Hotel with the poverty of a nearby "skid row" called Five Points. On a walk through these slums, Norton found human beings "so destitute of the means of comfort, as to be reckless of good or of evil." He sounded, indeed, like an angry socialist as he wrote:

> In the centre and very heart of this Christian city was a shame worse than barbarism, and an evil worse than adversity . . . It was a dangerous and detestable error; dangerous in any country, but more than in any other, in our own.[11]

Several weeks later, a series of five letters appeared in the *Cambridge Chronicle* (July and August, 1853) entitled "Letters on Poverty and Charity in Cambridge." They were signed by "N" and repeated ideas and even exact phrases from Norton's earlier writing. In these "Letters," he outlined a complete program of charity for the city of Cambridge. The first letter included a statement of principles: the well-to-do should recognize their duty to improve the lot of the poor. And, more practically, such moral duties would bring tangible profits to the benefactor. The happiness of the lower classes would reduce irritation in the social organism. Helping the poor to find employment would increase their economic independence and decrease the army of beggars. They would turn from a life of vice and crime and thereby help to lessen the expense incurred in running the local jails.

The next four letters described public and private means of attaining these ends. Regarding *public* responsibility, Norton urged that the municipality safeguard the health of the poor through close inspection of urban housing conditions. But the cornerstone of his plan was to be a program of public education. He advocated the enforced education of the poor, except those who were gainfully employed to support a family. Public schools should be "semi-industrial," preparing the student for a useful trade as well as teaching minimum lessons in good citizenship. Evening schools for adults and immigrants should be included in the public education system. And finally, a program of education should form an essential part of the rehabilitation of paupers in a properly supervised and tax-supported almshouse.

Letters four and five outlined a voluntary program of *private* charity, since there would be a natural aversion to government authority and taxation among Norton's readers. Norton offered two recommendations, which he explained in considerable detail. Briefly, he urged (1) that the leading citizens work together to establish districts in Cambridge for handling local charity cases as well as detecting impostors; and (2) that private citizens help to sponsor an autumn fair to be held annually to obtain funds for private charity.

The time for direct action had arrived. In the summer of 1853, Norton began to draw up a plan for a model lodging-house development in Boston. The project received support from other businessmen, and by winter he had obtained a sum of forty thousand dollars by subscription. Within two years, two five-story brick houses had been constructed and were immediately occupied by twenty families in each house. The rent for these flats ranged from $2.00 to $2.87 a week. He followed the progress of this experiment, and by 1860, Norton felt confident that the venture had been a success. He proudly described the first five years' business record of these houses: they had brought their investors more than thirty thousand dollars in rent; after repairs and depreciation, they had been operated at a profit of 6 per cent; and a new house had been constructed from the proceeds of the first three years. Norton explained the enterprise at some length in an article for the *Atlantic Monthly*. After reminding his readers of "the intimate connection between physical misery and moral degradation," Norton went on to describe the floor plan and architectural features of these lodgings, and to explain their expense and return during the first several years. The entire article carried a tone of satisfaction. It also carried an unwitting undertone of irony: Norton had illustrated for his readers that humanitarianism could be a profit-making business.[12]

Norton's pride in this initial attempt to rid Boston of slum conditions seemed entirely justified at the time. He found hopeful signs that the plan was being imitated by private builders elsewhere. One person had willed fifty thousand dollars to continue the construction of model lodgings. An editorial in the *Boston Advertiser* of September, 1864, acclaimed Norton's housing development a success. At the time, it is true, the pecuniary profit and the admirable conduct of the tenants in these dwellings seemed to promise nothing but good fortune and continued expansion into other housing areas. Yet the unhappy truth is that today Norton's housing development has vanished and the area of Boston at Pleasant Street and Osborn Place continues to be a tenement district. Why did the enterprise eventually collapse? The main reason was probably financial. America was entering a period when men were speculating for much more than 6 per cent. Later experience has shown quite conclusively that low-profit housing developments have no appeal to the American capitalist. Without municipal sponsorship, they could not exist at all. Norton's point about the moral effects which accompanied better housing for the worker is also rather dubious. Either by design or by accident, the occupants of these dwellings were not recruited from the oppressed classes of European immigrants. (Norton endorsed the aims of the Know-Nothing Party, organized in 1853, which called for more stringent naturalization laws as well as the exclusion from public office of foreign-born or Catholic citizens.) Norton himself pointedly observed that "the tenants have been, with few exceptions, Americans by birth, and they have taken pains to keep up the character of their dwellings." [13] Norton's scheme, then, did not prove to be an attractive business venture in later years, nor did it actually support his premise that proper housing would have salient effects on the character and citizenship of the lowest classes of society. It did, however, call to public attention one of the degrading aspects of American society. It also provides a later age with an excellent example of an American businessman who could not enjoy the comfort of a drawing room while he knew that other men lived in desperation and squalor. True, Norton's "humanitarian" concern for workingmen's housing came a bit close to outright Yankee shrewdness. While he preached charity as a social and moral duty, he was at the same time selling charity as something commercially attractive. Or had he sized up his audience and decided that the pursuit of the dollar was the governing motive in their lives — and perhaps a pardonable sin when directed toward a good result? These conjectures aside, Norton deserves to be recognized as one of the first Americans who wrote and worked for more civilized living conditions among the poor.

Improving the lives of the poor through better housing and wider public education was Norton's chief effort in this period of humanitarian reforms. He felt deeply the suffering of the lower classes; but socially he identified himself unmistakably with the aristocracy of New England. The heart of his message, more than anything else, was *noblesse oblige,* realistically blended with enlightened self-interest. He had become a conservative businessman since his college days, and now reminded an Anglo-Saxon ruling class that it behooved them to ease the life of the poor in order to keep the wheels of a stratified society well greased. If on certain occasions he might shame the conscience of the well-heeled, his intonations were not to be mistaken for those of George Ripley, Orestes Brownson, and other disciples of Fourier and St. Simon. In fact, Norton clarified his social philosophy in 1853 by writing (anonymously) his first book, *Considerations on Some Recent Social Theories*. In its pages, he denounced the social doctrines and experiments of St. Simon, Fourier, Pierre Leroux, Robert Owen, Etienne Cabet, and the current popularity of such European political figures as Kossuth, Mazzini, and Louis Blanc.

Two themes dominated the *Social Theories:* (1) Leadership, the locus of power, should rest with an elite rather than with "the people"; and (2) social and economic progress among the lower classes must come slowly in the social order through the moral improvement of man rather than by rational planning.

Norton began with an attack on the political assumption of Mazzini and others that "wisdom and power are derived directly and immediately from the people, — that is, from the great mass of any nation; and consequently, that political liberty is an inherent right of mankind, and that a republic is necessarily the best form of government." Norton regarded this faith in the masses to be painful evidence that "the old doctrine of the divine right of kings has been supplanted by one not less absurd, — the divine right of the people." The masses (Norton wrote) were still without "counsel, restraint, education"; therefore the wisdom of leadership should come from the few rather than from " 'the people' ": "Their progress must be stimulated and guided by the few who have been blessed with the opportunities, and the rare genius, fitting them to lead." The social revolutions in Europe, Norton believed, had accomplished one important result by putting a scare into the aristocracy everywhere and arousing their social conscience:

They have begun to learn the true tenure of [their] possessions, and to understand that no selfish claim to them is sufficient, that no exclusive right to them can be sustained; and that no title to earthly advantages, however ancient and hedged round it may be, is valid, unless it be supported by clearly acknowledged responsibilities and well-performed duties.

As in Disraeli's England (Norton said in effect), so in America could one distinguish "two nations" — the rich and the poor. Norton saw the need "to diffuse the satisfaction of material wants as widely as possible," but the socialist plan "to distribute to each and to demand from each his due proportion, must be the work of some *authority*." Thus Norton's remedy, like Disraeli's, lay in rousing the aristocracy to a sense of its obligation as the born leader of society.[14]

At this point, Norton's second theme bears on his argument. Social and economic reform and "progress" among the poor must be accomplished not by revolutionary change in the "forms" of economic and political control, but slowly through a change in the "spirit" of society from top to bottom:

It will only be when nations learn that Liberty depends not on forms, but on the personal character of the individuals who compose them; that it rests on the virtue, the power of self-government, of each one of the people; that the disadvantages of physical condition must be overcome by continual effort, and not by any sudden impulse or impetuous and quickly exhausted burst; and that freedom is to be preserved only by moral excellence, — it is then alone that they will possess Liberty, for they will have learned that "where the spirit of the Lord is, there is Liberty."

The recent social theorists had adopted an oversimplified view of man and society. They failed to recognize that human society was a complex organism of unequal, interdependent but yet independent, members. And that this organism, without the enlightened leadership of an elite, could only grope about blindly without direction or intelligence. The future of America (Norton concluded) depended on the responsi-

bility of the upper class in rising to the call of duty — to
accept its traditional role as guardian and leader of the nation.

> The trust committed to the hands of the intelligent and the pros-
> perous classes . . . [will insure] the future of their country. It is for
> them to provide against the evils which threaten it, by spreading and
> improving education; by laboring to throw open freely every opportun-
> ity for advantages that may be shared by all; by checking every injustice
> and every corruption; and, above all, — including all — by endeavoring
> to carry into daily life and into common action the spirit of Christian-
> ity.[15]

Considerations on Some Recent Social Theories was Norton's confession of faith in the early 1850's. After several
years of troubled searching, he had temporarily sided with
those who looked for social reform not in granting of more
political power to the masses, but rather through benevolent leadership by the "intelligent and prosperous classes."
Since he did not allow his name to appear on the title page,
the book did not produce the reaction in America which it
otherwise might have. That it created a minor stir in some
other quarters can be inferred from a review which appeared
in the *London Critic*:

> It is certain that the appearance in the great western republic of a
> book essentially, though not avowedly, anti-republican — at best but dis-
> tantly civil to liberty, hostile to equality and absolutely disdainful of
> fraternity, and casting scorn on all the institutional machinery by which,
> according to theorists, any given quantity of ignorance and misery is to
> be spun out into good government and universal happiness — and with
> all this earnest, dispassionate, and evidently not the work of any Catholic
> ecclesiastic or other person interested in the prevalence of arbitrary
> power — is, for the United States, a very noticeable phenomenon.

The appearance of the book during these years of political
revolution and utopian experiments was strategic and gives
it a special historical significance today. Norton's *Considerations on Some Recent Social Theories* deserves more attention from the historians of American thought than it has yet
received.[16]

THE END OF A BUSINESS CAREER; BEGINNINGS OF SCHOLARSHIP

The impetus toward serious scholarship which Norton received from the writing of *Social Theories* might have been slowly dissipated. But on September 18, 1853, after a long illness, Andrews Norton died, and his son, fulfilling a wish of fifteen years, began to edit his father's works. With the assistance of Ezra Abbot, Norton devoted the end of his working days during the next year or more to the tedious job of preparing editorial notes out of manuscript papers, and establishing a table of variant readings. He sent the proofs of *A Translation of the Gospels*, in two volumes, to the printers in 1855, followed by a small book of *Poems* and a larger volume of *Discourses*.

Never short of "projects" in these years, Norton was promoting social causes in one guise or another. In 1854, he served as treasurer for the School of Design for Women, an institution which had been established some two or three years before. Although he complained of public apathy and a depleted treasury, Norton was content that the School was helping women to gain their own economic support. He was also continuing to work for the Evening School. In a letter to Francis Child (who had succeeded E. T. Channing as Boylston Professor of Rhetoric at Harvard), Norton mentioned a public lecture he had given recently to some two hundred Cambridge citizens: "The best result of it is the pouring in of teachers for the Evening School, — and a general flutter of life rattling among the dry bones." [17] To these educational activities can be added one more: on Sundays Norton taught a class at the Unitarian church in Cambridge. He edited two books for the church — *Five Christmas Hymns,* and *A Book of Hymns for Young Persons.*

Probably as relief from a winter of editorial and other labors, Norton traveled south in the spring of 1855 to visit

the plantation of his friends the Middletons of South Carolina. They had met at Newport, Rhode Island, the fashionable
resort where the Nortons had recently built a summer home.
The trip south brought Norton face to face with the slavery
problem in America which, up to then, he had met only in
newspaper accounts of Missouri, Kansas, and Nebraska, or in
the appearance of a random fugitive slave in Boston. His reactions clearly echoed the central themes of his *Social Theories.*
The main issue in the South, Norton held, was not freeing
the Negro. It was the burden of leadership and the effect on
the master who bore the responsibility of a subjected, ignorant laboring class. The plantation system, in short, was oppressive not to the slave so much as to the master. Norton
wrote to his friend Child in Boston:

> If I ever write against slavery, it shall be on the ground not of its
> being bad for the blacks, but of its being deadly to the whites. The
> effect on thought, on character, on aim in life, on hope, is, even in this
> five days' experience of mine, plainly as sad as anything can be — and
> among the women not less than the men.[18]

Norton had even decided, in his second thoughts on India,
that the people of India were better off under British im-
perialist rule than they would be with a "native democracy."
In an article which he was writing for the *North American
Review,* he insisted that the British pattern of government
had been "in the end of greater advantage to the conquered
than to the conquerors." [19] For the South, he concluded
that the master-and-slave relationship was not a political
problem, but a moral one; nor did the solution lie in immediate freedom for an ignorant, leaderless Negro population.

> For my part I see no remedy but gradual and slow progress of the
> true spirit of Christianity, bringing together black and white, quicken-
> ing common sympathies, and by degrees elevating both classes, the one
> from the ignorance and brutality in which it is now sunk, the other from
> the indifference and the blindness of mind in which it rests content.
> But this is a work of ages. I am losing all confidence (if I ever had any)

in the idea that any immediate compulsory measures would improve the condition of either masters or slaves.[20]

The South, however, held its attractions, and Norton, arriving home again in May, wrote to Tom Appleton (Longfellow's brother-in-law), "After the delight of the softest of climates, of indolence, of the most hospitable of friends, we return to — BOSTON." [21]

Andrews Norton's death was decisive in steering the son away from a business life and toward mature scholarship. This progress was natural from the beginning of his business career. He had read widely and by 1855, already had written a respectable number of magazine articles and reviews. Most important, he had lived at Shady Hill amid the intellectual storms that had swept over Cambridge for twenty-five years. He had also become an American host to British writers visiting America. Arthur Hugh Clough, in need of literary employment, had come to America in the early 1850's and lived at Shady Hill. Norton helped to get Clough's poetry published in America, and read the proofs of Clough's *Plutarch* until business affairs forced him to pass them on to Frank Palfrey. Clough wrote back to England in these years, "[Charles Norton] is the kindest creature in the shape of a young man of 25 that ever befriended an emigrant stranger anywhere." [22]

Norton's literary acquaintances in America already included nearly all the great figures of New England's flowering — Longfellow, Whittier, Holmes, Emerson, Hawthorne, Lowell, Parkman, and countless others. There were limits, however, in his literary tastes. He may not have read Thoreau seriously by this time and apparently never met him.[23] American writers outside New England seldom found any favor at Shady Hill in these years. But Norton did read Walt Whitman. We now know that Norton was the anonymous author of one of the most perceptive, and favorable, reviews of the *Leaves of Grass* in 1855.

Leaves of Grass

In the summer of 1855, *Putnam's Monthly*, perhaps at the suggestion of Norton's friend George W. Curtis, who was one of its editors, asked Norton to review *Leaves of Grass* and probably sent him a copy of the poems. The September issue of *Putnam's* carried Norton's review of "this gross yet elevated, this superficial yet profound, this preposterous yet somehow fascinating book." Whitman's "barbaric yawp" sounded, to the son of Andrews Norton, like a New York fireman shouting his own version of some old-fashioned transcendentalism; yet these incongruous elements (Norton wrote) "seem to fuse and combine with the most perfect harmony . . . while there is an original perception of nature, a manly brawn, and an epic directness in our new poet, which belong to no other adept of the transcendental school." [24] As in his vacillations with respect to India and European political revolutionists, Norton's reception of Whitman suggested again the rather violent ups and downs of a disturbed political imagination. Author of the aristocratic *Social Theories* just two years before, Norton now was praising a poet of such lines as "I give the sign of democracy, /by God! I will accept nothing which all cannot have their counterpart of on the same terms."

The depth of Norton's experience in reading Whitman can be measured by an even more unlikely result: inside the cover of his personal copy of *Leaves of Grass*, Norton pasted a poem in his own hand, with interlinear revisions. The verses are striking in several ways. In the first place, the stanza is free verse. Norton had been moving in the direction of free verse for some time. He had visited with Horatio Greenough in Florence during the previous trip to Europe and had read Greenough's ideas of the "organic principle" in art in Tuckerman's *Memorial*. In a letter to Clough, Norton had criticized Matthew Arnold's recent poetry as "too chiselled

and cold, too sculpturesque for our hot and hasty demands." [25]
In addition to being written in free verse, Norton's musings
about a "leaf of grass" echo clearly the cosmic overtones of
transcendentalism:

> In it is the order of all things, in the narrow stem is
> enclosed the mystery of life and of death.
> Its slender flag is the banner on which the names of God
> are inscribed.

Finally, in the lines describing "the boy in the mine, cold,
dirty, hardworked, low-browed, cruel & mean," and again
in the "I go to a factory" stanza, Norton writes with a moder-
ate Whitmanesque empathy for the industrial worker. (See
the Appendix for the full text of the poem.)

Norton may have composed the poem for Lowell. The two
had met some two years before, and had become close friends.
Lowell had now left for a year of study in Germany before assuming Longfellow's chair in Modern Languages at Harvard.
Norton wrote to him shortly after the review of Whitman
appeared and was still deeply moved by the poetry. "There
are some passages of most vigorous and vivid *writing,* some
superbly graphic description, great stretches of imagination
. . . [despite] passages of intolerable coarseness." "I have
got a copy for you," he told Lowell.[26] Lowell's reply was discouraging enough to paralyze Norton's muse in mid-flight
and probably accounts for the semirevised state of the poem:

> No, no, the kind of thing you describe won't do. When a man aims
> at originality he acknowledges himself consciously unoriginal, a want
> of self-respect which does not often go along with the capacity for great
> things. The great fellows have always let the stream of their activity
> flow quietly — if one splashes in it he may make a sparkle, but he mud-
> dies it too, and the good folks down below (I mean posterity) will have
> none of it.[27]

Travel and Study in Europe

Norton might have continued to feel strongly the spirit of
Whitman's America, in spite of the icy reception Lowell had

given the *Leaves of Grass*. But a rapid decline in his health
weakened this mood and altered the direction of his interests.
(When he presently turned briefly again to versifying, the
lines were in regular pentameter, all properly rhymed.) He
had overtaxed his strength in these years, and the month after
his review of Whitman appeared, Norton, accompanied by
his mother and sisters Jane and Grace, left America to spend
nearly two years of travel and rest — and study — in Europe.
William S. Bullard (of Bullard and Lee) who had married
Norton's oldest sister, Louisa, took care of Norton's business
accounts and investments as Norton officially took leave of
the world of business in order (he said) to continue the work
on his father's unpublished papers. In a letter to Bullard,
he explained this decision to abandon the life of a businessman, and sometime philanthropist, for the calling of the
scholar: "Of course I would like to be richer, that I might
gain more power for good; — but I believe that if I live I
shall be able to gain as much influence through other means
as I could through riches." [28]

Just how rich Norton was on the eve of his departure for
Europe is hard to determine. His success as a businessman
certainly had not been spectacular. He had invested an unknown sum of money in an independent business, possibly
cotton, and had seen the entire investment disappear in a
business failure. The experience apparently made him a
timid speculator. In 1854, G. E. Squier, the archeologist-diplo-
mat and also something of a Colonel Sellers, twitted Norton
for lacking the adventurous spirit of an entrepreneur. He had
urged Norton (without success) to become a partner in a projected railroad company to cross Central America from ocean
to ocean. Norton's assets at the time of his sailing in 1855
were probably not large. To meet travel expenses, he planned
to draw on an income in Calcutta goods through Bullard and
Lee, and advised Bullard to put Mrs. Andrews Norton's
property income into account. If the expenses exceeded these

resources, Norton intended to borrow on his insurance policy.

The Nortons landed in England in October, 1855. James Jackson Jarves had given Norton a letter of introduction to Ruskin in order that Norton might see Ruskin's collection of Turners. Although Ruskin soon forgot the meeting, they were to see each other again on the Continent and begin what was to become a significant literary relationship. After a fortnight in London, spent mainly with the Cloughs (he had married after his return to England), the Nortons set out for the Continent. During three weeks in Paris, Norton met Dickens for the first time (at Ary Scheffer's) and renewed his friendship with the Brownings, who were briefly residing in Paris. The Nortons continued their trip southward in a hired private carriage. By late November, 1855, they had progressed to southern France. Their destination was Italy, which Mrs. Norton had never seen and where Norton hoped to find a climate more congenial to his sagging health than the bitter winters of New England. Portions of his travelogue, however, make it clear that the trip would become more than a mere convalescence. It was to be a sentimental pilgrimage into the past — a search for his spiritual home. In the mood of the American exiles who were migrating to Italy in the mid-1850's, Norton described the journey from Nice across the initial heights of the Riviera into Italy:

One of the first of these promontories is that of Capo Sant'Ospizio. A close grove of olives half conceals the old castle on its extreme point. With the afternoon sun full upon it, the trees palely glimmering as their leaves move in the light air, the sea so blue and smooth as to be like a darker sky, and not even a ripple upon the beach, it seems as if this were the very home of summer and of repose. It is remote and secluded from the stir and noise of the world. No road is seen leading to it, and one looks down upon the solitary castle and wonders what stories of enchantment and romance belong to a ruin that appears as if made for their dwelling-place. It is a scene out of *that Italy which is the home of the imagination, and which becomes the Italy of memory.*[29]

Norton's excursion into the Italian past started within days after his arrival in Italy. At Pisa and Florence, he found art works which had faded under the ravages of time and were badly scarred by weather. But in the reverent gaze of an American pilgrim, such scars of time only added to "the solemn beauty and sacred interest . . . which come only with age, softening and harmonizing all that was rough and incongruous." His previous trip and subsequent reading had acquainted Norton with Italian art. But his senses were now quickened anew by the immediate experience in Italy, and he began for the first time to formulate personally his impressions of Italian art history. He found in the paintings at Florence a reflection of the early civic pride of the citizens, and the purity and power of those days "when men painted . . . from their hearts, and the figure of the Saviour stood for the real image of Him who died on the Cross. Those were the days when Florence was capable of the noblest things, — the days just before Dante's time, just before Giotto began to build his Campanile." [30]

Norton's meditations on art clearly were following some of the same paths marked out by Ruskin and the Pre-Raphaelite Brotherhood in England. In addition to *Modern Painters,* which insisted on the "spiritual" basis of art, Norton by this time was probably familiar with Ruskin's other published works, *The Seven Lamps of Architecture* (1849) and *The Stones of Venice* (1851–53). *The Seven Lamps* approached architecture as a history of the national mind as well as an art form capable of producing social change. *The Stones of Venice* again underlined the relation between art and national morality, and analyzed "The Nature of Gothic" to the disparagement of Renaissance art.

In January, 1856, the Nortons had reached Rome. After a visit to the Sistine Chapel, Norton pronounced Michelangelo a genius and a good draftsman, but not a deeply spiritual artist. Along with Titian and Raphael, he was a "forerunner of decay," whose "genius gave just expression to

the character of the Papacy in its period of greatest splendor."
The earlier simplicity and modesty of Giotto and Fra An-
gelico had grown incongruous amid the pomp and world-
liness of Renaissance Italy:

> Instead of being the minister of truth, the purifier of affections, the
> revealer of the beauty of God, art was degraded to the service of ambi-
> tion and caprice, of luxury and pomp, until it became utterly corrupt
> and false.[31]

Thus from the beginning Norton approached art mainly
as an expression of the moral temper of an age. With the
same spirit which inspired his humanitarian programs, he
studied great works of art as moments in the social and moral
advancement of a nation. The decline in modern Italian
art, he found, had resulted from the immoral forces which
acted upon the people of the Renaissance world and were
still alive in Italy. The political despotism and papal corruption of Michelangelo's time persisted in Italy. Norton's social
conscience could not rest "while Milan and Venice are
hemmed round by Austrian bayonets, and Florence is dis-
contented under the stupid despotism of an insane bigot,
— while Rome stagnates under the superstitious priests, and
Naples under the brutality of a Bourbon. . ." He loved the
soft Italian speech of the people and the gentle southern
climate. Cities like Rome were still beautiful with the works
of devoted artists and the eternal regard of nature. But the
present rulers of church and state, "the priests, the princes
and the churches," he found "all alike, untouched by the
sacred genius of the place." Vanity and gaudy spectacle
characterized the Vatican. In an outburst of particularly bad
temper, Norton confided to Lowell, "I think I could roast a
Franciscan with pleasure and it would need only a tolerable
opportunity to make me stab a Cardinal in the dark. . ." [32]

Norton's most vicious attack on the Catholic Church was
political, centering on its suppression of fundamental human
rights. In short, the Roman Church was "un-American":

No theories of government and of religion can be more diametrically in opposition than those prevalent at Rome and in America. As an American, born into the most unlimited freedom consistent with the existence of society — trusting to the result of the prevalence of general freedom, as affording a moral check upon the excesses of individuals, — believing in freedom in the fullest extent, as the divine rule for individual development, — regarding feeling, thought, and speech as having a natural privilege of liberty, — honoring the right of private judgment in all matters, — it is difficult, even at a distance, to regard the system of the Roman Church as being other than a skilful perversion of the eternal laws of right . . .[33]

So Norton, who had recently endorsed the Know-Nothing Party, which would suppress the political liberties of immigrants and Catholics, now assailed Catholicism for suppressing the "natural privilege of liberty" among the people. The switch was characteristic of his uncertain political sympathies in these years. Moreover, it accommodated his interpretation of Italian art history. Norton traced in the rule of a despotic church and state the decline of art in Italy during the Renaissance and after. But his theory of art was not yet clearly defined. It required some ideal referent or symbol which could embody all at once sincerity in art, purity in religion, and an expression of popular will in society and government. Norton soon found what he needed in the architecture of the medieval church.

The Gothic cathedral represented for Norton not only a lifelong devotion of craft to the glory of God, but also the "expressions of the popular faith":

Cathedrals . . . were the work neither of ecclesiastics nor of feudal barons. They represent, in a measure, the decline of feudalism, and *the prevalence of the democratic element in society*. No sooner did a city achieve its freedom than its people began to take thought for a cathedral . . . When the democratic element was subdued, as in Cologne by a Prince Bishop, or in Milan by a succession of tyrants, the cathedral was left unfinished. When, in the fifteenth century, all over Europe, the turbulent, but energetic liberties of the people were suppressed, the building of cathedrals ceased.[34]

For a specific instance of his argument, Norton chose the

Duomo at Orvieto. In the story of its construction during the fourteenth century, he found confirmation for his thesis. The constitution of the city, he observed, "seems to have been democratic, except in so far as the powers of the elective magistracy were subordinate to the authority of the Pope, or of his delegates." Only a popular government, and a deep religious fervor, could have impelled the citizens to erect this colossal monument to their faith. Some of the carts filled with stone and marble were pulled by buffalo from landing points on the Adriatic and Mediterranean. Others came from north and south, over mountain passes and down barren slopes to the valley below Orvieto. The final distance up the hill to the cathedral site was then pulled by "voluntary labor." The popular faith inspired the Orvietan artists — the master builder, the painters and sculptors — and these artists, in turn, helped to direct and elevate the overflowing religious energies of the people. "The work of the artist was not so much to embody his individual imaginings in independent and original designs," Norton wrote, "as to give to the common and accepted types such elevation, such power and beauty, as lay within the compass of his genius to conceive and to exhibit." The same devout spirit of craftsmanship pervaded the lesser decorative arts of mosaics and wood-inlaying, and continued throughout the many years when the piety of the citizens remained at full tide. Near the end of the fourteenth century, however, a decline in this spirit began to appear at Orvieto. Gothic art was failing at Orvieto and throughout Italy, "not more through the inability of her artists than through the change in the spirit and the decline in the temper of her people, of which this inability was one of the marked consequences and indications." [35]

Through the image of the cathedral, Norton had begun to renew his hope in the "democratic element in society." Also, he was able to give precision to his critique of Italian art and society. He showed only mild discomfort over possible contradictions in the hypothesis that the cathedral was a "democratic" monument of art inspired by an age of faith. He noted in passing that Orvieto's self-government was in fact subordinate to papal authority; that citizens received "special incitements" in the form of indulgences for "voluntary" contributions of labor and money; that enforced contributions were obtained from legacies, and in tributes exacted from towns and feudal lords subject to the town of Orvieto; and that "minor" motives of personal ambition, and of civic rivalry (with Siena, which was building a cathedral during the same century) may have contributed to the enthusiasm and success of the undertaking. But these qualifications of the spontaneity and extent of popular will were only minor difficulties which Norton admitted and then dismissed. In the story of the medieval cathedral, he had found rich source material for later scholarship and social criticism.[36]

Norton's health was improving, and in April, 1856, Lowell came down from Dresden to join Norton and two other friends on an arduous two-hundred-mile mule trip in Sicily. On their return to Rome in late May, the year was running out for the Nortons. They made plans for the trip northward, and in early summer Norton had moved his family to Switzerland. In July, in the cabin of a steamer sailing down Lake Geneva from Vevay to Geneva, they met the man whose writing had played the most important part in Norton's aesthetic and historical understanding of painting and architecture — John Ruskin. In his later autobiographical memoirs (*Praeterita*) Ruskin described this meeting with Norton as the two families sat near each other in the ship's cabin: "I noticed that from time to time the young American cast somewhat keen, though entirely courteous, looks of scrutiny at my father and mother." Since Ruskin had not remembered their meeting during the previous October, Norton reintroduced himself and his family to the Ruskins. The two families immediately engaged in a friendly and spirited conversation which lasted until the boat docked at Geneva. Ruskin's account of the meeting gives an interesting description of Norton's appearance and personality. Physical traits Ruskin later remembered vividly were "the bright eyes, the melodious voice, the perfect manner . . . [and] the sweetest quiet smile I ever saw on any face (unless, perhaps, a nun's, when she has some grave kindness to do) . . ." They arranged to meet again at St. Martin's, for Ruskin had discovered what for him was the most unlikely of friends — an American who was generous, acute and urbane:

[He was] a man of the highest natural gifts, in their kind; observant and critical rather than imaginative, but with an all-pervading sympathy and sensibility, absolutely free from envy, ambition, or covetousness: a scholar from his cradle, nor only now a *man* of the world, but a *gentleman* of the world, whom the highest born and best bred of every nation, from the Red Indian to the White Austrian, would recognize in a moment, as of their caste.

He regarded Norton as his superior "in every branch of classical literature" and found that the young American had not only read, but had also *tested* the theory of *Modern Painters* with "all the sympathy, and all the critical subtlety" of his scholarly — though nonimaginative — mind. Ruskin ended this portrait of Norton in 1856 with affection and praise: "And thus I became possessed of my second friend, after Dr. John Brown, and of my first real tutor, Charles Eliot Norton." [37]

After Norton arrived in London the next month, he consulted a doctor and was advised to spent another winter in Italy. He had hoped to sail with his family to America where the slavery issue was dominating the fall political elections. But England offered compensations. He toured once more the cathedral towns, the castles with their Italian art treasures, visited often with Ruskin, the Storys (whom he had met in Rome), and the Cloughs, and met Matthew Arnold, Thackeray, and Thackeray's daughters. In November, shortly before departing for Paris, Norton had an experience which

brought new conflict to his unsettled political and social outlook. He attended a lecture given to the London working
classes by the Chartist leader, John Ernest Jones. Eight years
before, it will be remembered, Norton's sympathies had leaned
toward the social revolutionists in Europe and the supporters
of Chartism in England. But in the years between, he had
seen India and Europe and had developed a more complex
view of human nature and the social organism. He shared
with Ruskin the concept of art as a moral force in an industrial society, and recognized the desperation of England's
laboring classes; yet he could not quite identify himself with
them and their leaders, or with the political aims of socialism.
He set down his impressions of the Chartist meeting in a
letter to Lowell which revealed the conflicting sympathies in
Norton's social philosophy:

> The hall was full of a dirty and ill-looking audience; there were
> some of the burly brutal pothouse and gin-palace set, some of the thin,
> sickly excitable workmen, with pale wives in tawdry dresses. It was
> rather a sad sight, . . . and [the crowd's] appearance was a bitterer
> denunciation of the social system than anything which Mr. Ernest Jones
> or any other ranting orator could utter against it.[38]

Within weeks, Norton was on his way south to live one
more winter under the warmer skies of Italy. His health was
failing, it seems, from no more specific ailment than the loss
of physical strength. Poor health did not seem to enfeeble
his energies for study, however. His mind had been quickened by the stimulation of his travels and the long talks with
Ruskin. He had written to Lowell:

> I go back to Rome as to a dear old friend; we have not got to get
> acquainted; no tedious preliminaries, no uncertainties; we know each
> other's hearts. I mean to go to Ravenna, to Ancona, to all named and
> unnamed places in Italy; to leave nothing that is worth seeing unseen,
> and if on my return I find that anybody has seen things in Italy that I
> have not, I shall be sure that they were not worth seeing.[39]

The return to Rome marked the beginning of another
aspect of Norton's future life as a scholar — his studies and

translations of Dante. A notebook which he kept in December, 1856, contains the words "Vita Nuova," together with references to the poem. In Rome once again, he began to collect books on Dante, and on New Year's night of 1857, he wrote to Lowell:

> I am amusing myself with making a translation of the "Vita Nuova." The more familiar I become with it, the more lovely does it seem to me, and the fuller of an exquisite spirit of tenderness, grace, and simplicity. One can hardly appreciate rightly the "Divina Commedia" without knowing this first.

During these final months in Italy, Norton was able to express more clearly than before his feelings toward Italian society and post-Renaissance art. He saw with renewed despair the enervating effects of political intrigue and a totalitarian church. The poverty of the lower classes, and their political impotence, was so hopeless that even the attempt at revolution was impossible. Small wonder that the Italian imagination had dried up: "A modicum of liberty is essential for the development of literature and art. When political and spiritual despotism combine, a vacuum is produced in which thought and imagination die out, and all the qualities of manly character dwindle and decay." In the age of Giotto and Dante, Norton wrote,

> when Italy contained great men, capable of great works, the political life of the people had not ceased, and the authority of the Church had not pinned up their minds within its narrow walls of creed. Florence, which, during a period of three centuries of political turbulence and activity, produced a succession of the most distinguished poets, historians and artists, has not, during the last two hundred years of political servitude, given birth to one genius of the first order.

Norton again skirted the difficulties in his theory. For were not the minds of men also being liberated in the fifteenth century from the narrow medieval world, with its confining boundaries of heaven and hell? In Norton's reconstruction of the age, this dispersal of religious authority had created only an atmosphere of "aimless restlessness." The medieval Church had ruled the lives of the people only to the extent of directing into productive channels the religious energies released during the age. The expanded boundaries of the Renaissance world had only served to shrink the imagination. The invention of printing in the fifteenth century seemed "rather to have depressed than to have stimulated the development of original thought." The medieval imagination with its innocent freshness and vitality had vanished with the corrupting influence of Renaissance immorality and a prodigal taste for the literature of "pseudo-classicism":

> The immorality of the period found not only a stimulus, but an excuse, in the old literature now extolled as divine. The authority of antiquity was invoked in favor of a looser code of morals, and of a more accommodating philosophy, than those which had Heaven and Hell for their final terms.[40]

Again, was not the fifteenth century also the time of Lorenzo the Magnificent, the poet and patron of the arts? The age of Lorenzo, Norton affirmed, was "a gilded rather than a golden age. Lorenzo is called the patron of letters and of art; but when letters and art need a patron, it is because they have lost their natural vigor." In that age of pampered luxury, Italy (in Norton's opinion) had lost her rugged spirit — the "rough sincerities" — which had found expression in the Gothic style:

> Passions were becoming subjected to the control of manners, expression was losing its force under the relaxation of refinement, enthusiasm was yielding to indifference. The rough sincerities, the hard fights, the hearty loves and hates, the coarse life, the brilliant shows, the long romances of feudalism and chivalry, were drawing to an end.

Norton's other comments on Renaissance "dilettantism," its "vulgar" and merely decorative art, and the lack of genuine passion in artist and audience — all these themes foreshadowed his commentary on art during a later "gilded age" in his own country.[41]

In mid-April, Norton bade farewell to the Storys, Aubrey de Vere (Irish poet and Catholic convert whom he had met

at the Storys'), and other friends in Rome. He accompanied
Mrs. Gaskell and her daughter northward as far as Venice,
where they parted, Norton staying behind to study the paintings at Venice and Verona. In May, he left Italy and passed
through Germany, which he found dull in comparison with
Italy. (Lowell's opposite opinion forms an interesting contrast. Returning to Dresden after their mule expedition in
Sicily, he wrote to Norton: "When I saw the firs and pines
and mountain ashes, I felt what a Northern and homely soul
I was, and that the South is, after all, only an exile to me." [42])
After a brief stop at Paris, Norton crossed the Channel to
spend the summer months in England. New literary friendships formed in London during the summer: Coventry Pat-
more, the Rossettis, and at the Brownings' (living in the home
of the late John Kenyon) two young men named Morris and
Burne-Jones. Before he sailed to America, he attended the
Manchester Exhibition and a semi-private showing of Pre-
Raphaelite paintings. His enthusiasm for the work of Dante
Rossetti was instantaneous. He commissioned the Society's
leader to do a painting (for fifty guineas) as well as a portrait
of Ruskin. Most important of all these friendships in future
years, of course, was the one with Ruskin, whom Norton
visited at Ruskin's home, Denmark Hill, and again during
long hikes together at Oxford.

The friendships Norton had formed during these two
years helped to stimulate his interest in the history and principles of art, but as Ruskin remarked, Norton tested earlier
theories of art by making his own original investigations.
Norton was neither a "hero-worshipper" of the literary men
of Europe nor the "satellite" of Ruskin and his circle, as later
critics have alleged. That his relation to Ruskin (his senior
by eight years) was anything but servile is proven decisively
in Ruskin's own words:

. . . Norton saw all my weaknesses, measured all my narrownesses,
and, from the first, took serenely, and as it seemed of necessity, a kind

of paternal authority over me, and a right of guidance, . . . and to me, his infinitely varied and loving praise became a constant motive to exertion, and aid in effort: yet he never allowed me in the slightest violation of the laws, either of good writing, or social prudence, without instant blame, or warning.[43]

Ruskin's dependence on Norton as a friend was at times excessive. During the fall of 1856 in London, Norton recalled that "few days passed in which [Ruskin] did not send me a note . . . or come to my parlor, laden with books and drawings for my amusement, or carry me off in his brougham for an hour or two at Denmark Hill." Ruskin's letters after that time show that his need for Norton's friendship could become almost obsessive: "Dear Norton, — Glad, and glad, and glad again have I been of your letters —" and "I wish you would come here once again — I *need* you now. I only enjoyed you before." [44]

Another English writer whom Norton saw frequently on this European trip, Mrs. Elizabeth Gaskell, held his learning and his friendship in the same high regard. They had met often in Rome in the spring of 1857 at the home of their mutual friend, William Wetmore Story. Meta Gaskell (the daughter) remembered Norton's custom on these meetings of bringing flowers "with the true American generosity and courtesy." But his main role was that of a tutor: "He constantly joined us in our sight-seeing, and we learned from him, more vividly than any book on art could teach, all the deep principles of painting and sculpture." When the Gaskells returned to Italy some years later, they carried along as a guidebook the *Notes of Travel and Study in Italy,* Norton's first attempt to formulate a moral and "democratic" explanation of art history.[45]

Norton's progress from business to scholarship covered eleven years of widely varied activity at home and abroad. Like many another young American in his twenties, Norton was restless and apparently adrift in these years. Certain patterns begin to take shape, however. His interests in education — the Evening School, the School of Design for Women, the Unitarian Sunday School — all point to a humanitarian sense of public duty. So, too, does his agitation for improved housing for the lower classes. Though his concern for the poor remains strong, we notice a shift in his ideology from the "republican" sympathies of his early twenties to a more traditional family conservatism. The shift accompanies his advancing career in business and explains his second thoughts on European revolutionary figures, British imperialism in India, Chartism in England, as well as his approval of Know-Nothingism. His anonymous *Considerations on Some Recent Social Theories* (1853) sets forth his social philosophy of leadership through an enlightened aristocracy. The sudden enthusiasm for Whitman, however, serves a warning that these social opinions may not yet be settled convictions. Beginning contributions to scholarship appear early in his editorial help on *The Oregon Trail*, the articles in *North American Review,* and the editions of Andrews Norton's works. Equally decisive in drawing him away from the business world are the many new friendships he forms in America and during the two extended trips abroad. The list includes virtually every major writer in England and New England. These relationships also give important clues to Norton's character and temperament. During these years he is frequently stern and severely honest with those who are closest to him, for he was by temperament inclined to adopt a paternal role in his friendships, even with older men like Ruskin, Lowell, and George Curtis. That he later was to become literary executor of all three reveals the high value which they placed on his friendship. For his occasional severity with them, aside from giving the measure of his faithful concern as a friend, was to provide the stimulus for some of their best efforts.

Finally, these eleven years shape Norton's opinions on the world of art. The social conscience which guides him as a businessman-humanitarian also determines his approach to art as primarily a reflection of the moral climate of an age. His growth can be measured by contrasting his deference to Browning on matters of taste in 1850 and the confident pronouncements which impress Ruskin during the second trip. So in 1857, after nearly two years of intensive original study in the history of art, Norton was coming home to begin a long career of art criticism and instruction in a young country sorely in need of both.

III

THE JOURNALIST AND CIVIL WAR OPTIMISM

We shall come out of this war with . . . new reason for
trust in the political instincts and intentions of an instructed
and intelligent people. We shall have given proof of the
possession by a free popular government of those very qualities which it has been commonly though erroneously supposed such a government was incapable of exhibiting.

(Norton writing in the *North
American Review*, October, 1864)

THE ATLANTIC MONTHLY

Norton had left Italy and was on his way north across
Europe in May, 1857, when he received a letter from Lowell
announcing the plan to found a new magazine in Boston. In
the same month, Lowell and other Bostonians, including
Francis Underwood, Cabot, Motley, Longfellow, Holmes,
Emerson, and Phillips (the publisher) had gathered at a
dinner to discuss the enterprise. Underwood, the prime mover
of the plan, had just persuaded the wary publisher Phillips
to underwrite this doubtful venture. Underwood nominated
Lowell to be the first editor and offered to serve as Lowell's
office assistant.

Norton replied from Paris and offered his services both
as a contributor and as a solicitor of articles from British
friends. But like some of the others connected with the venture, he could see only faint hope that it might last in the
land of novelty and change:

It would be a great thing for us if any undertaking of this kind could live long enough to get affections and associations connected with it, whose steady glow should take the place of, and more than supply, the shine of novelty, and the dazzle of a first go-off. I wish we had a Sylvanus Urban a hundred and fifty years old. I wish, indeed, we had anything so old in America; I would give a thousand of our new lamps for the old one, battered, but true magical light.[1]

In England during July, Norton encountered Clough, Mrs. Gaskell, Rossetti, Morris, and others and obtained a trunk of manuscripts to send to Lowell. Upon his return to America in August, Norton learned that the trunk had been lost. The new magazine, presently christened the *Atlantic Monthly,* was therefore compelled, by a lucky accident, to rely on American writers for the success of the first number. Eight or nine months after its disappearance, the trunk was discovered intact among a pile of baggage in a Liverpool hotel. But meanwhile the *Atlantic* had begun to establish its reputation for drawing on some of the foremost literary and editorial minds in America.

Norton's intimate connection with the birth of the *Atlantic* marked the beginning of a ten-year period of influence in American journalism. During these crucial years in America's history, Norton exerted all the energies of his mind and heart to the shaping of public character and popular opinion, first as a writer for the *Atlantic* and editor for the Loyal Publication Society; then as co-editor (with Lowell) of the *North American Review* during and after the war; and finally as a founder of the *Nation.*

Norton's contributions as a writer for the *Atlantic Monthly* were sporadic for several reasons. Weak health continued to plague him after his return from Europe in the summer of 1857. He was unable to join his fellow members of the Adirondack Club, a small camping group which included Lowell, Longfellow, Emerson, Agassiz, William J. Stillman (the artist and editor of *The Crayon* art journal), and Samuel G. Ward (the Boston banker). Throughout 1858, he lived as a semi-invalid in the family's summer home at Newport and was, for the most part, out of touch with the magazine. Despite his convalescence, however, Norton managed to have an article for virtually every number of the magazine during these months. His offerings in 1859 were slim, for he was seeing through the press both his *Vita Nuova* and the *Notes of Travel and Study in Italy*. Thereafter, he steadily contributed articles and reviews until 1861, when Lowell stepped down as editor of the *Atlantic*.

Norton's main writings in the *Atlantic Monthly* during its first years fell into two divisions: essays and reviews on art and scholarship; and articles on the war crisis and its effect on the character of the American people.

American taste in the arts had not occupied Norton's attention in his earlier years of humanitarian reform. On his first European trip, he had resented the superior attitude of foreign travelers who ridiculed the crude tastes of his countrymen. Norton wrote to his family from Milan:

> We hear much about the taste and reverence for works of art among the lower classes on the continent, — and we have heard much also about the ridiculous passion among our own countrymen to write their names upon all conspicuous or noted places. — Now the desecration of works of Art . . . and the amount of scribbling that there is upon all public buildings here . . . quite equals, I was about to say much exceeds, anything I have ever seen at home.

He was a chauvinist and freely admitted, "I like to defend my countrymen even from the smallest of unjust accusations." [2]

A steady maturing of his own taste brought about a change in his attitude five years later on the second trip to Europe. "I am fond and proud of my countrymen," Norton wrote (to Tom Appleton), but he was annoyed at seeing them in art galleries, as well as in shops and cafes, for they spoiled a "pure taste" of Europe.[3] The next year he wrote with even stronger distaste for American tourists, "utterly ignorant of art," who came to Europe and were promptly hoodwinked into buying fake "originals":

It is no matter of surprise that our best artists find but little encouragement, and that Art is considered among us generally as a matter of little importance, when one sees, by such evidence as is afforded by American travellers in Italy, the average level of American taste and the depth of American ignorance.[4]

Several months afterward, he referred again to American ignorance of art, though a recent incident had made him feel somewhat more kindly toward his countrymen. In Rome he had accompanied the Storys to an opera (Donizetti's *Roberto Devereux*), and found the Italian opera-goers more judicious than Americans, but also more "brutal." In true European fashion, the Italian audience had hissed and groaned after the prima donna missed a critical high note:

If one has to pay for an audience with fine critical ears the penalty of seeing them cruel to a woman because the artist in her fails, let me rather have our dull unmusical, uncritical American audiences who know nothing and care nothing about art, but are tender to a woman's efforts and cheer her failures.[5]

On Norton's return to America in August, 1857, he was struck once again by the contrast between life in Europe and the "deficiencies" of life in his own country. His love for America remained constant, but he recognized the work which had to be done. He wrote to Child:

The contrast between America and Europe never struck me so forcibly as it does now. The grandeur of our opportunities is proportional to the immensities of our deficiencies, — so that one may rejoice to be an American even while seeing how far we fall short in many ways of what is accomplished elsewhere, and how much we have to do to make life what it ought to be and might be. But to be contented here one must work.[6]

Two of America's chief deficiencies, Norton believed, were neglect of the arts and meager results in scholarship. His efforts to remove these shortcomings in American life appeared in the pages of the *Atlantic Monthly* during the next several years.

The initial number of the *Atlantic* carried Norton's criticism of the Manchester Art Exhibition, which he had attended just before sailing to America. The opening paragraph of the article revealed Norton's intention — to instruct his readers on the function of art in society. After passing through the scenes of dirt and ugliness in bustling Manchester, he had entered the Exhibition hall and was there immediately engulfed by the rare world of the artist. Point by point, he contrasted the eternal beauty of the artist's work to the fleeting impressions of life and beauty in the industrial metropolis outside. Continuing in this didactic vein, he turned to a criticism of the individual paintings. The later Raphael was well represented, but not his early works, which, Norton pointed out, were executed during Raphael's years of deep moral sincerity. The Bolognese school was overly plentiful and reflected a time when religious feeling — and therefore artistic power — was at a low ebb. From the later schools of painting in England which were represented, Norton singled out the Pre-Raphaelites, and praised especially their union of nature and religion. None of Rossetti's work was displayed, so Norton discussed Rossetti's absent paintings. He concluded with the premonition that the future of the Pre-Raphaelite school, and all modern art, would be very bleak:

> The times in which we are living are not fitted to develope [sic] and confirm the qualities on which the best results of art depend. Ours is neither an age of composure nor of faith. It urges speedy results; it desires effective, rather than simple, truthful work.[7]

Several months later, Norton resumed his teaching Americans the facts of art history, and in particular, the lesson of art in the depraved Renaissance times. The moral deterioration of the age had left its stamp even on the works of such men of genius as Michelangelo:

> The decline of religious faith . . . [can] be predicated from the

"Last Judgment" in the Sistine Chapel; . . . the luxury and pomp of the Papal Court and Church are manifest in the architecture of St. Peter's, whose dome is swollen with earthly pride; the ceiling of the Sistine Chapel betrays the recoil toward heathenism from the vices and corruptions that then hung round Christianity; and the Sacristy of San Lorenzo is the saddest and grandest exhibition that those days afforded of the infidelity into which the best men were forced.[8]

Not Michelangelo, but Dante, illustrated the sincerity, the modesty and simplicity of art that Norton was preaching to American readers of the *Atlantic Monthly.* In January and February of 1859, the magazines carried two portions of Norton's translations and commentary on the *Vita Nuova.* During this earlier age, said Norton, the bursting energies of commercial Florence had been directed by men of integrity and genius. The simple grace of the *Vita Nuova* reflected the age's integrity and sincerity of feeling. Norton contrasted Dante with the writer of "sentimental" literature in nineteenth-century America who "steadily exhibits the influence of factitious feeling, of self-conscious effort, and of ambitious display." [9]

Norton's criticism took one further turn in 1859. The modern spirit in America, he asserted, appeared not only in deficiencies of her literature and painting, but also in American architecture. In his review of *The Oxford Museum* by Henry Acland and John Ruskin, Norton bemoaned the absence in America of a single building capable of "stimulating the imagination to new conceptions, and nerving the will to large efforts." Foreshadowing his famous later criticism of Harvard architecture, Norton cited the Museum of Comparative Zoology that was being built at Harvard, and compared it unfavorably to Oxford's. At Harvard, mere utility had been the overriding concern. External beauty (by which Norton probably meant the Gothic form and embellishments of the Oxford Museum) had been ignored in a building which might have inspired later generations of Harvard men to emulate the lofty conceptions of their forefathers.

In America, monuments to inspire national pride were being erected in the form of "extravagant stores and steamboats, — in the lavish and selfish adornment of drawing rooms and chambers." In this bad humor, Norton wrote America off as a land "barren and naked," adding, "We exhibit in our civilization neither the taste nor the capacity for any noble works of art." [10]

What conditions were lacking in America for a full play of the creative powers? Norton was moving toward an answer some months later in his review of Lord Vernon's latest Dante studies. The primary need in America, Norton felt, was a body of scholars capable of the higher criticism which "makes thought accurate and perception fine." Norton was telling Americans what Matthew Arnold four years later in his famous essay would say to England — that mature criticism was urgently needed to provide a spiritual and intellectual setting in which the artist could live. "[Such criticism] adds truth to the creations of imagination by teaching the modes by which they may be best expressed, and it thus leads to fuller and more appreciative understanding and enjoyment of the noblest works of the past. There can, indeed, be no thorough culture without it." Norton concluded with an appeal to his readers to help establish this atmosphere of learning in America by turning from the pursuit of wealth to the cultivation of their minds. The futility of his plea can perhaps be imagined:

> To restore the balance of our lives, in these days of haste, novelty, and restlessness, there is need of a larger infusion into them of pursuits which have no end of immediate publicity or instant return of tangible profit, — of pursuits which, while separating us from the intrusive world around us, should introduce us into the freer, tranquiller, and more spacious world of noble and everlasting thought.[11]

In another review of the same year, Norton lamented England's uncontested superiority over America in scholarly studies. Certain native philosophers (he did not name them) had pioneered in the old fields of error and had upturned the soil on "the fallen leaves of decayed beliefs." But America, he asserted (pursuing the metaphor), had failed to supply a disciplined band of scholars "who are to follow the pioneers and do the higher and more lasting constructive work of civilization. In tones strongly echoing Emerson's "American Scholar," Norton regretted America's reliance on foreign thinkers:

> Now, as in past times, we must be content, so far as we may, to have this work done by the thinkers and scholars of other lands. But how long is this to last? Is the same sort of makeshift to be allowed in the processes of American thought, which in the expanse of our territory we have allowed in the processes of material labor? [12]

The same theme dominated his writing for the next issue when he reviewed an English edition of the unpublished minor works of Roger Bacon. Such a volume might have discouraged another reviewer. Not so for Norton. He extended the review into a fourteen-page essay on the life and work of this astonishing thirteenth-century scholar. Despite the ignorance of his times, the lack of materials for scholarship, the bad translations or none at all, Bacon's learning was encyclopedic. He deserved the respect of more fortunate students in America whose opportunities for sound and thorough scholarship were far more favorable than Bacon's. For Bacon, with all these impediments to learning (and unlike men in a later age), had been willing to forsake wordly gain in favor of the pursuit of knowledge.

In Norton's articles and reviews during the first four years of the *Atlantic Monthly,* one begins to sense the capacity and rapid development of a scholarly, critical mind. His tenacious memory, which would astonish some of his later contemporaries, had already enabled him to master in detail a wide range of subjects. When called on to review any work containing careless errors of fact, his precise criticism could also become particularly trenchant. Books which were inattentive to truth or displayed shoddy learning brought from him the angry epithets of "ignorance," "disgrace," "fraud," "incompetence," and "dishonesty." His praise of scholars could be as impassioned as his censure. The ideal man of intellect, however, he found not among his contemporaries, but in the age of Bacon and Dante. The latter's significance to a modern age, Norton told the readers of the *Atlantic,* lay in his blend of the poet, scholar, and statesman. Here was a learned poet also active in the political affairs of his time. The magnitude of Dante's character and achievement seemed to dwarf, by contrast, the stature of modern man:

> The tendency of modern civilization is to diminish rather than to strengthen the originality and independence of individuals. Autocracy and democracy seem to have a like effect in reducing men to a uniform level of thought and effort.[13]

Norton's second major service as a contributor to the *Atlantic Monthly* was closely related to this concern for the personal character of citizens in a "democracy." As war became more imminent, Norton grew increasingly convinced that the survival of the union rested upon the character of the people rather than on any superiority of American political institutions.

To his political articles for the *Atlantic,* Norton brought a ripening judgment gained from years of close attention to domestic politics. During February of 1846, while yet a student at Harvard, he had made a trip south into New York, Baltimore, and Washington, and was particularly aroused by the issues of the Oregon question, which was then being debated in Congress. Three years later, he had traveled to Washington to attend the inauguration of President Taylor. Also on this trip, he had heard John Calhoun debate the slavery question on the Senate floor. Norton's interest in the slavery issue probably was sharpened during the trip, for in the 1850's the South frequently occupied a central place in his writing. He took an early stand against slavery, but this opposition was complicated by the family's friendship with the slave-holding Middletons of South Carolina. It was further complicated by his attraction to Southern society and tradition. During his trip into the South in 1855, he admitted a strong attachment to the charming atmosphere of age and leisurely repose which he found in Charleston. This was not America with her "compact and uniform" cities and restless acquisitive instincts. It was Italy:

The climate, the southern habits, the social arrangements all give a picturesqueness in their separate ways, and there is a fine air of age, and dusty decay which invests whole streets with the venerableness of the past. — It is like Italy in the feeling that belongs to it, — and ought to have painters and poets. The air is full of indolence, and the sense of repose finds everywhere a gratification to which it is unused in our sharp driving, restless North.

But after living a few days on the Middleton's cotton plantation on Edisto Island near Charleston, Norton realized that the way of life in the South, for all its attractiveness and apparent contrast to the Northern commercial spirit, rested finally on the unfeeling exploitation of the Negro race. In his second thoughts on plantation life, Norton regarded the price of its leisure and refinement as too costly. The "sense of repose," in fact, seemed rather like a "moral miasma" which hovered over the society. It was most deadly in the effect on the Southern gentry, for they were growing steadily more blind to all the dictates of humane reason.[14] Norton's reaction was strikingly similar to Henry Adams' ambivalent response to the prewar South. Adams wrote:

Slavery struck him in the face; it was a nightmare; a horror; a crime; the sum of all wickedness! Contact made it only more repulsive . . . ; and yet the picture had another side. The May sunshine and shadow had something to do with it; the thickness of foliage and the heavy smells had more; . . . and the brooding indolence of a warm climate and a negro population hung in the atmosphere heavier than the catalpas.[15]

Norton's opposition to the "peculiar institution" was based

on humane if not strictly egalitarian feelings. His work for the *Atlantic Monthly* in 1860 and the year after, reflected the complex development of his outlook on the impending war against slavery. Subjecting one human being as the legal "property" of another in a Christian society deadened the moral feelings of slave and master alike. But the prospect of seeing the free Negro in American society chilled Norton's enthusiasm for emancipation. In a review of Anthony Trollope's *The West Indies and the Spanish Main* (March, 1860), Norton underlined the problems arising from emancipation of the Negro in the West Indies. The Negro's initiative to work, his responsibilities and privileges as a free citizen — these were concerns that now faced the West Indian society.

In another review, Norton was even more restrained in discussing emancipation. Commenting on a new book, *The Laws of Race, as Connected with Slavery,* Norton supported the view that "the black is in many of his endowments inferior to the white," though humane feelings urged the white to improve the moral and intellectual condition of the Negro. Norton objected not to the subjection of the Negro; he felt merely that the slave system in the South was an amoral form of subjection. A further objection to the slave trade was that it appeared to be propagating an inferior race in America at an alarming speed: "It is the question . . . whether the country shall be occupied a century hence by a civilized or by a barbarous race." [16]

Norton, then, was no champion of racial equality, and he dreaded the Negro's eventual freedom; still, he held the unwavering conviction that slavery was morally wrong and must be abolished. The political and social problems of emancipation, however, would have to be solved in their own time. Norton's immediate concern was the psychological readiness of the North for the war he now believed to be inevitable. Several months after John Brown's raid on

Harper's Ferry, Norton reviewed for the *Atlantic* James Red-path's biography of Brown. Norton now turned to instruct an irresponsible North on her proper role in the critical months ahead. He regretted the tone of the fire-eater which Redpath had adopted, nor was he willing to condone the lawless methods which Brown had employed. But Norton did recognize in Brown an instance of noble character in a man of the people. The violent raid on Harper's Ferry was a wrong committed by a good man, he wrote. Brown's cause was just, and his life taught a moral lesson to all his country-men severely in need of "more manliness, more uprightness, more courage and simplicity in our common lives." In Brown, Norton found one trait in particular which was noticeably absent in the lives of Americans — a capacity for suffering: " 'Suffering is a gift not given to every one,' wrote one of the Covenanters, who was hanged in the Grassmarket in Edinburgh, in 1684." [17]

The redemptive power of suffering was a theme Norton had developed briefly in his studies in the Italian Renais-sance. Italy had declined in art and character during the fifteenth century because "she had lost the capacity of moral suffering, and she sought relief from harass in self-forgetfulness among the delights of sensual enjoyment." [18] When Norton had returned to America in 1857, the country was in the middle of a depression. The Renaissance parallel may have been alive in his mind then as he wrote to Clough, "I am glad of the present difficulties. They make men stop and consider, and they will, for a few years at least, check the social extravagance which had reached a ridiculous, and sometimes pathetic, excess." To Clough again now before actual war with the South, Norton hoped that "the nature of these difficulties, the principles involved in them, and the trials that accompany them, will develop a higher tone of feeling and a nobler standard of character than have been common with us of late." Norton expressed his deepest sorrow over the tragedy and desolation which imminent war would soon bring. Would the people be able to meet the demands of sacrifice and courage required by a war? He wrote to Clough:

How is it all to end? I believe, somehow for good. But the commercial spirit is very strong with us at the North, and the corruption of long prosperity very manifest. We have need of a different temper from that which prevails, before we can reap much good from our present troubles.[19]

The test began two days later. On April 12, 1861, the Confederate Army fired the opening shot of the war at Fort Sumter. Almost immediately, Norton sensed a change in the spirit of the people. In slightly more than one month he wrote again to Clough describing the pervasive bond of unity which had suddenly formed in the North. This spirit was not "the sudden contagion of a short-lived popular excitement," Norton now confidently asserted. Rather, Fort Sumter had awakened all of the best qualities which had lain dormant in the American people. The letter revealed how thin the line was between Norton's affirmative view of America and his fearful misgivings. Clough himself might well have questioned the permanence of this sudden confidence in the American people whose character his friend so recently had censured. For Norton was now writing, "All their self-respect, their intelligence and conservative love of liberty, and their sense of responsibility for the safety of the blessings of freedom and of popular government, were stirred to their very depth." [20]

Within two months, Norton's new faith in the people had grown even stronger. After the Northern defeat at Bull Run, he watched the Union temper harden with greater resolution to wage a victorious war. "I believe the people will save the country and the government," he wrote to George Curtis; and to Mrs. Gaskell in England, "If the further course of the war should be very difficult its results will be the greater. . .

We are at the beginning of a most difficult but also a most inspiriting period in our history." [21]

The next number of the *Atlantic Monthly* (September, 1861) carried Norton's "The Advantages of Defeat." In the article, he publicly praised the American people for the reasons he had mentioned in his private correspondence. The defeat at Bull Run had been a test of their (Puritan) virtues — of their discipline and courage, and their ability to endure the suffering of war with a determined will and voluntary denial of luxuries which they had so recently enjoyed. He found that the people had passed this test admirably. Norton concluded the article in the emotional rhetoric of a war pamphlet, by ringing out the names of old heroes and traditional champions of freedom, from Launcelot and Bayard, to Sidney and Milton and Cromwell.

Norton, in fact, did write a war pamphlet at this time for the "Army Series" being published by the American Unitarian Association. *The Soldier of the Good Cause* (Boston, 1861) was a pep-talk to the Northern army, urging obedience, courage, honor, and brotherhood. The fight for "liberty," he wrote, had created a spirit which erased the distinctions between the various classes of men:

> Our army is the representative, in its heterogeneous composition, of the people itself. Native-born and adopted citizens, laborers and mechanics, students and ploughmen, men tenderly nurtured and men roughly bred, stand soldier to soldier in the ranks, each equally ready and eager to do his part in the work for his country and for liberty. [PP. 4–5]

In weeks to follow, the war began to reach a stalemate. Apathy had begun to settle in the North during the two months of inactivity after Bull Run. Norton's article in the *Atlantic* had been an attempt to maintain excitement and patriotism at a high pitch in the North. But in October, he could sense a growing popular indifference toward the War. "Pray that we may have suffering enough," he wrote "to make us a nation nobler and worthier than we have been, worthier of our unexampled opportunities and our unbounded hopes." [22] A visit to New York did not change his opinion. There he found men preoccupied with petty affairs of the moment, heedless of the tragic war which was separating the nation. Several months later his faith in the people had begun to evaporate still more. He confessed in a letter to Curtis: "I can hardly help wishing that the war might go on and on till it brought us suffering and sorrow enough to quicken our consciences and cleanse our hearts." [23]

Norton contributed little to the *Atlantic* after Lowell's editorship ended in May, 1861. He reviewed Beaumont's edition of the work and correspondence of Tocqueville (whom he had met in Paris during the first European trip). And after Clough's death in November, 1861, Norton prepared a memorial sketch of his friend which appeared in the *Atlantic* during the following spring. A letter from Lowell in late 1860 to his future successor (then publisher), James T. Fields, may explain why Norton's offerings became fewer. Fields had complained that the magazine had become too "heavy" for popular consumption, and had cited Norton's extended review of the new edition of Bacon's minor works as one instance. Lowell's slightly irritated reply defended Norton's review and asserted the editorial policy which both men shared:

> I think you are wrong — not merely about that article which seemed to me as interesting as it was thorough — but on the general question. I hope I need not say that I never let any personal feeling influence me consciously in editing the magazine — so do not think it is Norton I am defending. I stick to the principle. If we make our Magazine merely entertaining how are we better than those Scribes and Pharisees the Harpers? We want to make it interesting to as many classes of people as we can, especially to such as give tone to public opinion in literary [matters], if there be any such in America.[24]

Norton's association with the *Atlantic Monthly* in its infant years gave him a valuable introduction to American journalism. In its pages, he reached the homes of forty thousand subscribers (and an actual reading audience which presumably would be even larger). As a writer, he revealed a gift for graceful style, a lucid prose which seems to have been a natural acquirement of Norton, Lowell, and others born into intellectual Cambridge and schooled in the rhetoric classes of E. T. Channing. The hortatory mood at times did lead Norton into lengthy, grandiloquent involutions (shades of Andrews Norton). His aim throughout his writing clearly was to *instruct* — that is, to shape mass opinion in matters of art, scholarship and national character. His reviews of the current works on Bacon or Michelangelo went beyond an opinion of their accuracy and value, and became short histories of the Middle Ages and the Renaissance (and their relevance to contemporary America). "The Manchester Exhibition" gave American readers an introduction to post-Renaissance art history — with the moral implications heavily underlined. "The Advantages of Defeat" taught Americans the exalted spirit of patriotism in all ages, though Mrs. Gaskell read it in England as a bona fide description of the American spirit: "I have circulated [it] far and wide among my friends, — and I only wish I had more of the same kind to show, — in order to make us English know you Americans better." [25] His close association with Lowell as editor gave Norton additional experience in the ways of the press in America. At times, in fact, it was Norton who offered personal advice to Lowell. The Birdofredum Sawin letters, for example, Norton told Lowell, were freighted with too much detail to influence popular opinion: "One blow must be struck, not ten." [26] Within two years, the relationship hinted at here — Lowell the gifted writer and Norton the student of the American conscience — was to culminate in their joint editorship of the *North American Review.*

THE LOYAL PUBLICATION SOCIETY

In 1862 and the year after, most of Norton's activities were concentrated on aiding the Northern cause. Even though his feeble health disqualified him for army service, he voluntarily furnished a substitute at the cost of five hundred dollars. Meanwhile, he looked about for other forms of war service, large or small. At the City Hall during the early months of 1862, he supervised women who packed boxes for the soldiers. He contributed to a subscription fund for "Cambridge Volunteers." And he devoted many months of preparation for a course of twelve medieval lectures which he delivered in the winter at Lowell Institute. The Institute was then only twenty-three years old but already able to boast courses of lectures by such figures as Sir Charles Lyell, Palfrey, Felton, Sparks, Silliman, Asa Gray, Curtis, Lowell, Holmes, Agassiz, Benjamin Peirce, Francis Bowen, and E. P. Whipple. Norton's lectures on the age of Dante were relevant to the war, he announced, for they illustrated "the efforts, failures and successes of men who were called to hard service, and gave themselves to it with an earnestness which has since been rare in the world." But through it all, Norton had recurring doubts that his activities were helping the progress of the war. "Nothing will do for the country, —" he wrote to Curtis, "neither Clubs nor pamphlets nor lectures, nor Conscription Bills (three cheers for the despotism necessary to secure freedom) nor Banking Bills . . . nor Institutes, — nothing will do us much good but victories." [27]

Norton's private and social life at this time was marked by two important events — his marriage to Susan Ridley Sedgwick, and his joining the Saturday Club. The Sedgwick family of three girls and one boy had moved to Cambridge from Stockbridge in 1860 after the death of both parents. Cared for by two aunts, Anne and Grace Ashburner, they soon became regular visitors at Shady Hill. After a short engagement, Norton married the eldest daughter, Susan, in May, 1862. They lived in a portion of the Norton home during the next six years of the marriage which was to end tragically in Mrs. Norton's early death.

The Saturday Club had been formed earlier as an outgrowth of such "conversations" as those held at the Nortons in the 1840's, when the gifted talkers of Cambridge and Boston had come together on evenings at Shady Hill. In 1856, while Norton was abroad, the Saturday Club was initiated, with Emerson, Lowell, Agassiz, Motley, Dana (Jr.), Judge Ebenezer Hoar, Benjamin Peirce, and the banker Samuel G. Ward among its first members. They met for dinner one Saturday each month, from 3:00 P.M. to 9:00 P.M., at Boston's Parker House in a second-story front room looking out across to the City Hall. The membership increased slowly to include Longfellow, Holmes, and Felton the next year; Prescott and Whittier in 1858; and Hawthorne, Tom Appleton, and the businessman John Murray Forbes in 1859. When Norton was added in the following year, the Club totaled twenty members.

The war roused the Saturday Club to a deep sense of duty, even though the actual scene of battle was hundreds of miles further south. (The same patriotism cannot truthfully be claimed for many a Harvard student and Boston citizen at large.) Virtually all of the Club members were anti-slavery and took important roles in the war effort. As a group, the Club backed Lincoln's administration, supported the invaluable work of the National Sanitary Commission, and helped to organize the Union Club, a group of two hundred patriotic civilians in Boston united to support the war in every possible way. The war personally touched every member of the Club. Holmes, Forbes, Hoar, and Longfellow had sons who fought for the North. The younger Holmes and Longfellow both were wounded. Lowell saw three nephews commissioned who were later killed in action. Emerson, Whittier, and Holmes wrote war verses to stir the people. Judge Hoar went to Washington as mediator on behalf of the Massachusetts military detachment. Benjamin Peirce became consulting astronomer for the Coast Survey, a job which involved him in the naval engagements of the war. Forbes used his wealth and influence in various ways. Through his interests in the railroads, he helped to speed the transportation of war supplies. He acted as the government's emissary to England to secure a loan from Baring's and to try to dissuade pro-Southern sympathies in England. He helped to raise $100,000 in subscription money to recruit and support two Negro regiments from Massachusetts. And he was the prime mover in the forming of the Loyal Publication Society, an organization which brought him into close relations with Norton.

In January, 1863, Norton received from Forbes the appointment which exactly suited his talents. He was engaged as editor for the New England Loyal Publication Society. The purpose of the Society was to print broadsides designed to influence and mould public opinion. These broadsides were distributed free of charge to nearly one thousand editors in the North. The job of selecting short articles, most of them previously published elsewhere, was entirely Norton's. He recognized at once his enormous opportunity to initiate and guide Northern thinking on the crucial issues of the war. In April, he wrote to Mrs. Gaskell, "It is not without interest to circulate through a country and among a people like ours the opinions which are the expression of one's own principles and faith. On the whole our cause makes progress, and the war is accomplishing a good work." The broadsides covered such diverse topics as Negro citizenship, English opinions of slavery, government security, and the complex problems of financing the war. Norton estimated that the total newspaper circulation of these articles was a million weekly through the remaining years of the Civil War.[28]

The Loyal Publication Society was the forerunner of the syndicated column — or perhaps more accurately, the wire service — of modern journalism. In this early form of "mass communication," as our age has dubbed it, Norton in his quiet, inconspicuous role as editor, planted propaganda throughout the North and gained a personal influence over public opinion which was rare in American journalism up to that time. The job suited him, he discovered, and he took to the duties of an editor with all of the relish which had characterized the editorship of Andrews Norton in earlier years. Writing to one of the small-town newspaper editors in Indiana, J. B. Harrison (who became a lifelong friend of Norton's), he discoursed on the role of the newspaper editor: "Moral cowardice is a common fault of editors. Pray avoid it. Fight the majority when it is wrong. Be sure that the ground you stand on is firm [and rests] on right principle and then never mind who attacks you." Norton saw the power of the newspaper in a free society either to vulgarize or to enlighten the mass mind. The responsibility rested with the editor. "He is one of the chief instruments for promoting the education of the community," Norton wrote again to Harrison:

There is a great deal of worth in our country press generally, but it is often connected with a vulgarity of tone, and a fear of public opinion . . . The higher education of the country finds little expression in the newspapers, and this is the more to be regretted from the fact that our people often read scarcely anything besides the newspaper.[29]

THE NORTH AMERICAN REVIEW

The summer of 1863 saw the Union forces winning the momentous battles at Gettysburg and Vicksburg, and the autumn, at Chattanooga. But the victories were sobering. The Massachusetts Twentieth Regiment had been virtually annihilated at Gettysburg. The mood in Boston was hopeful, but mingled with grief as the bodies of dead soldiers returned home to remind the city of the tragedy and destruction which the war was bringing. The public mind, in short, was prepared to listen to the stern principles of faith and duty which Norton was circulating in the Loyal Publication broadsheets and elsewhere. What he needed was a wider outlet for these ideas, an established journal of public opinion through which he could promote the Northern cause.

Fate stepped in once again to provide Norton with the opportunity at the right moment. In mid-October, the publishers Crosby and Nichols called Norton to their office and offered him the editorship of the *North American Review* and the challenge of trying to liven up America's oldest quarterly. With Lowell as co-editor, he set out at once to solicit articles for the January issue, drawing on some of the earlier contributors to the *Atlantic Monthly* and such non-Bostonians as George Curtis and a recent acquaintance, Frederick Law Olmsted. For their own writing, Lowell would receive five dollars a page and Norton three dollars.

The greater share of editorial labor was borne by Norton from the beginning. Lowell's name gave prestige to the *Review,* but he performed very few of the tedious chores which had plagued him as lone editor of the *Atlantic.* Financial details, make-up, and proofreading were largely managed by Norton alone. Their correspondence establishes beyond any question that the content of the *North American Review* during the next four years was a reflection largely of the purpose and mind of Norton. In July, 1864, he was making up the magazine at his newly purchased summer home at Ashfield in western Massachusetts. He wrote to Lowell requesting that the article Howells had sent to Lowell (on "Recent Italian Comedy") go to the printers at once: "I want it to stand as the second article in the October number . . . I mean that the October number should be a lighter one than that for July." He asked Lowell to read the proof if he had an opportunity. "If not, let them send it to me as usual." [30] After the *North American* passed into the hands of Ticknor and Fields in October, 1864, Norton confided to George Curtis, "I am glad of it, for I retain as absolute control as ever." [31] To Aubrey de Vere, he wrote, "The weight of editing falls upon me, and at times I am fully occupied by it." [32] From 1864 to 1868, Norton, then, was properly editor rather than co-editor of the *North American Review*.

Lowell turned his own talents to writing for the magazine. As he told Howells, "[Norton] 'makes up' the *Review* as he likes, for I have not time to do anything about it." [33] Norton's training as a businessman served him admirably in handling the endless details which went into the management of the rather bulky *Review*, while he looked to Lowell for help in trying to make the *Review* readable and, if possible, even entertaining. "All our authors are destitute of humour," he complained to Lowell. "Nobody but you knows how to say weighty things lightly; nobody but you has the art of light writing." [34]

Throughout his editorship of the *North American*, Norton kept alive the same idealism which characterized his policies as editor of the Loyal Publication Society columns. These critical war months, he felt, would soon bring the people to a deepened sense of what America might become. The ground was ready and an editor had only to scatter the seeds. "There is an opportunity now," he wrote to Olmsted, "to make the 'North American' one of the means of developing the nation, of stimulating its better sense, of setting before it and holding up to it its own ideal, — at least of securing expression for its clearest thought and most accurate scholarship." [35] As editor, he hoped to make the magazine "a powerful instrument for affecting public opinion on the great questions now at issue here, and . . . to raise the standards of criticism and scholarship among us." [36]

To reach the widest audience, Norton tried to find men

who could write on subjects having an appeal "alike for the great public and for the critical few." [37] That he succeeded in securing some of America's finest literary men and scholars for the pages of the magazine cannot be questioned. Lowell wrote on current government affairs and contributed literary essays on Shakespeare, Rousseau, Carlyle, and others. Howells, who had served as American consul at Venice during the war years, wrote essays on modern Italian literature. On Howells' return to America, Norton became his friend, helped him to buy a home in Cambridge, wrote a flattering review of *Venetian Life,* and welcomed Howells as a fellow lover of Dante during evenings together both at Longfellow's and at Shady Hill. Other literary contributors to the *Review* included Curtis, who offered an article on Hawthorne; Emerson, his essays on "Character" and "Originality"; and Henry James his, as he put it, "very first awkward essay in criticism." [38]

Several leading historians contributed to the *Review* during Norton's editorship. Parkman wrote on Indian life; Henry Adams on earlier American and British history; Charles F. Adams, Jr., on railroads in America; and James Parton, biographical portraits of Henry Clay, John Calhoun, and other political leaders. Norton's interest in mid-century humanitarian activities had not disappeared, for he solicited articles from F. B. Sanborn on such social problems as prison reform, education of the deaf, and care of the poor in New England. Religious essays and reviews came from Andrew Preston Peabody and H. C. Lea, and essays in defense of political democracy from E. L. Godkin. Norton also hoped to gain a popular audience for articles on "Property Rights of Married Women," "Ocean Steam Navigation," and the unhappy state of painting and sculpture in America. This last essay, "The Condition of Art in America," which appeared in the issues of July, 1865, and January, 1866, was written by Russell Sturgis, Jr. But a letter from Sturgis to Norton

(September 20, 1865) suggests that Norton revised the proof so closely that he was virtually a co-author.[39]

Norton also put his own pen to work, writing reviews and essays on an astonishing variety of studies. Whatever the subject, however, he tried to keep one eye on the American scene. The office of the critic in America was to act as "public instructor of correct taste." After flaying the shabby scholarship of E. H. Gillett's *Life and Times of John Huss,* Norton discovered that other critics had praised the book warmly. In a rage, he condemned in one sweep both the author and his critics. "The success of democratic institutions," he wrote, "depends on the intellectual and moral training of the people, and the training is greatly influenced by the character of the books afforded them." Inaccuracy in scholarship and criticism, especially in America was, in Norton's opinion, a "moral offense." [40]

The same issue (July, 1864) carried a review of "Beadle's Dime Books." Norton was aware of the tremendous popularity the dime novel had gained among the soldiers and the masses of people. In April he had received a parcel of books from Beadle and Company. He acknowledged receipt of the books in a letter carrying suggestive overtones. "They have made themselves the instructors of a large portion of the community," he wrote to O. J. Victor, "and it is of the highest importance that the instruction they afford should be fitted to cultivate the taste, to stimulate the intellectual development, and to improve the moral tone of the people." [41] Norton's experience with the Loyal Publication articles made him excited over the opportunity of the press to supply good reading for the nation. He had recently suggested that J. B. Harrison print in his Indiana country newspaper the essays of Bacon, Emerson, and other literature containing "what the best men have thought and felt in times past." [42] He continued, in his letter to Victor,

In order that . . . the principles of true democracy . . . may produce their best results in character and institutions, the intellectual and moral culture of the people must keep pace with the material progress of the nation . . .

His suggestion: the experiment of printing Shakespeare's plays in an inexpensive dime edition for the firm's five million patrons. Norton offered his services in providing the textual details and footnotes which might be needed. With growing enthusiasm, he went on to suggest that "should the issue of Shakespeare's plays in this form prove a success, it might be followed by other works of interest of the great English authors." [43]

The review of the Dime Novels in the *North American* was written not by Norton but by William Everett. That Everett was thoroughly indoctrinated by Norton, however, is sufficiently clear in the following passage of the review, and the suggestion in the final sentence:

> With such established popularity as they have obtained for their publications, a serious responsibility rests upon them. They are wielding an instrument of immense power in education and civilization . . . By discarding poor works, by publishing books of real excellence and interest, exact in statement, careful in style, and true to nature, they may do much to form a correct public taste, and to supply with sound information a vast body of readers not likely to be reached by any other literature . . . They can find no more honorable employment than that of supplying at a low cost to their immense constituency the popular masterpieces of English literature both of the past and of the present time.[44]

Beadle and Company angrily replied at once to this criticism of their dime novels and authors. Norton defended the review, regretted that the novels were not better literature, and informed the publishers that during his reign the *North American* would not puff inferior writers. His parting courtesy carried a hidden barb: "I shall follow the course of your publications with interest, and shall be glad at some future time to have occasion to speak with justice in unqualified praise of them." [45]

During the first year of his editorship, Norton wrote a number of patriotic essays for the *Review*. His optimism at the beginning of the war had begun to reassert itself by mid-1864. His articles were deeply tinctured with a mounting faith in American institutions and the good sense of the individual citizen. In July, 1864, Norton observed that "the purifying and elevating influence of hardship and suffering" had engendered in Northern soldiers a "noble patience, endurance, courage, and all manly virtue." He recalled the prewar years when "the temptations of prosperity had already misled us; the love of ease had already begun to work corruption; we were stagnating in selfishness and losing the sense of virtue." [46] In October, he reviewed the works of the English historian, Goldwin Smith, lately a guest at Shady Hill and a supporter of the Northern cause (unlike Ruskin, who had stopped corresponding with Norton during the war). In the review, Norton made ample digressions on the American crisis. The war had produced a salutary effect on national character: American people were growing "more enlightened and virtuous," he declared. "We shall come out of this war with . . . new trust in the political instincts and intentions of an instructed and intelligent people." He confidently foresaw in postwar America "the possession by a free popular government of those very qualities which it has been commonly though erroneously supposed such a government was incapable of exhibiting." [47]

The next number of the *North American* carried Norton's essay on the man whom he credited with the greatest single contribution to the success of the war — Abraham Lincoln. Norton had not always admired the President. When this backwoodsman from the West first came to Washington, Norton had thrown up his hands in dismay. Lincoln lacked both the moral stature and the elevated style of expression necessary in the leader of a nation during its most crucial hour in history. But as the war progressed, Norton's attitude toward

Lincoln changed. He hailed Lincoln's reelection as a triumph of popular government. "I had never a doubt that the good sense, the intelligence, the sense of honor, and the attachment to principle of the mass of our people would triumph over their opponents," he wrote to Aubrey de Vere.[48] In early 1865, Norton still expressed certain doubts about the course Lincoln had steered, and also about the President's "disadvantages of imperfect culture, of self-education, and of little intercourse with men of high breeding." But these were minor reservations. In the discipline of Lincoln's pioneer life, in his simplicity, honesty, common sense, and moral earnestness, he had become a model "American in the best sense." The source of Lincoln's strength came from his confidence in the American people:

> The nation was worthy of this confidence; and the past four years have done more than any similar period in our history to develop its trust in itself, and to convert not merely our politicians, but the whole people, from theoretical democratic republicans into practical believers in the rights of man, and in the power and virtue of an intelligent democracy.[49]

The most striking passage in all of Norton's writing during the war years — striking for the distance he had traveled since his criticism of the European social reformers twelve years before — appeared in the Lincoln essay. The Civil War, he declared, was above all a struggle to protect and extend the rights of *labor* (not of property) in a free society.

> The freedom, the dignity, the intelligence of labor, are the tests of the true civilization of a community. Great refinement, great moral elevation, may be attained by individuals, even by classes, in a society where these rights are denied and withheld. But a society in which such a condition exists rests upon foundations that will assuredly prove insufficient, and will in time crumble away, to the destruction of whatever superstructure rest upon them. The excellence of a political society may be judged by the degree in which the rights of its humblest member are protected, and in which the benefits which flow from it may be shared by him.[50]

Norton's optimism was at its peak in 1865. Though he

awoke on certain mornings to question the blessings of popular government — the Negro vote, the disregard for old-world traditions, the absence of distinguished leadership (with the rare exception of men like Lincoln) — his outlook toward the close of the war was predominantly hopeful. Both in private correspondence and the pages of the *North American Review*, he continued to believe that America was approaching an ideal form of society. This ideal state would never be attained, but America had now caught a glimpse of the promised land. "From the height of our Pisgah," he proclaimed in the *Review*, "we have beheld the promised land, not as in a dream, but in actual vision, and the cloud of the Lord by day and his pillar of fire by night have led us on our way." [51] The striking similarity of other passages, all ringing with the accents of Emerson, shows how pervasive Norton's optimism had grown during these months. In the North American of April, 1865:

> We shall constantly come short of our ideal; but our interests will continually combine more and more closely with our duties to compel us by faithful and strenuous exertions to become worthy of our splendid and unparalleled opportunities.
>
> ["America and England," *NAR*, April, 1865]

To a friend in England:

> I believe that we have really made an advance in civilization, that the principles on which our political and social order rest are in harmony with the moral laws of the universe, that we have set up an ideal which may never be perfectly attained, but which is of such a nature that the mere effort to attain it makes progress in virtue and in genuine happiness certain.
>
> [Letter to Meta Gaskell, October 2, 1865]

In October, 1865:

> Every year has taught us — these last five years more than any others — that the crimes, the wrongs, the miseries which deface the ideal of our state, — the inherited errors of the past, the selfishness of materialism, the mass of ignorance, the corruption of politics, the atrocities of slavery, — that these and *all else of evil in their train were capable of*

removal, were not natural and inherent results of our system, were excrescences upon it which might be, which in time would be, got rid of, so that the actual commonwealth should assume slowly, imperfectly always, but ever more and more nearly, the image of the ideal.
["American Political Ideas," *NAR,* October, 1865.
Italics added.]

And again in October, 1866:

It is only within a few years that we have passed out of this stage of immaturity. There is still much that is raw, imperfect, and barbarous in our civilization; but the ideas and principles which inspire us as a nation have gradually been moulding us to their own likeness. We are getting rid of old-world things, and gradually become accustomed to the new. We are forming new creeds, new judgments, new manners; we are becoming a new race of men.
["Harvard Memorial Biographies," *NAR,* October, 1866]

Thus had Norton altered, and in some cases reversed, his earlier aristocratic view of the social organism. Each month toward the end of the war had given him new proof that America was growing into a mature nation. He could even stop worrying about the problem of leadership in government, society, and the church. "The average quality of character is the last and the best test of the influence of political systems and social relations," he now wrote. "We are getting beyond leaders in America. A moral, thoughtful community does not need them. Mr. Lincoln has shown us the example of a great popular statesman, not a leader. It is a new era in politics." [52]

But about Lincoln's successor, Andrew Johnson, Norton was not so hopeful: "His democracy does not extend to the black." Lincoln might have obtained Negro suffrage quickly at the end of the war and thereby secured "a truer social order than has hitherto existed at the South." Under Johnson, the fight for equal Negro rights would be harder. "He holds that [the Negro] is inferior to the white man, that the white man is to govern, the black to be governed." [53]

And what of the tyranny of the press over mass opinion in

America? Norton found evidence that American people were becoming more critical readers of the newspaper: "When the Tribune goes right the people take it; when it goes wrong they drop it. They don't take their ideas of right and wrong from it, any more than they take the manners of Mr. Greeley as their model." [54] His faith in the masses continued to grow in the next year. In an article, "Religious Liberty," Norton translated his own developing agnosticism (doubtless strengthened by talks with Chauncey Wright and with two recent English visitors — Goldwin Smith and Leslie Stephen) into a general argument against institutionalized religion. An enlightened populace need not be shackled by the formalized creed of any organized church. America was entering a new era when men would become free from all established forms of thought control and be bound only by the humane ties of brotherly love. When the political atmosphere grew turbulent in the Capitol, Norton observed that politicians lost their tempers while the people remained calm and rational. "It is a good thing to see the temper of the people so calm and steady," he wrote to Lowell. "It is an indication of our growth in national manliness and confidence during the last few years." [55]

FOUNDING THE NATION

Norton's experience with the *Atlantic Monthly* and the *North American Review,* and with the Loyal Publication Society articles, prepared him for a fourth major contribution to American journalism. In 1865, he was one of a small group of men who worked to establish the *Nation* magazine. The idea had probably begun two years earlier when Frederick Law Olmsted informed Norton that an able newspaperman, E. L. Godkin, was coming to Boston to discuss with Norton the idea of founding a new weekly. No further correspondence has come to light, but the visit did not accomplish its main purpose. Norton apparently was impressed by this stranger whose political views he shared, however, for Godkin later became a contributor to the *North American Review*.

In 1865, Olmsted again wrote to Godkin, this time urging him to come west. Olmsted could raise $150,000 in San Francisco to begin a new daily newspaper and wanted Godkin to become its editor. Godkin replied in April, declining the offer. He preferred to wait for an opportunity in the East. Meanwhile, Norton asked George Curtis, then with *Harper's Weekly*, if he was interested in taking control of a new paper. The war was just over, and the country needed a new magazine to voice the important issues of postwar reform and reconstruction. Curtis was skeptical. The fifty thousand dollars Norton could raise did not seem to be enough, Curtis wrote, and any audience interested in "liberal reform" could be reached by the established periodicals — the *Atlantic, North American Review, Harper's,* and the *Evening Post*. Curtis's biographer concludes that "nothing came of the project." [56]

Something did come of the project, however, for the proposed magazine was undoubtedly the unborn *Nation*. In Philadelphia, a group of men, including the abolitionist, James Miller McKim, had been planning for some months to establish a "freedmen" paper. When McKim learned of Godkin's hope to edit an eastern journal, he proposed his plan to Godkin, and in early May a merger of interests took place among the friends of McKim in Philadelphia, Godkin in New York, and Norton in Boston. Forty stockholders invested $100,000 in the enterprise, and in July, the first number of the *Nation* appeared.

The prospectus of the *Nation*, according to its first publisher, Joseph H. Richards, included the following objectives:

—— To champion the equal opportunity of the "laboring class at the South," and follow the social progress of the Negro
—— To provide information on Southern business (capital and labor)
—— To discuss legal and economic issues with less bias than the daily press

—— To stress the importance of popular education in the United States
—— To spread "true democratic principles in society and government"
—— To offer "sound and impartial" literary and art criticism [57]

So began the long and honorable history of one of America's most vital weeklies. From the beginning, the *Nation* had a turbulent career. In his first month, Godkin learned that America had some sacred cows and vested interests which an editor criticized at his own peril. Men accused him of having the "Englishman's" hereditary dislike for things American (he had come to America in 1856). Stockholders of the *Nation* informed him that no man in his proper senses criticized Jay Cooke in the pages of a national magazine. Discouraged by these rebukes in the first few weeks, Godkin wrote to Norton, "You are the only man of the whole body of projectors with whom I know I am in thorough sympathy." [58]

Godkin's woes continued in the succeeding months. He gloomily accepted the impending failure of the *Nation,* but he told Norton, "If it failed to-morrow, I should feel myself abundantly repaid in having by means of it been brought into such close relations with so kind and sympathizing a friend as you have been." The *Nation* held up under the abuse from its critics and stockholders, however, and on its first anniversary, the two friends exchanged mutual congratulations. "If the paper succeeds," Godkin wrote to Norton, "I shall always ascribe it to you, as without your support and encouragement I do not think I should have been able to endure to the end." Norton replied, "You are making the paper more than I ever hoped it could be. . . *You* are the *Nation*; without you it is not worth supporting." [59]

Norton's encouragement and support of the *Nation* continued in following years. " 'The Nation' is a weekly comfort and satisfaction . . . ," he told Godkin. "It seems like a personal message from you to me; as if printed for my sake. I hear nothing but good of it." He offered to advance Godkin one thousand dollars a year for three years or longer if the

Nation should need additional funds. "This I would do in the belief that as long as you live the *Nation* is a good investment." [60] The friendship weathered the stormy decades of reconstruction and political conflict in the later nineteenth century. In 1895, Godkin dedicated his volume of collected essays to Norton. The dedicatory note read: "To CHARLES ELIOT NORTON, to whom the foundation of the *Nation* was largely due, in grateful acknowledgment of a long friendship." [61]

Norton wrote for the *Nation* from its opening numbers, and, as Frank L. Mott has rightly said, Norton's name should head the list of writers for the early *Nation*. For Norton, the pages of *Nation* became an outlet for certain reservations about American life which he had omitted in the *North American Review* for fear of dampening the wartime spirit in the North. The *Nation,* however, had announced the intention to deal critically with postwar issues. Norton put away his patriotic banner and began to examine seriously some of the problems of the future. He wrote on deficiencies in American education, including education (and suffrage) for women. He goaded the readers mildly with essays on the native lack of refinement and good taste. Some of the titles tell their own stories: "The Paradise of Mediocrities," "Waste," and "Good Manners." His complex attitude toward America — the conflicts which plagued him even in these months of soaring optimism — appear in these articles for the *Nation*. Contrapuntal themes recur insistently: America had no hereditary lower class — and no distinguished higher class; snobbery was absent in America — and so were "good manners"; in America every man had "a chance" to become wealthy — and after obtaining wealth, to squander it in tasteless, barbaric extravagance. The terms "equality," "democracy," and "mediocrity" clashed with "cultivation" or "culture."

After pointing out these shortcomings in American life,

however, Norton could still conclude: "A nation where men start on a level, where 'every man has a right to be equal with every other man,' where every man has 'a chance,' is not likely to remain forever the 'Paradise of Mediocrities.' " [62] Though Americans too easily ignored European traditions in art, learning, and good manners, Norton also noted that such traditions "were part of the laws by which the false distinctions among men were maintained." For a model of good manners, America needed to look back no further into the past than to her own late president:

> Mr. Lincoln possessed the essentials of good manners. He showed us what manners an American "railsplitter" might have. They were the manners of a good heart, that trusted itself and other men. Upon such a foundation we may build whatever superstructure of beauty, grace, and art we choose. And though our manners be uncouth and unconventional today, they shall to-morrow — a hundred years hence — be the noble manners of men not only gentle in heart but of refined and elegant cultivation.[63]

The optative mood prevailed through the coming months, despite occasional doubts. In 1867, Norton flatly confessed that "with all the crudeness and roughness of our new state, with all its deficiencies of *culture* and its want of those historic traditions and memorials which give grace, dignity and beauty to life in the Old World . . . we see glimpses already, nay more we already enjoy something of truly Christian manners and society. . . *It is hard not to be an optimist here.*" [64]

THE EDITOR RESIGNS

By 1868, the constant exertion of these years of journalism had begun to weaken Norton's health. In addition to his activities with the *Atlantic Monthly,* the Loyal Publication Society broadsides, the *North American,* and the *Nation,* he had also borne the strain of various public lectures, his always voluminous correspondence, and the reception of scores of guests at Shady Hill. In 1868, he resigned his editorship of the *North American Review* and prepared for a second convalescence in Europe. How successful had the *Review* grown in these four years? Financially the magazine had obviously not thrived. Norton shared the publisher's anxiety over subscription figures and made every effort to combine high quality with some measure of liveliness. His letters to Lowell reflected this continual fear that the *Review* was too "heavy" for a large audience of readers. Once he even suggested to Thomas Wentworth Higginson that the magazine might rather have been named "The 'Senile Review.' " [65]

Although the *North American* did not make money, it did establish certain admirable precedents in American journalism. Howells praised the *Review* in these years, noting that "while it kept the scholarly attitude in its treatment of topics, it dealt with current events as courageously, vigorously, conscientiously as if they had been matters of history." [66] Although bankruptcy frequently threatened, Norton was the first editor to pay writers of the *Review* more than one dollar a page. In doing so, he secured the leading (New England) authors of the day as contributors to the *Review*, and welcomed the early efforts of Godkin, James Parton, Henry Adams, William Dean Howells, Henry James, and other young writers. Through the war years and after, Norton tried to hold up to the nation an image of its best self. And he almost convinced himself that the vision had become reality.

A few days before his sailing, the publishers of the *Review*, Ticknor and Fields, sent Norton their regret that "even for the present, the Review is to be deprived of your connection with it." In view of the magazine's meager profit, the publishers paid Norton high tribute:

It is true, as a business enterprise the Review has but little to commend itself; nevertheless, the admirable manner with which the editorial department of it has been conducted [has shown] on the part of its editors so much judgment, taste and rare scholarship, that we have felt that to be simply its publishers was an honor to our house, and its publication worthy of our attention.[67]

In July of 1868, Norton, accompanied by his wife (also in fragile health) and four small children, together with his mother and two sisters, sailed for England. Lowell recorded the event, and his own sense of loss after Norton's departure, in the "log" of the *North American*:

11 July. Lat 42°1′, the first officer, Mr. Norton, lost overboard in a fog, with the compass, caboose, and studden-sails in his pocket, also the key of the spirit-room.[68]

IV

EUROPEAN INTERLUDE: DISILLUSIONMENT

In memory I see you generally as you were in the war
years. We were all immature at that time; enjoying our
Emersonian June.

(Norton to S. G. Ward, March 9, 1903)

ENGLAND

W HEN Dickens visited the United States in 1868, Norton
delivered a short speech at a dinner held in New York in
Dickens' honor. In the heart of his speech, Norton presented
a contrast between the "two Englands":

There is the actual England — the England of *The Times,* the *Book
of Snobs,* and *The Alabama,* — the England that we do not like; and
there is the real England — the England of the imagination and the
heart, — the England to which no thoughtful and sensitive American
can go without rapture in visiting the scene of the old and glorious
memories of our race . . . He will come back with firmer convictions,
eager to do his best in carrying out those principles which are the vital
spirit of America, and which the real England holds in her heart, rever-
ences in her faith, places first in her religion, — the principles of justice,
liberty, and humanity.[1]

This ambivalent feeling grew even stronger during his return
to Britain in the late summer of 1868. After brief visits with
Dickens, Ruskin, John Simon (Ruskin's physician), and the
Gaskells, Norton moved with his family into a house at
Keston Rectory near Bromley, Kent. His neighbors included
Darwin and Frederic Harrison. He made a new acquaintance
— George Lewes — and renewed old ties with Morris, Burne-
Jones, and Goldwin Smith. The landscape in Kent abounded

with associations of England's past and dizzied his senses. He walked again in a nostalgic reverie through "grandmother's garden," with its meadows, fields, hills, dales, Roman villas, farms, sheep, partridges, rabbits, sparrows, finches, and starlings in all the hedges, "and everywhere that old world look and those old world things," (he wrote to Lowell) "which in spite of their novelty and strangeness have for me, — and for you too, — a deeper familiarity than the very things that have lain before our eyes since we were born." [2] He confided to Howells, "I am gradually getting rid of some American angularities and drynesses. My roots feel the refreshment of unfamiliar waters flowing from the deep old-world springs of culture and imagination." [3]

But at the same time that his roots were drawing nourishment in the "old home," Norton had grown acutely disturbed by the price modern England was paying to maintain her "old-world springs of culture and imagination." He found an upper class reclining on the lap of plenty while England's poor were groveling in their cellars of filth and starvation. "A traveller may venture to let his selfishness have sway, and to enjoy [himself] without pricks of conscience," Norton wrote again to Howells, "but to live here would be intolerable; and I shall come back to the barrenness of America more American at heart than ever." [4]

Norton's concern over lower-class poverty and ignorance in England, and his renewed fear of the dangerous consequences, increased in proportion to the complacency of the Englishmen whom he met. A captain of industry in Manchester blithely assured Norton that labor was properly subdued and would cause no disturbance. John Stuart Mill also promised Norton that England would have no social revolution. Norton's fears did not subside. The more he saw, the more apprehensive he grew. He was alarmed not only by the numbers of unemployed, but also by the "ignorance and hopelessness" of agricultural and mining laborers. "When your discussion of such questions as those of property in land, of the limits of income, etc., once begins in earnest, —" he warned Mill, "and this discussion seems near at hand, [the laborers] . . . can hardly fail to be roused, and their excitement becomes dangerous in proportion to the ignorance and dulness of their minds." [5]

Norton moved his family to London to spend the winter of 1868–69. Living there amid the company of such friends as Ruskin, Browning, Leslie Stephen, Morris, and Burne-Jones, he was constantly impressed by "the advantages of culture and thorough discipline" of the intellectual class in English society. New acquaintances included George Eliot, John Forster, Froude, and, in March, the seventy-four-year-old Carlyle. (Largely through Norton's good graces, a young, homesick Henry James, recently arrived in London, became a part of the Nortons' "international set." Norton introduced him to Ruskin, Morris, Rossetti, and other members of the English society whose conventions James would come to cherish above all others.) In London, however, he again felt class conflict imminent. "England grows richer and poorer," he wrote to Lowell, "as riches collect together in a heap on one side, and poverty huddles together in a mass on the other, and there seems to be scarcely a passageway of communication between them. . ." [6] He was forced to confine such observations to private correspondence. During conversations, Norton found to his dismay that many Englishmen who listened to his worries about English social conditions, and his praise of life in America, regarded him as another boastful Yankee. "Even the genuine liberals can not conceive of the virtue of our practical democracy," he complained to Curtis. This was not Yankee pride, said Norton; it was "the just confidence of an enlightened American in the principles of our system . . ." [7]

In May, he was ready to admit that an American observer in England was perhaps tempted "to overestimate the dangers resulting from the apparent division of classes, the unequal distribution of power and wealth, the wretched condition of the mass of the productive portion of the population." Still, he heard unmistakable rumblings in the distance. This cleavage between rich and poor in England could not go on indefinitely without tragic results:

> I cannot but believe that . . . the question is imminent whether the nation is to decline into a state of chronic decrepitude, or to be redeemed by a more or less violent revolution which shall complete the work left unfinished by the Cromwellian period, and restore vigour and common life to the various classes which are now arrayed against each other . . .[8]

Norton repeated these warnings in a long article, "The Poverty of England," which he sent to the *North American Review*. The essay appeared under the guise of a review of British Annual Reports of Public Health, Poor Laws, and Agricultural Labor. In the article, Norton angrily condemned the overcrowded housing in Britain, the apathy of the well-to-do, and the cynical attitude of the British capitalist, who bargained for his labor according to the merciless principles of Adam Smith. Norton defended the laborer who tried to fill the vacuum in his life with the desperate pleasures of alcohol and aimless reproduction. Unless the ruling classes awakened to a sense of responsibility, Norton warned, the masses would change the face of English society, not through the slow cumbersome process of majority vote, but more suddenly by violent revolution.

SWITZERLAND AND ITALY

In early summer, Norton and his family left England to live from June until late autumn in Switzerland. On the Continent, as in England, he was preoccupied with the turmoil of political events. More significant, his misgivings about modern society in Europe were also beginning to have a counterpart in America. While in January he had praised Grant, the army-general-turned-President ("so simple, so sensible, so strong, and so magnanimous"), by July, he was dismayed to hear that abuses of privilege and the beginnings of corruption were creeping into the Grant administration. He pronounced some of the President's political appointments "disgraceful," but felt the trend could be checked and the nation saved when the current Jenckes Bill to establish civil service reform would be passed (it was not).[9]

His gloomy forebodings about contemporary politics increased during the summer meeting in Switzerland of a "Peace Congress" of revolutionary political figures, including Victor Hugo. Norton attended the meetings and sent his observations to Godkin and the *Nation*. The article marked the initial decline of Norton's war-inspired faith in popular sovereignty. Revolutionary change in social or political institutions, Norton affirmed, would not automatically bring peace, liberty and justice into the world so long as the "moral dispositions" of men remained vicious. In a single long sentence, deeply tinged with irony and pessimism, Norton gave renewed emphasis to his reservations on the "democratic form of government":

> It was curious and instructive to listen, day after day, to the various expressions of this doctrinaire faith in forms and institutions, not as the evidences but as the sources of human progress, and to hear the virtues of the people exalted, as if the establishment of a democratic form of government, based on universal suffrage were synonymous with the abolition of selfishness and all evil passions — as if men and women were bad because of imperialism and the government of kings, and nothing were needed for the millennium but popular liberties.[10]

Depressed by conditions in Europe, and by reports he heard from America, Norton longed for the south. "Switzerland is not Italy," he wrote to Ruskin during the summer, "and Italy is the country where the American, exile in his own land from the past record of his race, finds most of the most delightful part of that record." [11] In the late fall of

1869, Norton returned to Italy. He settled during the winter in Florence. But presently he discovered that the impulses current throughout America and the rest of Europe had reached Italy as well. Not only was she seeking the "panacea" of a popular constitutional government; but she was also losing her historic charm through economic prosperity, and had begun to imitate the low commercial tastes of modern materialism, "the taste of New York and Paris, — the taste for what is fashionable and fresh and showy." Walls dear to Norton's memory were being torn down and replaced by glittering new façades. Railroad construction was under way, and the common school was springing up with ambitious hopes of advancing popular enlightenment. "Happy country! Fortunate people! Before long they may hope for their Greeleys, their Beechers, and their Fisks." [12]

He reappraised the social order in America, as well as in Europe, and wrote to Chauncey Wright, "Whether our period of economic enterprise, unlimited competition, and unrestrained individualism, is the highest stage of human progress is to me very doubtful." One of two results was inevitable — either a violent and destructive revolution in the social order, or an approaching cycle of decline, fall, ruin and revival. He welcomed either. "No man who knows what society at the present day really is, but must agree that it is not worth preserving on its present basis." [13] Several weeks later, he wrote with increasing bitterness, "I hate Americanism out of America . . . Here all that reminds me of Imperial Paris, or of Democratic New York is detestable, out of harmony with the nature of the land and with the spirit of the associations that belong to it." [14]

During the winter in Florence, Norton's health suffered another reversal. He had been studying Dante and Michelangelo and, characteristically, he had overworked himself into a state of exhaustion. When spring arrived, Norton and his wife journeyed south to spend several weeks in Rome, leaving the rest of the family behind in Florence. (The vacation in Rome would be a needed rest for his wife, too. In January, she had given birth to a fifth child, Margaret.) But he could not rest. "Rome . . . resists with steady persistency the flood of 'American' barbarism and of universal materialism which is desolating Europe," he wrote to Ruskin. The odious tyranny of church and state, however, made Rome's "immobility" hardly more desirable than the "progress" he had observed in Florence:

> It is conservative not only in good old ways, but in bad ones also. It clings indiscriminately to what has been, — it cherishes (not alone in the physical world) dirt, ruin, and malaria . . .

Norton dispelled the rumor that he had grown overly depressed during his winter illness. He had become more "sober" than in previous months, he told Ruskin, but tried not to be "sad." "I believe cheerfulness to be part of godliness, part too of the best humanity. And of all men I have least excuse for sadness." To put on a cheerful mask, however, took strenuous effort. In addition to the duties of a husband and father ("the care that comes with love") he felt continual frustration from a "desire to be of service to one's world and inability to fulfil one's desire, the sense of the useless and needless misery among men, the living in a time in which one is out of sympathy with the ruling motives of the mass of men and women who surround them . . ." [15] Contributing also to his gloom was a report from Godkin on the alarming rise to power of immigrant races in postwar America. Norton praised a recent article by Godkin, which contained the following opinion of the masses:

> Their rush into the forum and into the temples and palaces and libraries is not an agreeable sight to witness, and it would be foolish to expect that under their ruthless touch many gifts and graces will not be obscured, many arts will not be lost, many a great ideal, at whose shrine the best men and women of three generations have found courage and inspiration, will not vanish from the earth to be seen no more.[16]

Norton's health was far from vigorous when in June he traveled north from Rome to begin studying the cathedrals at Siena, Florence, and Venice. In Siena during the summer of 1870, his failing strength hindered the progress of these studies. He was forced to interrupt his work from time to time and convalesce, as he said, in the warm Italian sun "free from the taint of the ten per cent stockbroking age." Like a leitmotiv, the tug of war continued in Norton between exile and retirement into the past (Europe), and a life of service in the future (America). "If the world were not so bad," he wrote to Curtis, "and if America in especial were better, — I could be content to live here.

But with you attending Educational Conventions, with my dear friend Godkin editing "The Nation," and every friend I have in the pell-mell of the fight with the devil and his allies, I am now only waiting for the opportunity to rush in at a fair moment for dealing a good blow, and getting out of breath like the rest . . .[17]

More evil days followed. On July 19, the Franco-Prussian War began. "The prospect of this — of the long train of miseries that it opens — makes me very heavy-hearted," he wrote to Chauncey Wright.[18] Also in the summer of 1870, Norton mourned the death of his friend Dickens whom he had counted on "in case of any sudden terrible overflow of the ignorance, misery and recklessness which the selfishness of the upper classes has fostered . . ." [19] Reports from America gave few signs of a serious temper at home. "Really the 'Nation' and the 'North American' are almost the only evidences of thought in America," he wrote, "and they drag out a difficult existence in the midst of the barbaric wealth of the richest millions of people in the world." Emerson had been her foremost thinker, but America's industrial age, Norton believed, had created social problems which Emerson's philosophy could not solve. A new spirit in criticism was urgently needed, with the exercise of rational minds rather than the "intuition." Emerson's message had belonged rather to "the pure and innocent age" of Monroe and John Quincy Adams.[20]

Norton's last months of study in Italy — at Florence during the winter and spring, and Venice in the early summer of 1871 — only deepened his sense of conflict between the past and the present. "Prosperity, independence, and the rail-road" were daily changing the beauty of old Florence. "I am glad I first saw Europe before the days of California," he wrote.[21] At Venice, where he completed his studies of the medieval church, the spectacle was equally melancholy. He found no trace left of the old Venetian spirit and character. The palaces remaining from her period of greatness had been converted into hotels and shops, all pandering to the taste of the modern tourist.

GERMANY

In the summer of 1871, Norton left Venice and Italy and turned northward to Germany on the last phase of his European travels. In the fall, he settled in Dresden, where once again he noted the spread of material prosperity and the influx of *nouveaux riches* American tourists, "many of whom are of a sort whom one does not see at home, and does not wish to see abroad." He discovered that standards in German society, as well as in scholarship, were being determined by a practical and scientific materialism. From the growing prestige of a prosperous middle class, he traced the same standardization of values in German as in American society:

> Berlin is acting upon Dresden and other small cities within its range much as New York acts on New Haven, Hartford, and Springfield. It takes its independence and individuality from it; forces it into imitativeness and provinciality and ruins "society" by depriving it of an original, native flavour, and self-sufficing standards.[22]

In spite of this aversion to German society and the American tourist, Norton and his family could not leave Germany.

His wife was pregnant, and further travel was thought unwise. They spent the winter in Dresden, and in February, the sixth child and third son was born to the Nortons. But the labor had seriously weakened Mrs. Norton, and, several days afterward, she died.

Norton had seldom mentioned the details of his married life, for he did not care to have his private life become the business of others, particularly in the age of a scandal-mongering press. He bore this bitterest experience of his life alone, with the same acceptance and toughness of spirit which had carried him through earlier trials. He urged his friends not to burden themselves with sorrow on his account. Only in a letter to his classmate and longtime friend Professor Child, did Norton suggest briefly the rareness of the woman he had lost:

> Europe . . . had enlarged all her resources of giving and receiving happiness, — and had she come home with us you would have found her with all her youthful freshness of spirit undiminished, but with a fulness and richness of maturity added to it such as few women have the character to attain. The years never seemed so full of promise for us. — But we lived together with open and simple recognition of the uncertain tenure of our happiness. The thought of this was seldom absent from our hearts, — and the anxieties of life pressed often heavily upon her.[23]

HOMEWARD BOUND

Winter in London

With his mother and two sisters, and a family of six small children, Norton left Dresden in April, 1872. The lease of his home at Shady Hill would not run out for one more year, so the family moved to Paris and St. Germain during the summer, and, in October, to London. An occasional passage in his letters and private journal hints at his recurring grief over his wife's death. On his forty-fifth birthday (November 16), Norton entered in his journal the following brief note:

"The children gave me pretty presents, and their uncon-
sciousness of my loss and theirs almost breaks me down."

During the winter in London, Norton's health broke again,
and he spent one month in bed with pneumonia. The rest of
the winter passed quietly in a daily round of the children's
lessons, his Italian studies, and the frequent company of
English friends. He welcomed the almost daily visit of either
Leslie Stephen, Frederic Harrison, Carlyle, Morley, Ruskin,
Burne-Jones, or Morris. He wrote down the conversations of
Carlyle (mainly on literature and religion) after their long
walks together, and toured London art galleries with fellow
Americans Henry James and Emerson. His health had
strengthened in the spring, and in May he prepared to re-
turn to America. Lowell came over from Paris the week
before Norton's sailing and met Norton's guests, Carlyle,
Ruskin, and Morris — Ruskin and Morris, whom Norton
would not see for many years, and Carlyle, not ever again.
Carlyle noted the departure of Norton and his family:

> I was really sorry to part with Norton, and his interesting Family
> of little Motherless children, good Sisters and venerable Mother: he has
> been thro Winter the most *human* of all the company I, from time to
> time, had. A pious-minded, cultivated, intelligent, much-suffering man.
> He has been five years absent from America, and is now to return One
> instead of Two as he left! [24]

Emerson the Shipmate — Some Second Thoughts

Norton's voyage back to America became, like his previous
crossings, a symbolic journey. He had left America with a
heart full of hope for her people and institutions. He was
returning five years later to the land of his lost innocence.
And the one man who symbolized for him that hopeful and
innocent America accompanied him on the return voyage.
His shipmate was Ralph Waldo Emerson.

Norton's friendship with his father's famous adversary
dated back to the 1850's, and in itself hinted at the intellectual conflict in which Norton found himself as a youth. As

mentioned earlier, Emerson's doctrine of the Oversoul had been a liberating breath of air to young men who were being formally schooled in the strict rationalism of Andrews Norton. In the 1850's, Charles Norton resisted the Emersonian logic and declared his misgivings about social progress and human perfectibility. But *Leaves of Grass* found its way to Shady Hill in 1855. Norton's sympathetic reading of Whitman was portentous, even though much of the excitement soon wore off.

In the 1860's, Norton's friendship with Emerson was cemented first in the Saturday Club and later by Emerson's agreement to write for the *North American Review*. If Norton's optimism in the war years was influenced by the written teachings of any single man, they were those of Emerson. He praised Emerson both as a poet and as a prophet "who has lived to the days of the fulfilment of prophecy, and finds his old inspiration become the common breath. How much we owe to him!" [25]

But the war years had passed. During his residence in Europe, Norton had an opportunity to reappraise American civilization. It had, he now saw, fallen woefully short of what he (and Emerson) had predicted. In his shipboard talks with Emerson, Norton soon discovered to his dismay that the Emerson of 1873 was still speaking in the blandly confident tones of the Emerson of the 1830's. In his journal of the voyage, Norton recorded some of the most incisive criticism ever leveled at the Emersonian doctrine. He found Emerson pitifully blind to the changes which were occurring in "the new and less childlike epoch of our modern democracy." For Emerson, American society remained essentially what it had been in the innocent days when

the Declaration of Independence, the common school, and the four years Presidential term, were finalities in political science and social happiness; of a time when society was simple and comparatively innocent; when our institutions and our progress were the wonder of Tocqueville and the Old World, and the delight of ourselves; when there were Peace Societies, and it seemed to the youth uninstructed by the past as if the Milennium were really not so very far off. His philosophy was of necessity one of hope; the gospel of prosperity; and it was settled so far as its influence on thought, action and character were concerned, before General Jackson was chosen President and we had entered on the new and less child-like epoch of our modern democracy.

Finally, Norton attributed to Emerson's facile optimism the "fatalistic indifference to moral considerations" in current American public and private life.[26]

The heat of these utterances betrayed Norton's own sense of guilt. For Emerson's influence had not ended at the Age of Jackson; Norton himself had fallen under the Emersonian spell less than ten years before. He had temporarily become one of those "youth uninstructed by the past," who suddenly had caught a glimpse of the New Jerusalem. Despite his own studies in the slow history of human progress, and his earlier distrust of popular government, Norton had mistaken the transient passions of a people at war for the signs of a permanent moral regeneration. His disillusionment after the war was equally sudden. It was, in fact, far more profound than any suffered by his friends. Curtis, Lowell, and Godkin, in particular, had shared Norton's admiration for Lincoln and had expected a new era of enlightened government in America. Although they were strongly disappointed with public affairs after the war, they were not demoralized. For they lacked Norton's brooding social conscience and his almost overriding concern with politics as a moral problem. Against the backdrop of European materialism and a social order in eruption, Norton's optimism had waned. His new broodings over the American "gospel of prosperity" were confirmed by reports of a corrupt Grant administration at home and the spectacle of "vulgar rich" American tourists in Europe. By 1873, Emerson seemed to Norton not only a god that failed; he had become a kind of scapegoat. In Emerson's person Norton subconsciously recognized himself as he had been only a few years before, and the conspiracy of which he too had been a part. By heaping abuse on Emerson, Norton was performing an act of atonement for the sins of his own past. But the spirit of Emerson in a man of forty-five refused to die so easily. In the years ahead it reappeared, even during moments of deepest pessimism, to lighten Norton's despair and give him renewed hope for America's future.

PART TWO
MATURITY
(1874–1908)

V

TEACHER OF THE FINE ARTS AT HARVARD

I have some ardours left — and no whit of faith in the good as good, and to be aimed at whether attainable or not, has vanished from my soul.

(Norton to Ruskin, January 10, 1874)

Professor Norton lectured in Italian 4 this afternoon. The dear old man looks so mildly happy and benignant while he regrets everything in the age and the country — so contented, while he gently tells us it were better for us had we never been born in this degenerate and unlovely age.

(*Diary and Letters of Josephine Preston Peabody*)

Norton's ship docked in Boston late in May, 1873. He returned to Shady Hill and a home filled with associations of a short, happy marriage and the bright promise of earlier days, memories which only sharpened his grief. He was further depressed by changes in Cambridge during the five-year absence. "When I recall it as it used to be," he wrote to Lowell in Europe, "I feel as if I had lived in prehistoric times . . . Everything seems strangely familiar, and yet to my heart strangely different. America never seemed to me so far from Europe as it does today; — and my past life is cut off from my present by a sea wider and deeper than the Atlantic." [1]

He soon moved his family to the Norton summer home at Ashfield. Again he was reminded of happier times, and the tranquil beauty of Ashfield's rural landscape deepened further his sense of isolation. He longed for England as he described his solitary life in America to John Simon: "The years to come will but close me more and more completely in a secret life of my own, while I lead a strange, unreal life in the presence of my friends and the world." [2] And to Carlyle he wrote, "My walks are now for the most part solitary, — and all life is likely to be solitary in America to one who cannot share that confident spirit of cheerful optimistic fatalism of which Emerson is the voice and the prophet." [3]

Many seductive voices in Europe beckoned Norton to return. Some of his closest friends lived across the Atlantic. By comparison with Europe's libraries and museums, America's resources in art and learning seemed hopelessly barren. The asperities of the New England climate alone were argument enough for leading a life of exile in the milder seasons of Italy. With Europe calling to him in a thousand ways, Norton elected to stay in America. In a revealing letter to Ruskin, he gave some of the reasons:

> My children must have a country, and on the whole this is best for them. I am bound here by duty to them and to my mother. For my life would doubtless be better in many ways in Europe; but I should be after all of less service there than here.[4]

THE OPPORTUNITY AT HARVARD

In the summer after his return, Norton tried briefly to regain his editorship of the *North American Review*. At the time, Henry Adams was at the helm of the *Review*, with T. S. Perry his assistant. Norton wanted the discipline of steady work, and asked Howells to inquire personally about Perry's future with the magazine, but not to mention Norton's name. He did not want it known that he was available for another man's job. Howells immediately arranged a meeting with the publisher, James R. Osgood. He discovered that Perry's position with the *North American* was only temporary, and therefore thought it proper enough to relay Norton's wish to edit the magazine once again. He then assured Norton, "I myself never thought it so good as when you had it, and heartily wish it was in your hands again," and without mentioning Adams, Howells added rather incoherently, "with Mr. Perry as your assistant, until Lowell's return." [5] Howells probably knew at the time that his mission had failed. The *Review* was flourishing under Henry Adams' guidance, and had been reduced to approximately one-half its former size. With his rather slender resources, Osgood obviously preferred to leave the magazine in Adams' care (Henry Cabot Lodge became the new assistant in 1873). Later, however, Adams would have been happy to hand the magazine back to Norton. Adams wrote to Lodge:

> As for Norton, I sincerely wish he would take the *Review*. My terror is lest it should die on my hands or go to some Jew. If Osgood can shove it off on Norton, I advise him to do so, and will negotiate myself with Norton for the purpose. He is not my enemy, but if he were, I would like no better than to shove him into such a trap and jump out myself on his shoulders.[6]

Meanwhile, in the late months of 1873, the faculty at Harvard and its president, Charles W. Eliot, became aware of Norton's unemployment. E. W. Gurney, then professor of history, suggested to Eliot that Norton might be attracted to the college by an offer to establish a chair in the Fine Arts. But Eliot, who was nothing if not a practical administrator, worried over the problem of finding money to finance a new department. An alternative occurred to him. The chair vacated by Lowell, who was on leave of absence in Europe, might be filled by Norton if Lowell resigned. In December, Norton wrote to Lowell and mentioned Eliot's proposal. Lowell had never shared Norton's fondness for hard work, and immediately abandoned his station at Harvard in favor of Norton.

When Norton officially returned to Harvard after a twenty-eight year absence, the college was pulling out of a slump under the leadership of President Eliot. Josiah Quincy had been succeeded by Presidents Edward Everett, Jared Sparks, James Walker, Cornelius Felton, Thomas Hill, and Andrew Preston Peabody, all gifted minds but ineffectual administrators. Yale, Princeton, and Columbia had been busily soliciting donations in the flush postwar era to bolster their professional and scientific schools, and Yale already boasted a graduate school. Harvard's slow growth was apparent in the relatively few buildings constructed since Norton's student days. Appleton Chapel (1858), Boylston Hall (1858), the Museum of Comparative Zoology (1860), and Grays Hall (1863) were the few prominent additions to the college. Norton's old dormitory, Holworthy, did have gaslights installed by 1855. Other buildings soon adopted gas also. Grays Hall (1863) had water taps in the basement, and within several years all Yard buildings were able to end their reliance on the Yard pumps. Coal heated the open fireplaces in the rooms. Plumbing had to wait until President's Eliot's administration. Outside the Yard, signs of change were far more noticeable during this interim. Horsecars appeared in the early sixties to make the vices of downtown Boston more easily accessible to the youth at Harvard. Norton himself complained that the new shops, new streets, and new immigrants were too rapidly transforming the old town of Cambridge into a modern city.

President Eliot rode in on the tide of this postwar change and expansion. A man confident of his ideas and determined to see them successfully carried out, he revolutionized the physical and academic character of the college. Between 1870 and 1872, Thayer, Matthews, and Weld Halls appeared, along with Holyoke House. Eliot rejuvenated the Law, Medical, and Dental Schools. He broadened the curriculum and made elective courses available even to freshmen. He banished the "Scale of Merit" and the last traces of the recitation system. Within a few years after his inauguration, Harvard had a graduate school. The most important part of this expansion was the outstanding group of teachers who were attracted to Harvard during the Eliot era. Only a part of the glittering list of Norton's colleagues includes Child, Wendell, Kittredge, Palmer, Royce, Santayana, William James, Shaler, Hart, Gurney, and Henry Adams. It has rightly been named the "golden age of Harvard."

In January, 1874, traces of Norton's earlier optimism began to appear, along with the old missionary zeal. He looked forward to his new role of teacher at Harvard, where he would be "brought into close relations with youths whom I can try to inspire with love of things that make life beautiful and generous. I have some ardours left, —" he wrote to Ruskin, "and no whit of faith in the good as good, and to be aimed at whether attainable or not, has vanished from my soul." His purpose was to teach the underlying unity of expression in all the arts, and their application to the American experience: that the arts cannot flourish "unless men have something to express which is the result of long training of soul and sense in the ways of high living and true thought." Then, characteristically, he added a gloomier note:

> I want to make them see that we have in our days nothing to say, that silence befits us, that the arts of beauty are not for us to practice; — and seeing this to resolve so as to live that another generation may begin to be happier than we.[7]

The position at Harvard was annual lecturer in the "History of the Arts of Construction and Design, and their Relations to Literature," at a salary of fifteen hundred dollars. As an enticement, President Eliot gave Norton virtual assurance that he would be made Professor of Fine Arts in the following year. So in the fall of 1874, Norton began twenty-three years of teaching at Harvard, continuing his fight with "the devil and his allies" by preaching the gospel of Art to future generations of Americans.[8]

WHAT NORTON TAUGHT

Norton brought to his teaching a preparation in mature scholarship which few members of that harried profession have equaled. At the age of forty-seven, he was author of a volume of Italian studies and a recognized authority on the age of Dante. In his reviews for the *Atlantic Monthly, North American Review,* and *Nation,* he had written on virtually every aspect of the fine arts, from wood-engraving to musical theory. During his five years abroad, he had studied the age of the great cathedrals from the original documents at Siena, Florence, and Venice. By 1874, the theory of art as the expression of a nation's highest moral aspiration had hardened into a personal doctrine.

Norton's ideas about the role of the fine arts in education perhaps were derived to some extent from his English friends Ruskin and John Stuart Mill. Mill, in his inaugural address upon assuming the honorary presidency of the University of St. Andrews in 1867, had emphasized the importance of art in the British curriculum. Mill's address helped somewhat to ease a conflict in Norton between the utilitarian and the aesthetic which he had discussed in his correspondence both with Mill and Chauncey Wright. On different occasions later in the century, Norton cited Mill and reasserted the belief that cultivation of the feelings and "imagination" through study of the fine arts should become a central aim of America's schools. In 1870, Ruskin had privately described his own plan of instruction at Oxford. Ruskin's letter, which has not come to light, deeply impressed Norton. He replied to Ruskin, praising his scheme of presenting the fine arts as an integral part of the Oxford curriculum.

Norton's program of fine arts at Harvard, then, was to have a triple purpose: to show the significance of the fine arts as the expression of moral and intellectual conditions of the past; then to illustrate, by contrast, the barrenness of the

American experience which, up to that time, had starved the creative spirit; and finally, to refine the sensibilities of young men at Harvard. This last aim apparently gave him some uneasiness. His studies up to this time had barely touched the aesthetic side of art. He suggested his plan of teaching in a letter to President Eliot wherein one suspects a certain amount of rationalization:

> The fine arts have been generally regarded as a sort of domain reserved for the dilettante. Too much has been written concerning them from the purely aesthetic side, and so much of this writing has been foolish and ignorant, that it is not surprising that their more important relations to history and literature have been more or less disregarded . . .[9]

Happily, a solution to the teaching of aesthetics was at hand in the person of Charles H. Moore, instructor in freehand drawing and water color. Moore supplemented Norton during the first year by offering "Principles of Design in Painting, Sculpture, and Architecture." This dual instruction was successful and established a pattern of cooperation in the department for future years.

What did Norton tell his classes at Harvard in these last decades of the nineteenth century? The answers are found in various places — in his own lecture notebooks and examination questions; in students' notebooks later given to the Harvard Library; in scattered correspondence both by Norton and his students; and finally, in Norton's published writings which grew out of the materials in his lectures. He was handicapped during the first years by the lack of suitable textbooks. He had acquired illustrative materials, including photographs, drawings, and small casts, but found them to be ineffective in the classroom and abandoned them. Not until 1896 was he able to introduce slides. Consequently, he was forced from the beginning to rely primarily on his vocal gifts — the precise diction and rich, expressive voice — and the personal impact of his quiet, intense manner. The early lectures were to a large degree eclectic. His lecture notebooks during the first three years are cumbersome with aesthetic and historical information gathered from authors ancient and modern. He soon learned where the richest materials lay, and the skimpiness of the later notebooks reveals the confidence with which he came to grasp the history of art. After the first years, Norton centered his courses heavily on the golden age of Athens, and the flowering of the Gothic style in Venice and Florence. The Renaissance he treated separately during one year only — in 1878. Otherwise, the Renaissance became the terminal point in Norton's survey of art history. For his purposes, there was no significant art after the year 1600.

The Athenian Age

Norton's earlier classical interests during his student days at Harvard did not disappear through the years in spite of his fascination with the Gothic and the friendship with Ruskin in the 1850's. Ruskin's opposition to the North during the Civil War had interrupted their relationship and weakened whatever influence on Norton he may have held. In 1869, Norton praised the early pre-Raphaelite painter Burne-Jones for progressing "from a narrow and exclusive field of art into the broad ranges of its complete domain which embraces Gothic and Greek, mediaeval and classic ideals." [10] In 1870, during his residence in Italy, Norton had planned to break off his Gothic studies at Siena in favor of investigating the Greek remains in southern Italy, but he had been unable to arrange the trip.

In the spring of 1874, Norton was reading intensively to refresh his knowledge of fifth-century Athens in preparation for his lectures in the fall. His studies centered on the Parthenon as a reflection of the "moral and physical elements of the Athenian nature." How could one account for this architectural miracle? he asked Ruskin. How should the Athenians at this particular moment of history have inherited "this sense of balance, rhythm, proportion, symmetry, — resulting in a sense of form very different from any that the modern world possesses . . . Why, and what did it mean?" He presently concluded that the principles of simplicity and beauty in the Parthenon were the same laws which governed the lives of the Athenian people in Pericles' time.[11]

Antecedent to human government, however, was the influence of the landscape on the Greek character and sense of beauty. The open-air life of the people brought them into close relation to the "friendliness and charm of nature," Norton said. The Greeks were therefore "in great part the creation of the land." For in Norton's definition, the imagination had its origin and derived its power from experiences in nature. Not only the people of Athens, but also Pericles and the Athenian statesmen were endowed with a healthy creativeness. The notebook jottings include the applications Norton drew from the Athenian character:

> Importance of imagination as a check to sensualism, materialism, hardness of heart.
> Its practical importance, in politics, especially in a country like our own; and in dealing with questions that affect international interests.[12]

In a society such as Athens had enjoyed in the fifth century B.C., the noblest work of an Aeschylus or a Phidias was possible. But even more, here was a time when every (free) man was an artist. In weaving, spinning, embroidery, metal work — in all handiwork, including the commonest utensils, the craftsman worked with an eye trained for beautiful design. "The hand was the instrument of the soul." The contrast between ancient Greece and modern America could be seen clearly in the "loss of sense of personal elegance as expressed in articles of common use, [the] lack of discrimination between the beautiful and ugly." The poetic impulse was absent in America for two reasons. First, the "uniformity of machine work" had dulled the perceptions of the worker and the community. The machine was bringing men down to its own level of indifference to beauty. It created abundance, but the value of an article had come to be judged only by the rules of a "money standard." Handiwork, on the other hand, made "costly but precious products, with something of human life in them." Second, the contrast included the difference between labor conditions in ancient Athens and industrial America:

> Habit of work may be delightful, there may be peace and pleasurableness of occupation; habit of work may be degrading, nay even corrupting; occupation in midst of roar of machinery may produce a barbarizing weariness of senses.

Greek civilization taught "the lesson of moderation, of self-control, of wise, sweet, simple, temperate living, of which we stand in need in these days of eager haste, of complex interests, of restlessness of spirit, of nervous over-excitement." In asides to his class, Norton tried to apply the example of the Greeks to the life of the students. One of his targets was the student rooms. Photographs taken at that time show these rooms as a clutter of banners, posters, stolen commercial signs, and professors' caricatures from the *Lampoon,* all nailed to the walls, while souvenir trinkets or tasseled pillows lay scattered on the high-Victorian-style furniture. On the mantelpiece, a skull fitted with horn-rimmed spectacles might be solemnly looking out on the jumbled scene. The following passage from a student's class notes in Ancient Art relates one of Norton's gratuitous comments on student taste, and also hints at the classroom response:

> The average student's room is evidence of a barbarism even beyond that which is exhibited in this room. *This is not a smiling matter.* It is a matter for shame that the standard of taste should be so low as is manifest in the rooms, which are the objects of your chief admiration. Consider how many of the objects in your room are ugly and vulgar! How many are really beautiful and ennobling? How many of the pictures on your walls have such a suggestiveness in them as would lead to a real enjoyment of life? . . . It is true we see many signs of a rudi-

mentary beauty, such as the savage sees in his tattooing; these are the tendencies toward something higher, something more noble.[13]

Medieval Venice and Florence

Norton found the Gothic age of medieval Florence and Venice as fruitful for his purposes as ancient Athens. The essay on the Duomo at Orvieto nearly twenty years before had established the pattern, and many of the conclusions, of his later medieval studies. In 1870, and during part of the following year, he was continuing these studies in the archives at Siena, Florence, and Venice. In the original documents from the era of the great cathedrals, he found increased evidence for the theory of art he wished to propound in America. When he was elected to the chair of Fine Arts at Harvard, therefore, Norton had acquired much of his raw material. What he told his students soon appeared in published form in the *Historical Studies of Church-Building in the Middle Ages* (1880). In the opening chapters of that book, Norton presents a general statement of his hypothesis. The subsequent chapters, relating the story of the cathedrals at Siena, Florence, and Venice, serve merely to document his previous conclusions. So, too, do his later studies of the cathedrals at Chartres and St. Denis.[14]

In Italy's Middle Ages (1150–1300), Norton traced the proper continuity of art history. Italy led all of Europe out of the Dark Ages, he explained, for in Italy the older Roman tradition had been preserved at fullest strength. In refinement and manners, in temperament and tradition, Italy was further advanced than any other country in Europe at the dawn of modern times. A sense of the world's beauty reawakened in the souls of the Italian people, and inspired her painters (said Norton), while the universal Church gave unity of spirit and a pervasive morality to the visual arts. In Venice and Florence, and also in Genoa, commerce had begun to thrive, giving to these communities a sense of permanence. All these impulses — the aesthetic and pietistic fervor of the artist aided by the civic pride of a flourishing community — had set the stage once again for a rebirth of the arts and, in particular, for a monumental architecture. In the spectacular and intricate beauty of the Gothic cathedral, this age reached its highest form of expression. Norton's question again was "Why, and what did it mean?"

The answer, for Norton, lay in the peculiar fitness of the Gothic style for the social and political, as well as the moral, atmosphere of thirteenth-century Italy. In the society of her chief cities there was "less caste and rank division"; the relation of classes was "more human" than elsewhere in Europe. A "republican spirit" dominated the city governments. In the general absence of "feudal chivalry," the people were able to express a measure of individuality.[15] In thirteenth-century Florence, the energies set loose by commercial prosperity aroused the "quick wit, the lively fancy, and the poetic imagination" of the people, who in turn aroused artists to seek perfection of form and expression in their work. As in Athens, the refinement and taste of the citizens stimulated the aesthetic sense of artists and workers alike:

> The spirit of art penetrated every department of life, and gave form to all the products of design. There is a solidarity in the arts; they do not flourish in isolated independence. So at this time art exhibited itself in the least no less than in the greatest things, in objects of common use as well as of display — in the weaving and embroidery of stuffs; in the shape and ornament of dress; in metal-work of all sorts — in the work of blacksmith no less than of the goldsmith; in armor; in jewelry; in articles of the table or the altar; in the wood-work of the carpenter and the joiner; in the calligraphy and illumination of manuscripts. Whatever the hand found to do, that it did under the guidance of artistic fancy and feeling.

This solidarity of the arts among the people was supremely embodied in the complex unity of the Gothic cathedral in the twelfth and thirteenth centuries. Earlier Romanesque art had been the expression of the clergy, Norton explained.

But Gothic art, especially in Italy, represented the imagination of the people and its lay artists:

It was mainly the expression of the piety of the citizens of towns in which wealth was accumulating, and of the spirit of a community with a sense of independence and of strength, and becoming confident of perpetuity. The new cathedral in an Italian city was the witness of civic as well as of religious devotion, of pride and of patriotism consecrated by piety.

The Gothic cathedral, for Norton, marked one stage in human history when a free society voluntarily channeled all of its religious fervor and civic energies into an art form — "the one that has alike the closest and widest relations to the life of a people — to its wants, habits, and culture . . . The lay democracy were the rulers in all that concerned it." [16] It was a time, Norton felt, when an ideal communion existed between the artist and the people. "It was truly said in older days, *picturae ecclesiarum libri sunt laicorum*. The change in the relation of painting and sculpture to the popular life and education is one of the chief differences between medieval and modern civilization." [17]

A last phase of Norton's instruction in art history concerned the ultimate decline of the arts in Athens and in early Renaissance Italy. His discussions of both periods are remarkably alike. The decline of literature and the arts in Greece had begun in Pericles' time and was signaled by a "change in religious feeling and beliefs," a weakening of the "moral temper." These changes were brought about by the growth of "unrestrained individuality . . . , increase of private luxury [and] selfishness. Intellectual life at Athens [was] no longer the life of the community." [18] In a later age at Florence, long years of prosperity had brought greater luxury, increased knowledge, and therefore a wider range of expression in the arts than had been possible in its earlier years; but there was also less piety and a thinner quality of imagination than before. At Venice late in the fourteenth century, the Gothic style had become laden with meaningless ornament, heralding "a change in the moral temper of Venice and a loss of fineness in her perceptions of fitness and beauty. She was growing luxurious, sensual, and prodigal." In Siena, the additions to the Duomo in the fourteenth century were "mostly monuments of the pride and wealth of special families or individuals, and no longer served as expressions of the spirit and devotion of the whole community." [19]

In the Renaissance, Norton saw the emergence of the modern world. Luxury and the diffusion of wealth had cheapened taste, encouraged sensuality, and vitiated the artist's sacred calling and devotion to craft. Renaissance neoclassicism was a travesty of the civilization of ancient Athens. Cold realism on one extreme was competing with shabby romantic sentiment on the other for leadership in the arts. Norton saw no reason to extend his History of the Fine Arts beyond the year 1600. The moral was clear, in the example of Michelangelo as in that of Euripides, and so was the application. In his lecture notebook, Norton inserted without further comment: "Use to Americans! 'Long may it wave.' " [20]

TOWARD A HARVARD LEGEND

Norton's fame at Harvard grew as the years passed. Enrollment in his classes mushroomed from 34 students in 1875 to 446 in 1895. Some of the students came because his classes were considered "snaps." A good coach on the night before examination could prepare a lazy student to pass the course. Other students enrolled out of curiosity. One of this group admitted later,

We knew that, outside the college, he was regarded as the outstanding celebrity on Harvard's faculty. He had been the intimate friend of such stellar figures as Oliver Wendell Holmes, George William Curtis, and wore the mantle of the last of the Cambridge Immortals. We knew that such English writers as John Ruskin, Matthew Arnold, and Thomas Carlyle regarded him as the leading American thinker, the greatest American scholar, the most cultured figure in American life.[21]

Many elected his courses not to learn art history but rather to see a college professor who dared to criticize all aspects of their national life, and even some of the sainted political gods. Norton's opinions were not designed to inspire pride in the national government. The only president he endorsed in the later nineteenth century was Grover Cleveland, though he doubted that even Cleveland possessed the strong character needed to rid the government of graft inherited from the big-business administration of General Grant. After Cleveland's Venezuelan war message, Norton abandoned hope even in Cleveland. Oswald Garrison Villard remembered Norton's political criticism and the reaction of fellow students.

> They sneered at Norton's priceless and caustic comments on men and affairs in our public life . . . Professor Norton deliberately included in his lectures discussions of the events of the day, of every phase of manners and morals and social happenings, [and] called politicians by their right names.[22]

Norton often had argued the importance of female suffrage and education in helping to raise the ideals and set the proper "tone" of society in America. He was an associate of Radcliffe College from its founding in 1879 as the "Society for the Collegiate Instruction of Women." When he repeated certain of his courses at Radcliffe or delivered the commencement address to the women graduates, he spoke as frankly as in his classes at Harvard. Josephine Preston Peabody recorded the following impression of one of Norton's side lectures in social criticism at Radcliffe in the 1890's:

> Professor Norton lectured in Italian 4 this afternoon. The dear old man looks so mildly happy and benignant while he regrets everything in the age and the country — so contented, while he gently tells us it were better for us had we never been born in this degenerate and un-

lovely age . . . that I remain fixed between wrath and unwilling affection . . .[23]

His trenchant criticism of architecture in America also became legendary. The buildings at Harvard were a particular eyesore to Norton. He complained of their ugly design and the incongruity of their different styles, and in 1890, wrote with mordant sarcasm in *Harper's* that someone should appear to render a "superb work of patriotism" — the destruction of most of Harvard's architectural monstrosities:

> If some great benefactor of the University should arise, ready to do a work that should hand down his name in ever-increasing honor with posterity, he might require the destruction of all the buildings erected in the last half-century, and their reconstruction with simple and beautiful design, in mutually helpful, harmonious, and effective relation to each other, so that the outward aspect of the University should better consist with its objective as a place for the best education of the youth of the nation.[24]

Some of the famous architects who figured in this wholesale condemnation (Norton did not name them) were Peabody and Stearns (Matthews Hall, 1872); Ware and Van Brunt (Weld Hall, 1872, and Memorial Hall, 1878); and H. H. Richardson (Sever Hall, 1880, and Austin Hall, 1883). The *Harvard Lampoon* quipped:

Remarkable

Visitor — What is this building famous for?
Student — Charles Eliot Norton didn't object to the architecture.[25]

A tall story circulated around the campus that Norton had died and was about to enter heaven. Suddenly he drew back and shaded his eyes: "Oh! Oh! Oh! So Overdone! So garish! So Renaissance!" He decided to enter hell instead. But presently he returned, informing St. Peter, " 'You are over-ornate here, but down there I found I was going to have to put in eternity looking at Appleton Chapel.' " Norton also criticized the old Romanesque Fogg Art Museum (now Hunt Hall) both in the planning stage and after its completion.

The architect was Richard Morris Hunt, who had ignored the suggestions offered by Norton and his Fine Arts Department. Norton declared that so ugly and ill-lighted a building had only a negative excellence: it demonstrated to Harvard students exactly what an art museum should *not* be. After Norton's feelings became well-known on campus, a prankster painted on the surface of the building the caption, "Norton's Pride." [26]

Norton gained a measure of campus fame for his strict stand on collegiate athletics. In June, 1882, the Harvard Faculty Committee on the Regulation of Athletic Sports held its first meeting, with Norton as chairman. Previously, Harvard teams had been left in student hands. Trainers from outside the college coached the players and became a general nuisance on the campus. Norton's committee ruled that the hiring of trainers in the future would first need the committee's approval. The committee also required that all students pass a physical examination before participating in college sports. The committee, and Norton in particular, also had serious misgivings about college football as a sport. The spirit of the game had begun to resemble the brutality of a Roman spectacle. In January, 1885, the committee took its next logical step: it withdrew the Harvard football team from intercollegiate competition for one year. Although Norton had taken a leave of absence in 1884–85, his opinions and previous work had laid the groundwork for the action. In succeeding years Norton continued to urge a more wholesome spirit of competition in football and other sports. In two separate articles he inserted the brave but futile plea that college athletics become "the sports of gentlemen who do not aim at professional excellence," and asked that the players and frenzied public alike try to regain a "sense of honor and of the sanctity of honesty in all competitions." [27]

Norton fully realized the magnitude of his task at Harvard. He wrote to a correspondent in England, "The rise of Democracy is for the time fatal to social accomplishments and arts . . . Even our Universities, as seats of social culture, suffer from the lack of appreciation in the world outside of this special element in civilization." [28] A glance around his classroom was sometimes enough to confirm his pessimism. A student in one of Norton's Fine Arts classes (enrollment: 446 students) entered in his college diary the notation:

November 24, 1894. A handful of men to hear Professor Norton on Monasteries, the rest being gone childishly to Springfield (for a football game).[29]

For an idealist to survive this "football generation" (as Norton called it) required a tough spirit. This Norton had, as well as a gift of ironical and sometimes caustic wit. He once began a lecture on the concept of the "gentleman" by blandly announcing: "None of you, probably, has ever seen a gentleman." [30] Another story describes an occasion when Norton arrived in class without his textbook. He asked to borrow a text from one of his students. (Silence.) Finally, a book was produced. (Applause.) "And now," he added, "if somebody will be good enough to lend me a paper-knife, we shall be ready!" ("This time the applause was uproarious.") [31]

His classes, as I have said, were oppressively large. And, as he knew only too well, they were often filled with young Americans who probably had little inclination toward the fine arts. "I should like to see an increase in the number of these idle persons," he once remarked with dry irony after surveying his overcrowded classroom at the beginning of a new year.[32] A former student has given an excellent description of Norton in one of these overflowing classrooms:

I recall how, seated on the small raised platform in the largest classroom in Massachusetts Hall, Norton would lean forward on his elbows, his eyes roving from one side of the room to another seeking, I have no doubt now, some gleam of sympathetic understanding from the half-baked students slouching in their seats.[33]

Some of the classes would shrink noticeably after the attendance had been checked. One student at Harvard in the nineties remembered the view from his dormitory window across Harvard Yard to Massachusetts Hall "with its ancient thick walls and incongruous modern fire-escapes, which at certain hours would be black with students retiring [after roll had been taken] from Charles Eliot Norton's course in fine arts on the upper floor." Some stayed the remainder of the hour only "to detach the large, round brim-stone heads from the matches then in use, place them under heel, and make diverting detonations." [34]

Along with such discouragements, Norton was plagued by the frequent return of poor health (in 1884 and again in 1893, he took an enforced leave of absence) and was also assailed with criticism from outside the college. Businessmen like Charles Francis Adams told Norton that the classical approach to education was unrealistic, outmoded, and therefore useless. The students at Harvard, said Adams, should be toughened for their future as American businessmen in the competitive warfare of industrial capitalism. Harvard should offer these young men a practical education:

> I think we've had all we want of "elegant scholars" and "gentlemen of refined classical taste," and now I want to see more University men trained up to take a hand in the rather rough game of American nineteenth-century life. To do that effectively they must, I think, be brought up in communication with that life. At least they should comprehend the tongues in which it talks. The fact is I don't admire Greco-Yankee culture in action, in art, or in literature. I prefer Hawthorne to Everett.[35]

Norton had his own doubts about the results of his teaching. I have mentioned the disheartening response he could detect in his large classes. Examination time gave him even graver doubts. In a notebook, he recorded "Idiotica" from the students' examination papers:

Morality was the most useful trait among the Greeks.
The beautiful eye of the Grecian saw that a perfectly round column would produce no shadow.
The difference between Gr. & R. architecture is that between a construction that displays its naked form of beauty, and one whose deformity requires covering.

Here was the sense of humor which saved him from taking himself too seriously, or from sinking into despair. John Jay Chapman once remembered a student's parody of Norton. The speaker imitated Norton's dress and platform manner, and spoke "in a musical, modulated, deliberate voice — 'I purpose this afternoon to make a few remarks on the hor-ri-ble vul-gar-ity of EVERYTHING.' " Chapman recalled that "Norton attended the lecture and enjoyed it as much as anyone." [36]

Jacques Barzun has remarked that the teacher in America is sometimes forced to put on an *act* to achieve his effect in the classroom. Norton's exaggerations and what appeared to others to be eccentricities were to some extent consciously practiced as necessary teaching devices. Only by exaggeration could he hope to implant certain ideas into the minds of lethargic students. Late in life, he confided to a former student:

> You used to think me almost ridiculous, I have no doubt, in the extremes to which I went. That was because I knew that my class could follow me only to a certain point, and that the higher I aimed the nearer they would approach to what I had in mind." [37]

In private correspondence, Norton confessed, "I am pretty solitary and do not care much for the days. I try to keep myself busy, but life is not very desirable to me. I find it hard to be interested in anything . . ." [38] In the classroom, however, he preached the supreme value of art with an enthusiasm and power that occasionally touched even the most boorish undergraduate. "One had to be a hardened Philistine indeed," a student of Norton's wrote, "to resist the charm of his stoop-shouldered, husky-voiced, but supremely urbane and gentle presence; and a high purity and resolution, as of saints and martyrs, that flashed through his gentleness at times must have awed even the slothful low-brow." [39]

Norton's warmth and "gentle presence" — his talent for friendship — were felt most deeply in the close relationship of the small class. In 1878, and for several years afterward, he invited a small group of seniors and young graduates into his study on Tuesday evenings. There, among Norton's rare books and collection of European art treasures, they read the *Divine Comedy*. Membership was voluntary and the spark of learning in these few students (one of them was George Woodberry) required little fanning by Norton himself. "It is interesting work," he told Lowell, "for they are a picked set, and all full of fresh interest and zeal in the study. By the end of the year, we shall have read the whole 'Divine Comedy,' and there will be eight more lovers of Dante in the land." [40] Another result of these meetings was the students' suggestion of forming a Dante society. The Dante Society of America was soon organized under Norton's direction and he served, after Longfellow and Lowell, as president of the group.

Students at Harvard felt Norton's personal warmth again when he invited into his home on Christmas Eve each year those students who were unable to travel to their own homes during the holiday season. Members of the group composed a cross-section of American immigrants. Some had come to Harvard from as far west as Indiana and California (one of these students once delighted Norton with the departing remark that the evening had been "just Western"). These informal Christmas parties, which became an annual tradition in the Norton home, included an evening supper and ended with Norton's reading of the Christmas story from Luke.

INFLUENCE

Such was Norton's teaching at Harvard in the last quarter of the nineteenth century. The range of his influence — the "unseen harvest" — is harder to describe. During his lifetime, Norton could find some concrete effects of his teaching in the achievement of the poet and scholar, George Woodberry; in providing the impulse (though not the method) of the art studies by Bernhard Berenson, who claimed Norton as a part of his "consciousness"; in the establishment, by James Loeb, of Loeb's Classical Library and the "Charles Eliot Norton Fellowship in Greek Studies" in 1901; and in the city-planning of Charles Moore, who attributed to Norton's fine arts class the beginning of his interest in architecture. At the end of Norton's teaching, Professor George H. Palmer estimated that fully ten thousand students had in some way felt Norton's influence.

Norton treated these younger men as equals, and infected them with a love for the same things he cherished. But he expressly challenged them to think for themselves. He disliked conformity in any field of study, and encouraged those students closest to him to become independent thinkers rather than Nortonian disciples. After his retirement some of Norton's former students wrote respectful letters describing his influence on them. He did not live to read many of these expressions, some earnestly given, but others written in a servile and faintly self-congratulatory tone. He would probably not have cared much to hear such testimony as the following:

> All that I have been and am was and is affected by his teaching and his character. He was the only *real* "master" I ever had . . . ; he implanted in me the seeds of a loathing of affectation and vulgarity; and he conveyed to me a minute part of his own exquisite scrupulousness of taste . . .[41]

Norton resigned his professorship after his seventy-first

birthday in November, 1897, but completed the year of instruction in Ancient Art and stayed on at the college for
several years after as professor emeritus with a small class in
Dante. During the closing months of his final year, he gained
nationwide publicity from an incident in his classroom. After
Congress had declared war in the Caribbean, Norton told
his students that the hostilities with Spain were avoidable,
barbaric, and criminal, and urged them to consider a better
way of serving their country than by enlisting in the armed
forces. For his remarks, Norton received the abuse of the
newspapers and the superpatriots of that day. These critics
were led by Norton's own former classmate, Senator George
Frisbie Hoar, who condemned not only Norton's stand on
the Cuban War, but also his habit, both in and out of the
classroom, of openly criticizing American political leaders
and public affairs.

Norton was prepared for the "pop-gun fire" of the press
and the declarations of the patriots. He weathered out this
new storm of abuse as he had the earlier ones. At Harvard
his courage had become well known. When he appeared on
the platform of the Fogg Art Museum for the last time, the
students answered his critics by purchasing a large basket of
crimson roses and placing them on his desk. A local newspaper reporter described Norton's final class at Harvard:

> The hall was packed, for not only had the members of the courses
> turned out to say farewell to Professor Norton, but many of the other
> undergraduates crowded into the hall and stood along the wall.
> The entrance of the professor was the signal for a burst of applause
> such as has been rarely seen at Harvard.
> Prof. Norton expressed his thanks to the boys for their thought of
> him, and then gave one of his characteristic talks, which have become
> so familiar to all Harvard men.
>   [*The Boston Advertiser*, June 1, 1898]

VI

THE AMERICAN SCHOLAR IN THE "GILDED AGE"

Longfellow was complaining the other day of the decline
in the interest in literature and in the taste for it. Nor was
he mistaken, — this generation is given over to the making
and spending of money, and is losing the capacity of thought.
It wants to be amused, and the magazines amuse it.

(Norton to Carlyle, November 16, 1873)

[Our scholars] have begun to discharge, even if as yet in
comparatively small amount, their debt to the old world
of learning; they are no longer mere borrowers and de-
pendants.

(Norton in the *American Journal of
Archaeology*, March, 1900)

AFTER Norton's retirement as a teacher, President Eliot
wrote, "His work in the University and his training for it
were both unique, and are not likely to be paralleled in the
future." [1] This unique intellectual training extended far beyond the bounds of his course in the history of the fine arts.
Norton possessed in many fields the spirit of curiosity and
independence which Emerson had encouraged in his essay
on "The American Scholar." On his European travels, Norton visited the ancient archives, galleries, and museums, and
formed firsthand impressions of the legacy of older civilizations. He became the respected friend of the leading men of
letters in England, and, on occasion, their severe critic as
well.

Norton parted company with Emerson, however, by preaching the need for a revitalized sense of the past and (contrary to Emerson) urging in America a feeling of humble gratitude for the products of earlier civilizations. In Norton's eyes, America's prosperity and industrial growth, and her accompanying "self-reliance," were leading the country into a spiritual desert rather than toward the oasis which Emerson saw. America could not spin mature wisdom and art from her own inwards, Norton felt. His purpose as a teacher had been "to quicken, so far as may be, in the youth of a land barren of visible memorials of former times, the sense of connection with the past and of gratitude for the efforts and labours of other races and former generations." [2] The handicap under which he labored during the early years of his teaching career was immense. America during the greater portion of the nineteenth century, he wrote at the century's end, lacked both the older materials necessary for the beginnings of scholarship and the newer books needed to keep pace with contemporary scholars in foreign lands:

> Our libraries were insufficiently stocked with older books essential for thorough investigations in any department of learning, and not one of them possessed the means of securing a regular provision of those new books which might enable the student at home to keep up with the progress of learning from year to year in other lands. There was not a single museum containing a collection of casts from which even an imperfect knowledge of the historic development of ancient art, or the character even of its chief works, could be acquired.[3]

THE USES OF THE PAST — THE COLLECTOR

Norton set out, therefore, both publicly and privately, to supply some of the needs which scholars in America lacked. Even in his early twenties while working as a countinghouse clerk, he had helped to raise funds to buy most of the library of George Washington for the Boston Athenaeum. In 1865, he had tried unsuccessfully to persuade Boston to purchase the James Jackson Jarves collection of Italian paintings.

The treasures went to Yale instead. Several years later during his conversations with Carlyle, Norton may have mentioned the barren resources for higher scholarship in America, since Carlyle in 1869 decided to send his books on Cromwell and Frederick the Great to America. He asked Norton to recommend a deserving institution for this library. At Norton's suggestion, the Carlyle collection, together with a cast from the mask of Cromwell's face (a personal gift from Carlyle to Norton), thus found its way to the Harvard Library.

Like his friends Jarves, Appleton, Henry Adams, and "Mrs. Jack" Gardner (whose Fenway Court museum was in large part a result of hearing Norton lecture on art), Norton had also been building his own collection of books and miscellaneous *objets d'art*. His precocious interest in old books and paintings as a boy has already been mentioned. The passion grew on each successive trip to Europe. The ardor with which he could pursue a rare book appears in the following description of a Dante collection belonging to Seymour Kirkup in Florence. After a visit in the study of this old Dante enthusiast, Norton wrote to Lowell:

> His books and manuscripts would make me envious, if envy were of any use. Eight editions of the "Divina Commedia," before 1500, I know not how many from 1500 to 1550. Three or four precious manuscripts of the "Divina Commedia," one dated in 1360 odd; — and innumerable rarities relating to the poet, the poem or the minor works, such as you and I know the charm of. I suppose his books will be sent to Paris or London for sale, — but I have, ghoul-like, inspired a worthy book-seller here with a zeal to get them that I may, if I survive, have some of them! This is horrible, — but one does not want the old women in the kitchen to burn them.

After his return to America, Norton wrote again to Lowell, who was then in Florence, and urged him to bargain for the mask of Dante which Kirkup owned. "I would give any reasonable sum for it," he told Lowell. "It would be a treasure worth having in America." [4]

The books and paintings which Norton brought back from

Europe to his library at Shady Hill he placed at the disposal of his friends and other American scholars. With evangelistic fervor, he loaned his paintings to art exhibitions in neighboring villages of Massachusetts. The words on his bookplate read *Amici et amicis* — Friends and for friends. The tribute which he paid to the generosity of his uncle, George Ticknor, could apply equally well to Norton himself. After Ticknor's death, Norton wrote in the *Nation,* praising

the generous freedom with which he placed his large and rare collection of books at the service of all who might be aided by it, to foster the love of letters and to qualify the force of the material tendencies in American life by the promotion of the better interests of intelligence.[5]

Norton's interest in wood-engraving and autotype photography stemmed from an awareness that these minor arts could acquaint large masses of people in America with great paintings, sculpture, and architecture. Since America had only a limited number of art galleries, and these were not accessible to more than a small fraction of the population, the development of wood-engraving and photography, he felt, became especially important. In addition, the printing arts in America could bring the works of eminent painters within the means of scholars who had little money to spend on works of art. He encouraged these minor arts in various book reviews in the *Nation.* In 1879, he wrote to his pupil George Woodberry that wood-engraving "is at this moment the one fine art that gives promise of value as practiced in America." [6] Four years later, Woodberry produced his first book, *A History of Wood Engraving,* written under Norton's stimulation. Norton lent his own woodcuts to Woodberry for a large number of the illustrations in the book.

In 1905, Norton's collection of rare books was purchased for the Harvard Library. The 581 contributors presented Norton with their autographs inlaid in a bound volume which carried the dedication:

To
CHARLES ELIOT NORTON
From
His Pupils Associates And Friends
In Appreciation
Of His Services To Harvard University
During Many Years . . .
In Gratitude
For His Hospitality Counsel Friendship
Inspiration
Felice te, che si parli a tua posta!

THE USES OF THE PAST — NORTON AND ARCHEOLOGY

The zeal that Norton gave to collecting he also imparted to his efforts to organize interest in archeology. He held that scholars should be sent to the Old World to acquaint themselves, and other Americans, with their indebtedness to the past. The country's intellectual independence, Norton felt, would come only after America could take her place among the other countries of the world, producing original scholars of civilization in times past. His own earlier travel and study abroad had taught Norton that to make America preeminent in classical studies, her scholars should return to Europe where visible memorials told the story of earlier races of men. Such investigations would also prepare teachers for their later contribution to higher learning in America. But even more valuable, this interest in humanistic learning would act as a corrective influence in American life:

At such a period as this, the need is great . . . [for] the humanities as the strongest forces in the never-ending contest against the degrading influences of the spirit of materialism, as the best means of development and discipline of the intelligence, as the source of the knowledge most useful for the invigoration and elevation of character, and most abundant in nutriment for the noblest intellectual qualities . . .[7]

The first step was to be the founding of an American school for classical study at Athens. In 1879, Norton drew up a circular to establish a society which would support such an undertaking. He obtained the signatures of eleven eminent men, and on May 10, 1879, a meeting was held and Norton made chairman of a committee to draw up the constitution. A week later, the Archaeological Institute of America was organized, with Norton elected as its first president; Martin Brimmer, the vice-president; and Agassiz, Ware, and Parkman members of the executive committee.

During the next year, Norton devoted time after his teaching chores and other public duties to promoting the interests of the Archaeological Institute. His chief object was to raise money for a projected fall expedition to be conducted by the young scholar, Joseph T. Clarke, to the ancient Greek site at Assos. He prevailed on Woodberry and Olmsted to write articles promoting the trip, and to solicit members for the Society at ten dollars apiece. An appeal for Harvard students to accompany Clarke on the expedition received an enthusiastic response. Some volunteers had to be turned away. Among the survivors was Norton's eldest son, Eliot.

In his own writing, Norton advertised the work of the Institute whenever possible. Reviewing a current book by the British archeologist, Charles T. Newton, Norton alluded to the expedition to Assos:

> There is great work yet to be done in classical regions in recovering from the earth the precious records of the history of the most brilliant race that ever occupied any portion of her surface . . . In our own country the first steps have been taken by the Archaeological Institute of America in the organizing of an expedition for the thorough investigation of one of the sites of Greek culture, which promises to yield an abundant harvest.[8]

The review ended with a plea to scholars and men of wealth to support this enterprise and to advance America's position in the fields of scholarship and archeology.

Later the references to Assos were inserted more openly. After praising the *Popular Introduction to a History of Greek and Roman Sculpture* by Walter C. Perry, Norton added: "In a new edition, which must speedily be called for, the remarkable additions which have been made to our knowledge of archaic sculpture by the expedition to Assos of the Archaeological Institute of America will demand notice." [9] And the next month, in a signed letter to *Nation*, Norton asked the subscribers to be alert in their reading of ancient history (?) for any mention of Assos, and to send in such information to aid J. T. Clarke's expedition in Greece.

In January, 1881, students at Harvard helped Norton's crusade in the humanities by staging Sophocles' *Oedipus Tyrannus*. Rehearsals took place in Norton's large study at Shady Hill. In a letter to Woodberry, Norton wrote expansively of these rehearsals, "It is a great gain for culture that this interest in a classic work should be so strong. Our expedition to Assos will help also. It has started with the best promise." After the play appeared in May, Norton described the evening as "the most interesting event in College life and studies for years." And with high expectations, he predicted, "It will have great effect in quickening the interest in classical studies." [10] He wrote a "review" of the play and prevailed on Thomas Bailey Aldrich to print it in the July issue of the *Atlantic Monthly*. Again the propaganda was transparent. Norton hoped that the proceeds of the play would be used to swell the fund for establishing the Institute's "American School of Classical Learning at Athens," and then warned the readers: "If we are not to be left behind in scholarship, whether in literature, art, or archeology, we too must have such a school." [11]

The Archaeological Society corresponded with the leading universities in the country to gain support for the School at Athens, and Norton, in January, 1882, traveled through some particularly grim weather to deliver a series of four lectures at Princeton to promote the project. A ticket to the lectures bears the following topics: I and II, "Athens and the Parthenon"; III, "The Building of the Abbey Church of St.

Denis"; and IV, "The Cathedral at Chartres." The Annual Report of the Archaeological Society in 1882 was able to announce that money contributions from American colleges had made it possible to open the School for Classical Studies at Athens in the fall, with Professor Goodwin of Harvard the director.

In later years, Norton allowed the management of the Institute to pass into other hands, but he followed its activities and wrote articles describing its progress. At the century's end, he proudly reviewed the achievement of the first twenty years. In addition to the Assos expedition and the School at Athens, the Archaeological Institute had established an American School of Classical Studies at Rome (at which Norton's own son Richard was professor in 1898); it had investigated the site at the Argive Heraeum in 1892 to 1895; it had sent an expedition to Crete and was currently carrying on investigations at Corinth. In the Archaeological Institute's own *Journal,* Norton could finally say on behalf of American scholars:

> They have begun to discharge, even if as yet in comparatively small amount, their debt to the old world of learning; they are no longer mere borrowers and dependants.[12]

LITERATURE IN AMERICA: REALISM AND THE WEST

In Norton's America, salvation would come chiefly through a renewed sense of continuity with Europe and the traditions of the past. Turning to his literary criticism, we find a natural conflict in his reception of the new postwar literature in America. It was a conflict which embraced the values of two generations — antagonistic attitudes toward subject matter in literature, the function of the writer, and his relation to his audience. Norton seldom endorsed the new "realism" and the literature of the West, nor did he bother even to recognize some of the foremost authors. What is important about Norton as a literary critic is that he devoted more time trying to come to terms with this new spirit in American literature than he did extolling Aldrich, Stoddard, Stedman, and other writers who imitated the older literary forms and politer tastes of prewar New England.

William Dean Howells

Shortly after he returned from Europe in 1873, Norton observed the dreary prospect of literature in America:

> Longfellow was complaining the other day of the decline in the interest in literature and in the taste for it. Nor was he mistaken, — this generation is given over to the making and spending of money, and is losing the capacity of thought. It wants to be amused, and the magazines amuse it.[13]

What Norton really was saying about American literature was that the interest in and taste for his own favorite poets — Longfellow, Lowell, and Emerson — were being replaced by the growing popularity of certain new voices in the land. His fears became more specific several weeks later in a letter to Lowell. Norton had seen his friend Howells, grown "plump and with ease shining out from his eyes," as befitted a man who was fast becoming a popular novelist. "He has passed his poetic stage," Norton wrote, "and bids fair to be a popular American author." In his own figure, Howells seemed to represent for Norton the surfeit and sensuality of American life. In the *Atlantic Monthly* (Howells was now editor) Norton found a departure from the literary quality of the earlier years when the genuine voice of New England had spoken in its pages. Norton wrote to Lowell, "As for art in American letters, — recent numbers of the 'Atlantic Monthly' forbid one to think of it. There are no artists left but Emerson and Longfellow and you!" [14]

Norton softened the criticism two weeks later by writing, again to Lowell, with slightly more approval of Howells' popularity. "He is in just such relations to the public that he makes the very editor needed for the 'Atlantic.' " But the *Monthly* was still below par. "There is not much in the magazine that is likely to be read twice save by its writers, and this is what the great public likes. There must be a revival of letters in America, if literature as an art is not to become extinct." Three weeks later, he again bemoaned the *Atlantic's* "common sackful of the most unnutritious chaff." [15]

A sensitive man like Howells could not help feeling that some Bostonians may have politely withheld their approval of an outsider — in this case a westerner — in the editor's chair of the *Atlantic*. "It is and always will be a deep regret with me," he wrote in these years, "that I have had so little regular education — I mean in the way of schools and colleges." [16] What had always been a slight diffidence in the presence of New England's venerated men of letters turned to acute mortification in 1877 at the *Atlantic Monthly* dinner. Most students of American literature have at some time read versions of what happened that evening. The dinner celebrated the twentieth birthday of the magazine as well as the seventieth birthday of John Greenleaf Whittier, and was attended by Norton and the rest of New England's most formidable literary men. Howells, who was master of ceremonies, suffered painful embarrassment during the dinner as a result of the speech delivered by his friend Mark Twain. Though short, the speech had been worked over with painstaking care by Twain, and he was prepared to receive a pleasant response. The guests had just finished a gigantic six-course dinner, including champagne and five separate wines, when Howells introduced Twain. With perhaps urgent hopefulness, Howells described Mark Twain as a humorist "whose fun is never at the cost of anything honestly high or good." [17] Twain then told his tall story burlesquing Emerson, Holmes, and Longfellow, all of whom were at the dinner.

Just how the audience reacted to the story of these three boorish strangers who ransack a western miner's cabin of food, drink, and clothing will perhaps never be clearly known. The newspapers reported that some laughed at the speech. "Whittier, Longfellow and Holmes seemed politely amused, but were slightly baffled and uncomfortable." Emerson, his mind by these years grown absent, paid little attention to the story. No doubt some of the guests had grown lethargic (or uncomfortable) from the food and drink. But to Howells and Mark Twain, sharply aware of being "outsiders," the polite reaction of the audience seemed the most painful rebuke possible. In their memory, the evening took on a nightmarish quality. As Twain remembered it, the hearers' faces "turned to a sort of black frost. I wondered what the trouble was. I didn't know. I went on, but with difficulty . . . always hoping — but with a gradually perishing hope — that somebody would laugh, or that somebody would at least smile, but nobody did." [18] So mortified was Howells when he recalled the incident that he could not remember any more of the evening, even though the program shows that he had introduced some eight more speakers. When he wrote to Norton two days after the dinner, Howells was still overwhelmed with humiliation and stricken by "that hideous mistake of poor Clemens's." [19]

After the *Atlantic* Dinner, Howells frequently looked to Norton for criticism of the later novels. Norton's role as a sort of elder guardian of Howells in literary matters had begun earlier when, as editor of the *North American Review,* he had welcomed Howells' return from the consulship in Venice. Howells had settled briefly in Boston, but was looking for a house in Cambridge (not an easy task immediately after the war). His landlady, meanwhile, was trying to buy such a house to sell in turn to Howells, at an appropriately high profit. Norton, when he heard that Howells was about to be victimized, took a special delight in thwarting the plan.

He sought out the owner of the house in Cambridge and then secured from his brother-in-law, W. S. Bullard, a loan which covered most of the payment. Norton himself endorsed Howells' note on the second mortgage. Norton also accepted Howells' articles at the outset of a promising career, and became one of his first literary counselors. In addition to Norton's editorial corrections, Howells asked for and received critical comment from Norton on the early sketches of Italian life. Their literary relationship continued into Howells' maturity as Norton exercised an influence on the reticent realist which has never been fully explained.

What did he tell Howells? At times, one can find explicit rules which he laid down for Howells to follow. The characters in American literature should reflect not the average, he told Howells, but the "ideal, that is the fully realized American man and woman, — of whom there are some very few." [20] Howells' characters were not heroic, said Norton. But they were perhaps innocuous, "at least not evil, not bad company, not whited sepulchres, and not corrupt at heart," he conceded, and therefore were "true to the great mass even of vulgar Americans." In the same vein Norton wrote again to Howells of Henry James' *The Better Sort* (1903), a book which Norton recently had read with "repulsion and wonder":

> If these people are his "Better Sort" what can the Worse Sort be? How can he spend his days and himself on such an unredeemed lot, whom he, no less than you or I, would shrink from, at least would not wish to associate intimately with in real life? [21]

At other times, one can infer Norton's warnings, as in the following conciliatory letter from Howells on the characters in his fiction:

> Some day I shall show that I have thought of you so much I could not help writing the kind of story you want. I have long confessed that it was a true story. The pleasant people are more familiar to our experience; you are entirely right; and I do not know why I should

have made so many unpleasant ones, unless it is because they are easier to do. I am glad when you like anything about my books.[22]

Howells' deference to Norton appears again in other letters. During his brief editorship of *Cosmopolitan* Magazine, Howells wrote to Norton in 1891, "I mean to conduct the magazine so that you will be willing to print something of your own in it." In 1895, Norton asked Howells to write a life of Lowell. Howells declined. "I wished very much to do it," he wrote. But he recognized in himself "some most serious disqualifications. Chief and irremediable of these is that I am not a New Englander . . . To my thinking . . . [you are the] one New Englander left." Howells acknowledged his "abiding unfitness for a task you alone could perform with innate and perfect intelligence." [23]

Throughout his mature period, Howells at various times sent his manuscripts to Norton for criticism, and, on one occasion admitted his older friend's influence by writing:

Whether you like it or not, you are always one of the half score readers I have in mind when I write: I don't write *at* you, but *for* you, and no doubt you sometimes save me from myself.[24]

In this attempt to please Norton, Howells sometimes succeeded. *The Undiscovered Country* (1880) Norton considered "charming"; *Annie Kilburn* (1888) "a novel in which America finds expression"; *The Day of Their Wedding* (1896) and *A Parting and a Meeting* (1896) were read aloud in the Norton home immediately after their publication; *The Kentons* (1902) was "just Western"; and in 1902, Norton was rereading *The Rise of Silas Lapham*. Howells' work as a whole Norton praised in 1902 as "the most faithful representations of actual life that were ever written." [25] Such unexpected acclaim was sweet fulfillment indeed for Howells. "I read what you say again and again," he wrote to Norton, "and am happier in it than in any other praise." [26]

During most of his career, Howells clearly needed the

approval of Norton and the Boston literary circle. How great this need was and in what ways it affected his writing — these problems have occupied critics for several decades. Certain lovers of Howells in recent times, however, have sidestepped these matters by peremptorily asserting Howells' disengagement from the New England literati. By discounting the evidence to the contrary, such critics have not helped to clarify the motives of Howells' life and art. Passions are the measure of disengagement. Howells' emotional reaction toward New England ranges all the way from submissive admiration to warm intimacy to stored-up resentment and private rebellion. I would suggest, too, that these emotions often may have been nearly simultaneous. One more instance shows vividly Howells' sensitiveness to the literary opinions of Norton. In 1902, Howells sent Norton a volume of stories by Edith Wyatt, a Chicago writer whom Howells and Henry James had liked. The book, *Every One His Own Way,* was published by McClure Phillips and Company (New York, 1901). Written with strong similarities to the George Ade manner of characterization and fable, the stories contrasted two sets of characters who reappear throughout the book. Richard Elliott and Henry Norris are refined young men with supercilious "Standards" of taste (they are scornful of novels like *Huckleberry Finn.*) By contrast, the Hoffmans and Einsteins are immigrant families who represent traditional human sympathies and goodness of heart. Norton read the book with mixed feelings of admiration and repulsion. He concurred with James and Howells in their praise of the spirit and technique of the author. But he objected to the characters (he didn't specify which set) who were "lacking in charm, in fact horribly true and ugly." He was willing to make one concession in regard to these people. While they seemed complacent in the dreary conditions of their barren lives, they had good intentions and marked an advance over the "Dime Novel level." These were not the people whom

Norton cared to champion quite yet, but he found them "possessing the rudimentary culture which in the next generation may perhaps develop into genuine refinement . . . , people to celebrate as products of democracy in America, but not yet as pleasant to be familiar with or to read about as those who have risen a little further." Norton planned to send the book to his friends in Europe, he said, "as a good specimen of democratic literature." [27]

Significantly, Howells did not choose to answer Norton's criticism directly. Rather, his reply came in an article for the *North American Review,* entitled "Certain of the Chicago School of Fiction" (May, 1903). In this essay, Howells hailed Miss Wyatt's writing as "the apotheosis of the democratic spirit." Then came a sentence which suggests a trace of the deep-seated resentment Howells more than once may have felt in the presence of Norton and other New England men of letters:

> If you yourself have been so distinguished by your maker as to have some essential difference from your fellow-creatures, you will think it very common; but if you are upon the whole not able to make out that you are better than most others, you will be disposed, as I am, to rejoice that the average of human nature is so apparently good, and kind, and beautiful as Miss Wyatt sees it. [P. 735]

Howells' outburst, on the surface, can be attributed to conflicting attitudes toward literary "realism." For Howells, an honest record of the commonplace was the proper domain of the novelist. Norton allied himself with the "romantics" whom Howells had attacked in *Criticism and Fiction.* Norton held that the imagination of the artist transformed the commonness of his characters into an ideal but believable extension of themselves. This conflict in literary theory does not alone fully account for Howells' defense of the Chicago characters in Miss Wyatt's fiction, however. Another part of the answer can be found in the conflict of Howells' personal life.

Since his early twenties as a self-educated youth in Ohio, Howells had looked east to New England, which for him was the promised land of the American writer. When he returned from Venice to live in Boston and Cambridge after the Civil War, his Italian interests made him a welcome addition to Norton's circle. But Howells was sensitive of a *difference* between himself and these others long after he had been cordially received into their group. (He was elected a member of the Saturday Club in 1874.) When Norton could not accept Miss Wyatt's characters as they were, the westerner in Howells made him defensive, and he imputed snobbery to critics such as Norton.

This disagreement over literary principles leads back finally to conflicting views of civilization in America. Norton's comments to Howells on the characters in "realistic" fiction were inspired not by self-esteem and exclusiveness. Rather, they reflect the high standards of his idealism. To accept, as Howells did, the current "average" in American character would have been for Norton the gloomiest of prospects. Howells praised the "democratic spirit" in Western writers of the time; Norton considered the restless, creative spirit of Western "democracy" as a means to "genuine refinement" in a later generation. What Norton was really asking from Howells the novelist was the depiction of characters who could rise from commonplace origins to an eventual cultivation of their tastes, manners, and intelligence — a development Norton could see in Howells himself. But Howells, perhaps enough of a determinist not to see in his own rise a pattern of "democracy," never understood Norton's optimism. Not until after he read the posthumous publication of Norton's letters did Howells fully realize that he, not Norton, had been more the pessimist in his view of American society. During their lifetime, an ultimate failure in communication prevented Howells from gauging Norton's profound idealism and the alternate discouragement and hope which came from his high expectations for Howells' "average" man.

In Norton's final years, Howells apparently continued to sense a gulf in their relationship which could never quite be spanned. In 1907, writing in the *Atlantic Monthly's* fiftieth-anniversary issue, he referred with awe and reverence to "the friend whom I cannot trust myself to praise except in naming him, Charles Eliot Norton." [28] Norton remained for Howells the guardian of New England refinement in taste, learning, and manners, the representative of an elite "culture" in a literary world of which Howells called himself "the latest if least citizen . . . ,that wonderful Cambridge world of poets and scholars which many centuries will not see again." [29]

Henry B. Fuller

Near the end of the century, Norton had a significant relationship with another writer, paralleling in some respects his connection with Howells. This was the Chicago novelist and social critic, Henry B. Fuller. The alliance began in 1890. The house of J. C. Cupples Co. in Boston had assumed the risk of publishing Fuller's first novel, *The Chevalier of Pensieri-Vani*. A copy of the work was sent to Norton, though at whose suggestion — Fuller's or Cupples' — Norton did not know. He read the book and was captivated by the Italian atmosphere which Fuller had evoked. He immediately took the unknown author under his wing and with well-meaning generosity, offered his critical services in a letter to Fuller:

> The book is so good that it is worth more trouble than you have given to it, and when the second edition is to be printed I wish you would allow me to play the part of a severe critic, — to score out here and there an epithet too "precious," a phrase lacking in simplicity, in —

Norton admitted his offer might seem presumptuous. But he wanted to assure Fuller that somewhere east of Chicago appreciative ears had heard the voice which spoke in the pages of *The Chevalier.* "I fear that your book may not be liked by the vulgar so well as it deserves," Norton commiserated. "How should they know that the sweep of the Arno at Pisa is a wonderful thing?"

Fuller replied at once. He was apparently somewhat nettled by the hint in Norton's letter that the novel had been carelessly prepared for publication. Norton, after a long correspondence with men like Ruskin, knew how to handle a hypersensitive writer like Fuller, and replied with ingratiating flattery. He had criticized the novel only "that you might feel that my praise was at least sincere." [30] He also enclosed a note in which Lowell had concurred in praising this first novel of Fuller's. What more could a young novelist from Chicago, himself attracted to the traditions of New England and the Old World, have hoped for after receiving the praise of this venerable pair of Bostonians? An introverted perfectionist, Fuller was gradually soothed and now was ready to admit the justice of Norton's criticism. In 1892, a revised edition of *The Chevalier* appeared, and bore a dedication to Norton.

In the same year, Fuller's second novel, *The Chatelaine of La Trinité,* repeated the mood and background of *The Chevalier.* Norton read it and exulted in a letter to Fuller: "It was a delightful product of Chicago, and gave me such hope for the city as a thousand Columbian Exhibitions could not do." [31] But in the next year, their relationship became somewhat strained once more, this time by the appearance of Fullers' satirical study of Chicago bourgeois society, *The Cliff-Dwellers.* Norton had just returned from the Chicago World's Fair filled with enthusiasm and hope for the new civilization in the West (see Chapter VII below). He sent his impressions of the Chicago Fuller had depicted in *The Cliff-Dwellers,* though he proceeded cautiously. Earlier criticism of Fuller had taught Norton to tread gently on Fuller's sensitive toes. He began by placing Fuller's "realism" on a par with that of Howells, though the praise in itself carried certain instructive overtones:

> The realism of "The Cliff-Dwellers" was implicit in "The Chevalier." It is the man of imagination, the poet, who alone sees things as they really are; it is the writer who has a natural genius for style who can present with equal worth the charm of Italy, or the repulsiveness of that aspect of Chicago which you depict. It is because Mr. Howells is essentially a poet that he sees and describes our American life with such insight and such worth. I put your work on the same shelf as his.

Norton objected to *The Cliff-Dwellers* on two counts. Both in tone and in subject the book had gone beyond the traditional limits of literary propriety and failed to attain the high moral office of great literature:

> I said, "that aspect of Chicago which you depict," — [Norton continued] because my recent visit there showed me another and a better aspect of it. I do not wonder that you detest the Chicago you have drawn, but . . . your disgust seems to me to have carried you too far in your book for its artistic perfection, and for its moral lesson . . .[32]

When Fuller finished his next Chicago novel, *With the Procession* (1895), he sent a copy to Norton, and wrote rather submissively, "I have tried to keep in mind the suggestions which The Cliff-Dwellers prompted you to make, and hope to have avoided the extreme of violence which you deprecated in the closing portion of that book." And he added with a slightly prodding note of irony, "Perhaps this second effort, too, is on a *fairer* social plane." [33] Reading *With the Procession* was a complex experience for Norton. "It is a painful book; hardly less so than 'The Cliff-Dwellers,'" he wrote Fuller, "but this is at once evidence of its worth and of its power." The book forced Norton to reconsider the nature of literature and the function of the writer in America. Should a novelist, in documentary fashion describe and then indict the life which he has experienced in his locale? Or should he depict *ideal* action and characters and thus offer the reader the vicarious experience of noble living? Norton raised these

Norton as a young man

Norton's summer home, Ashfield

The Norton home (Shady Hill) in Cambridge

questions to Fuller. He ended, however, by declaring his preference for the kaleidoscopic romance of the Italian *Chevalier,* rather than the hard, dry light and unrelenting focus with which Fuller had exposed the social and economic life of Chicago. Norton summarized his literary credo:

[*With the Procession*] raises a somewhat serious question, whether such life is fit subject for literary art, and whether the record of it is the best work which you can do for Chicago — for it is after all for Chicago that we are all working, — Chicago, or New York, or Denver City, however our democracy may call its palace-hovels. To be brief, I hold with the poets and the idealists; not the idealizers, but those who have ideals, and, knowing that they are never to be realized, still strive to reach them and to persuade others to take up the same quest. I believe that your "Chevalier" has done more for Chicago than any of the true Chicagoans whom you have given to us, "twice as natural" as life . . .[34]

Fuller's next work of fiction was a volume of stories with an international flavor, entitled *From the Other Side* (1898). This was undoubtedly the new book which Norton acknowledged from Fuller in March, 1898. The European setting, however, could not in itself redeem the tone of the book and the people in it. Fuller had lost the "poetic" quality of his earliest work. In a single sentence whose excessive length suggested the emotion with which Norton wrote, he berated not only Fuller, but American literature and popular taste in general:

I do not know whether to blame the prevalent disposition of the world of letters, or the special evil characteristics of literature and society in America, or the ill example of the most talked of writers of the day, or whether none of these are at fault, that you seem to turn from the paths of the *sacrosante Vergini,* the paths where the poetic imagination and the fancy can alone find full delight, to the dusty roads travelled by the crowd, where, if the Muses happen to stray, their voices are apt to sound faint and hoarse in the uproar and din of those who know them not.[35]

Fuller's reply to Norton was complaisant: "Nothing, I assure you, would give me more pleasure than to produce a work that would please *you*. . ." [36] But the friendship had reached a straining point and the correspondence between the two men ceased.

Other Voices of the West; Mark Twain and Whitman

Norton hoped to see in the western states an infusion of Old World refinement and tradition which might leaven the harsher realities and the primitive vitality of the new West. Howells and Fuller, both cultivated westerners, temporarily raised his expectations for the progress of civilization in America. When Norton turned to other writers of the West, however, he was more doubtful. In one year, he wrote three reviews of western verse, all concerned with the absence of any high standard of "culture" either in the authors or their poetry. In reviewing the work of two women rhymesters from the West, he attributed their inferior verses to the barbarism of western society:

> Culture is of slow growth, and cannot be forced — a fact that most Americans, loath as they have been to admit it, are gradually coming to acknowledge . . . If there were a high standard of critical judgment of women's work in our Western States, we should hardly be called upon to notice Mrs. Charles' poems, or those of Miss Minnie Ward Patterson of Michigan.[37]

With no greater charity, he dismissed the verses of a practicing Kentucky lawyer and popular poet named Theodore O'Hara. After presenting excerpts from one of O'Hara's poems, Norton dispatched it to literary oblivion:

> This is the elegy that is so much admired. It forces upon us the sense of the difference in contemporaneous standards of literary excellence, and impresses us with *the complexity of the problem of American culture*.[38]

The Ship in the Desert, by Joaquin Miller, filled Norton with similar revulsion. The author displayed "so little culture — so little knowledge of character and history." Norton made clear that in literature he did not disparage the backwoods life per se: the freshness of England's rustic verse was delightful to the lovers of poetry. But America lacked the centuries of tradition that endeared the English countryside to the hearts of Englishmen and Americans. In America, the West "comes to us indissolubly connected with associations of coarseness, vulgarity, and barbarism," he wrote. To compare the adventure and suffering of the Forty-Niners to the heroic action of the age of chivalry, as Miller had done, was "ludicrous rant." [39]

Norton echoed this criticism of Joaquin Miller later when Howells confessed a serious intention to write about the Ohio village life of his youth — in the manner of Crabbe's Tales. Again Norton fell back on the contrast between a rich English tradition and the undernourished poetic spirit in America. He warned Howells that such a poetic attempt on American soil would inevitably produce "a pathetic sense, not deep enough to be genuinely tragic, of the barrenness of life and the shallowness of the springs from which it was fed." In Norton's finest vein of ingratiating compliment, he reminded Howells that America, after all, was not England:

> Genius such as yours can indeed make human nature interesting under any conditions. But Crabbe had the advantage of life on an old soil, rich in suggestion and associations. His figures all have a background of generations.[40]

Howells accepted the advice and, for better or worse, abandoned his plan.

And what of Howells' friend from the West, Mark Twain? Norton, in his writing, never referred to any of Twain's novels, though it is safer to assume that he had read at least a few of them than to assume he had not.[41] His relationship with Clemens properly began some time before the *Atlantic Monthly* dinner of December, 1877. In Howells' letter of apology to Norton for Twain's "hideous mistake," Howells appealed the case to Norton "as you have more than once expressed a kindness for him." Howells tried to convince Norton that Clemens had a measure of gentility, "a good and reverent nature for good things," despite his indelicate burlesque of Emerson, Holmes, and Longfellow. A week later, Howells could report to Twain with some relief that Norton at least did not seem to think ill of the speech. "Mr. Norton left a note on my table the other day, expressing just the right feeling towards you about it." [42]

Mark Twain, along with Howells, was invited in the early 1880's to the annual village festival at Norton's summer home at Ashfield. But close relations between Hartford and Shady Hill never developed. Norton was "Professor Norton" in Twain's correspondence, and though Norton on certain occasions sent his personal regards to Clemens through Howells or Thomas Wentworth Higginson, one senses that Mark Twain represented the spirit in American letters which Norton had difficulty accepting. When Yale conferred the LL.D. on Norton during the college's bicentennial celebration in 1901, the degree contained little value, Norton complained, for this eastern seat of learning on the same day indiscriminately had honored two other Americans — Teddy Roosevelt and Mark Twain.

Norton's taste for Whitman declined, as we have seen, after the initial excitement of *Leaves of Grass*. His opinions of the later Whitman are hard to find. William Rossetti in 1869 recorded Norton's comments on Whitman's uncouth behavior:

> N says that Whitman is inconveniently rough in his personal appearance, etc. — will, for instance, call in a red shirt in a family where there are ladies; and that this made intercourse with him by cultivated people difficult, even including such a philosopher as Emerson . . .[43]

It is not clear whether this censure of Whitman's earthy appearance came after a personal meeting of the two men or after a report from Emerson. At any rate, Norton continued to recognize Whitman on the American scene. We know that in 1887, Norton traveled to New York and sat in a box at the Madison Square Theatre to hear Whitman read the annual Lincoln lecture. And in the same year, Norton contributed to a fund collected in Boston to build Whitman a summer home at Timber Creek, New Jersey. After *Leaves of Grass,* Norton's extant correspondence never mentions Whitman as a writer until 1900. A letter of that year suggests that Norton must have read a fair amount of the later Whitman. He wrote in mixed praise of Whitman after receiving a gift of *Gems from Walt Whitman*: "They, like the complete works of the poet, constantly awaken the regret that his literary taste and his critical faculty were not developed in equal measure with his poetic genius and his imaginative insight." [44] Surely it is a modern judgment of Whitman's excesses in form and expression. Moreover, it hints at a more sympathetic recognition of Whitman's genius than one usually finds among later critics. And it also affords added proof that Norton's admiration for the genius and spirit of Whitman, though less ardent than a half-century before, had not completely died away.

THE MODERN AUDIENCE AND THE ARTIST'S LIFE

Poetry and Privacy

Norton regretted the absence of the heroic spirit in modern literature. In place of the traditional hero whose life of exalted action and tragic suffering formerly had taught an ennobling moral lesson, the modern writer in America had chosen to depict what Norton termed "the great mass of vulgar Americans." He objected to this writing on still another score — that of technique or "method." In fact, he found the spirit and the technique of modern literature closely allied. Both reflected certain disquieting tendencies in modern American society. This new literature, with its method of documenting the surface details of ordinary life, and with its curiosity about personal lives and biological drives, had bared not only the most degrading aspects of American life but also some of the most sacred. The leveling of classes in America, Norton felt, had broken down necessary barriers in society which formerly had insured men some measure of privacy. The intimate affairs of men had become public property in an egalitarian society. Norton also blamed the newspaper — the sole reading matter of thousands of Americans — for its continual pursuit of private scandal and, perhaps even worse, for its seductive effect on man's last infirmity. ("I know no worse calamity that can overtake a man than to have a thirst for publicity, and yet it is the common vice of able men in this epoch of the newspaper reporter.") [45]

His aversion to a scandal-seeking reading public led Norton to various excesses in his literary criticism, the most unfortunate being an inability to appreciate poetry which dwelt on personal experience. He considered few poets worth reading "in this period of self-consciousness, of morbid introversion, of exaggeration of the interest of individual feeling and experience." [46] Among the worst offenders were the feminine lyricists, he wrote in 1876. With their new freedom in society and their common-school educational training, women in America had gained a fatal fluency in rhyming, and were displaying a lack of the "keen sense of self-respect" and "that reticence which comes of large experience and high breeding." [47] The modern poets, men and women alike, had grown accustomed to baring their naked souls to the greedy eyes of the public, and had lost "the modesty of reserve, and then, needing sympathy, are misled by vanity, fed by the admiration, flattery and curiosity of the public, into betrayal of themselves." [48] When he printed a volume of *Longfellow's Chief Biographical Poems* for a memorial celebration of the poet in 1907, Norton designed the selection to illustrate how poetry could be written in the first person without becoming an embarrassing confession. In Longfellow, the lyric was a personal moralizing on a general experience. Norton pointed out with regret, however, that even Longfellow could not escape the misfortune common to popular writers in modern times — the public intrusion into his domestic life. Longfellow's fame was "a penalty, exacted of the poet by the great democracy of America and England whose hearts he had touched, and who assumed that the notoriety of his works justified the treatment of their author as a public character." [49]

Norton and Carlyle

The repugnance which Norton felt for the modern craving to know every detail of a man's most sacred intimacies can be seen in his editing of the correspondence of Emerson, Carlyle, Lowell, and Ruskin, and his biographical sketches of Child, Longfellow, Chauncey Wright, and several other friends and writers. When Emerson wrote in late 1873 and asked to entrust his correspondence with Carlyle to Norton's care, he added the solemn note, "I please myself with believing that you will take care that his memory suffers no detriment on this side of the sea." [50] Such a request was unnecessary, however, to a man with Norton's distaste for gossip and scandal. He wrote to Carlyle of Emerson's proposal, and Carlyle heartily approved the bequest. "Lock it by in some drawer till I have vanished," he begged Norton, "and then do with it what to your own just mind shall seem best." [51]

Meanwhile, a villain entered the scene in the person of Carlyle's friend, James A. Froude, who was to act as co-executor (with Carlyle's brother, Alexander Carlyle) of the literary remains. Norton had disliked Froude from their first meetings, when he found the English historian "disagreeable from vanity and a style of somewhat cynical persiflage." [52] The relationship never improved thereafter, and upon Carlyle's death in 1881, Froude brought out his famous edition of the *Reminiscences*. With the appearance of this volume, and seven more which soon followed, Norton declared a private, and ultimately public, war on Froude's integrity as a friend as well as a scholar. Norton's first two volumes, *The Correspondence of Thomas Carlyle and Ralph Waldo Emerson, 1834–1872* (Boston, 1883), were the initial attempt to correct the false portrait of Carlyle which Norton found in Froude. Disappointment in Froude's handling of the biographical materials extended to Carlyle's own family, and in 1885, Mrs. Alexander Carlyle sent Carlyle's correspondence to America for Norton's re-editing. Included were the letters to and from Jane Welsh Carlyle which Froude had used for his intimate and damaging picture of Carlyle's courtship and early marriage. But Norton solemnly declared that these letters were "too sacred" for anyone to read:

> I shall not open the packages of them. Of course there is a temptation to print them, to correct Froude's misinterpretations and misrepresentations. But I think it is a less evil to leave these uncorrected than to violate for a second time the confidences and intimacies of husband and wife. At any rate I will not be he who shall do it.[53]

Later Norton's anger over Froude's biography increased to such a pitch that he broke this vow and opened the letters. In both volumes of the re-edited correspondence, which appeared in 1886, Norton openly criticized the inferences Froude had drawn earlier. The savagery of Norton's attack was felt on both sides of the Atlantic, and dealt a severe blow to Froude's reputation. The *London Times* had previously acclaimed Froude. But Norton's edition of the *Letters* had now forced the *Times* to do an about-face. Matthew Arnold wrote to Norton confirming the effect of Norton's work. The weight of popular opinion in England had now turned against Froude.

Norton opened his second round of accusations against Froude in the same year. In a signed article for the *New Princeton Review*, he set out to demonstrate Froude's diabolical handling of the *Reminiscences*. He accused Froude of treacherously exposing personal papers Carlyle had considered too intimate to be published. Carlyle had written a note on these manuscripts stating that their contents could best be thrown into the fire. In any event, Carlyle had implied that they were not to be published in their present form, and doubted that nine-tenths of the *Reminiscenses* could be properly edited after his death. (Froude maintained that he had been given oral permission by Carlyle to ignore these statements.) Norton hinted clearly that Froude's edition of the *Reminiscences* had been not only a breach of faith, but an outright attempt to calumniate the great Scotsman. "The only important omission," said Norton "is of the passage forbidding the publication." In an attempted *coup de grâce,* Norton rather foolishly printed a list of editorial errors Froude had committed. These were mistakes in punctuation, italics, capitals, the omission of words and clauses, and the printing of wrong words, all of which, said Norton, changed the sense, tone, inflection, and pauses in Carlyle's colorful style.[54] Norton repeated similar charges against Froude the next year in the preface to his own first volume of the *Reminiscences of Thomas Carlyle,* and again in his other later editions of Carlyle's personal papers.

The repercussions of this feud have led a number of scholars to review the history of the Carlyle papers. The most recent summary has exonerated Froude. The author calls Norton's criticism of Froude "spitefully malicious," "petty," and "motivated by a personal dislike." [55] He fails to mention, however, the central motive in Norton's scholarship here and again later as literary executor of Lowell, Curtis, and Ruskin. More important than any personal dislike and jealousy of Froude — and a case for the former can easily be made, though not for the latter — was Norton's enduring resentment toward modern society and its literary sleuths, with their fondness for peeping into the innermost privacies of a man's personal life.

Letters of Lowell and Ruskin

In handling the letters of Lowell and Ruskin, Norton again resisted this trend in modern life — the unbridled craving for gossip which he felt even scholars had fallen victim to. "We are losing the sense of the sacredness of the privacy of life," Norton wrote in a brief biographical sketch after Lowell's death; and in his edition of Lowell's letters, he expanded the statement, inserting a clear allusion to the Carlyle fracas:

> Portions of every man's life are essentially private, and knowledge of them belongs by right only to those intimates whom he himself may see fit to trust with his confidence. Vulgar curiosity is, indeed, always alert to spy into these sanctities, and is too often gratified, as in some memorable and mournful instances in recent years, by the infidelities of untrustworthy friends.[56]

Norton's crusade for privacy was severely hampered in his relationship with the erratic, free-speaking John Ruskin. First, Ruskin printed his own memoirs in the late 1880's (*Praeterita*), and drew a distorted picture of Norton's forcing an introduction with the Ruskin family during a boat trip on Lake Geneva in 1856. Actually, Norton had been formally introduced to Ruskin the previous fall (Chapter II above). "I do not like being represented . . . as trespassing on the privacy of a gentleman with whom I had no right to speak," Norton wrote to an English friend after Ruskin's version of the incident had appeared.[57] And to Ruskin, who had called Norton "my first tutor" in *Praeterita*, Norton said,

> I, the one man in America who have kept myself private, who have hated the publicity and advertising, and notoriety which, in these days even our poets have sought; who have believed it the disgrace and shame of the time that the Gods cannot enjoy their own felicity unless it be 'reported,' — I, the lover of seclusion, am suddenly to be brought before the public under the tremendous light thrown by your affectionate imagination! [58]

A long and frequently turbulent friendship had followed this early meeting. Their steady correspondence was interrupted only during Ruskin's anti-Northern stand in the Civil War, and briefly again during Norton's attack on Ruskin's friend Froude. The rest of the time, Norton had been the voice of sobriety and prudence, constantly trying to check his friend's stormy outbursts and guide his genius along the paths of respectability and convention. During Ruskin's illness in 1878, Norton wrote to John Simon urging that England "make a holocaust of [Ruskin's] correspondence. I dread the vultures that are already hovering over what they have long marked for their prey." [59] Norton became one of Ruskin's literary executors (he prepared the Brantwood edition of Ruskin's works in 1891), and upon Ruskin's death in 1900 was faced with the vexing problem of publishing Ruskin's private papers. "If it depended on me," he told Leslie Stephen, "there would be no further work of Ruskin or about him given to the public. Enough is known. He printed or allowed to be printed far too much." [60] Regarding the correspondence from Ruskin (and others), Norton had earlier resolved, "I shall never . . . prepare for publication the letters which have been written to me. I stand for the privileges and sanctities of privacy." [61] But when Ruskin's joint executors in England began to prepare the Library Edition of Ruskin's works, Norton noticed that the biographical prefaces showed a disregard for his own suggestions. He painfully came to realize that the public and the world of letters would not be denied the details of Ruskin's colorful and scandalous life. A large portion of that record still remained unknown in the letters at Shady Hill. In 1904, Norton personally supervised an edition of this correspondence (*The Letters of John Ruskin to Charles Eliot Norton*, 2 volumes). In this edition, he could take some comfort in restricting what history would report on his friend.

He had further satisfaction in knowing that only a few years before, another substantial part of the Ruskin story secretly had been removed forever from the prying eyes of posterity. For during his last trip to England, Norton, in a triumphant and symbolic act, had searched out and destroyed the bulk of his own correspondence to John Ruskin.

MAJOR CONTRIBUTIONS — DANTE AND DONNE

Even though Norton at times had a pitiably narrow understanding of the form and spirit of literature in the later nineteenth century, he did sense a number of the powerful, underlying conflicts of the age, and occasionally recognized their expression in literature. He was one of the first to perceive the essential conflict in Hawthorne's work, "the opposition that existed between his heart and his intellect. . . . He was always hurting himself, till he became a strange compound of callousness and sensitiveness." [62] Norton was also the first to bring Fitzgerald's *Rubaiyat* before American readers when he printed more than half of the quatrains in an essay for the *North American Review*. And in his scholarship on Dante and Donne, he anticipated the influence of the two most powerful voices of the past (excluding Shakespeare) who have spoken to the modern poetic consciousness.

The interest in Dante during the nineteenth century in America was due to several causes, Norton believed. It showed that the human spirit, starved by the triumph of materialism, was turning to poetry for nourishment. The Dante vogue reflected a widespread loss of religious faith in America. In Dante, the modern reader could respond to a poem which was "at once a work of art of supreme beauty and a work of didactic morals of supreme significance." There was comfort and security in Dante's comprehensive vision of human destiny and salvation at a time when science had slowly undermined these popular beliefs. Why Dante over Milton? Stylistically, Norton felt (anticipating certain twentieth-century critics), the *Divine Comedy* was more congenial to the modern poetic spirit than was *Paradise Lost*.[63] Our age can verify how well Norton recognized the shattered unity of the modern consciousness, and the importance of the *Divine Comedy* to the modern poet.

Norton aided the cause of Dante studies in America in countless ways. First he published his own translation of the *Vita Nuova* in 1859, and brought out a revised edition in 1867. His *Divine Comedy* appeared in 1891–92, and a painstaking revision in 1902. It remains today our standard prose version. In addition to his own translations, Norton was one of the foremost American critics of Dante scholarship. He wrote scores of critical reviews, aimed at a popular as well as scholarly audience. A critical notice by Norton might enlarge into a history of Dante's time, an essay on his current significance, a survey of all English translations of the *Divine Comedy*, an analytical comparison of two or three translations, or a minute criticism of textual errors in some recent Dante scholarship.

Another phase of Norton's Dante criticism is described in Howells' charming and nostalgic *Literary Friends and Acquaintances*. On Wednesday evenings in the winter of 1866–67, Lowell, Norton, Howells, and others gathered at Longfellow's to hear and comment upon their host's translation of the *Divine Comedy*. On Saturday evenings, Lowell and Longfellow, and sometimes Howells, in turn came to Shady Hill to help Norton revise his translation of the *Vita Nuova*.

The informal atmosphere of these meetings was renewed in Norton's teaching. In the late 1870's, he welcomed a number of older students of Dante to meet at Shady Hill in the evenings to read the *Divine Comedy* (Chapter V above). The stimulation of these readings prompted the students in 1880 to approach Norton with a proposal to form a Dante society in America. Norton told them that such a club would need Longfellow as president to insure its success. Longfellow consented, and on February 11, 1881, the Dante Society of America held its first meeting at Craigie House. After Longfellow's death the following year, Lowell became the nominal president (he was abroad during most of these years). When Lowell died in 1891, Norton, by then considered America's foremost Dante scholar, served as president of the Society for the rest of his life.

After 1891, the Dante Society met annually on the third Tuesday of May at Shady Hill. Norton briefly summarized the Dante scholarship of the past year, discussed the entries in the annual Dante prize-essay contest, and outlined the work of the Society during the coming year. The achievements of the Society included publication of native and foreign Dante studies, the printing of the Dante Concordances, and acquisition of a Dante collection at Harvard Library to be serviceable to all Dante scholars. The group acknowledged Norton as the primary influence in stimulating excitement for Dante studies in America, an influence felt by T. S. Eliot and which, through him, has been transmitted to scores of young poets down to the present day.

Norton's scholarship also anticipates the twentieth-century discovery and apotheosis of John Donne. Unlike his studies of Dante, Norton formed this interest in Donne late in life, perhaps from a feeling of obligation to complete an edition of the poems which Lowell had left unfinished and disorderly. Under Norton's exacting scholarship, this task soon mushroomed into a close comparison of all the editions of Donne in the seventeenth century. In 1895, Norton's (and Lowell's) two-volume edition of Donne appeared. Norton's taste for Donne at this time is surprising after his practiced comments of disgust for obscurity and romantic passion in poetry. His criticism of the harshness of Donne's metre was Johnsonian; but he praised the satires for the mingling of deep feeling and shrewd wit. In the love poems he found

such a combination of rapturous passion with delicate sentiment; of sensualism with spirituality; of simplicity with mysticism; of vivid imagination in conception and expression with lively wit and charming fancy, as to set them above all others of their kind.

He singled out for praise "that exquisite poem *The Ecstasy*"! Much of Donne's obscurity, said Norton, was only apparent on a first reading and "due to Donne's own tendency to subtlety of thought." He concluded that "the lover of poetry will find himself in agreement with Ben Jonson in esteeming 'John Donne the first poet in the world in some things.' " [64]

Here was the extra dimension of Norton's aesthetic response which he stubbornly suppressed, a capacity to enjoy the robust or sensual in art, which reappeared once in an unsigned review of some reproductions from Hogarth. Many were too coarse for the "refined modern woman" and her son and daughter, he wrote, but

the lover of humor, the reader of Fielding and Smollett, will turn to them constantly, not only as the best graphic illustrations of the London of George II and George III, but as among the best English delineations of human nature in its prosaic and often ugly aspects.[65]

Norton made a partial recantation of his praise of Donne several years later in a review of Edmund Gosse's *The Life and Letters of John Donne*. As a poet "giving exquisite expression to refined and, at the instant, sincere sentiment," Donne was still pre-eminent. "But alas," Norton regretted, "no poet of rank has surpassed him in preference for conceits to simplicity, and of obscure subtilties to limpid clearness of expression, and none has sunk lower in grossness." [66] In 1905, Norton put his conscience at rest: he issued an edition of Donne's love poems, this time properly expurgated before publication.

THE HUMANIST IN A SCIENTIFIC AGE

In Norton's view, the purpose of art was ultimately moral. He regarded the imagination as a shaping spirit or "crucible" which fuses "the facts that Nature affords it." But he inserted a necessary restriction. " 'In art one must not only report fact, but must choose the right kind of fact to be reported,' " he said, significantly quoting Howells. But he advanced one step past Howellsian "realism." The artist goes beyond mere selection and surface reporting of fact; out of his materials, he develops an ideal beauty, related to, but larger than, real life. "The imaginative poets are the true realists," he told his Harvard classes. By this act of the imagination, the artist realizes his lofty aim — the achievement of the beautiful and the good. Norton added in his notes that he sided with Mill rather than Plato in the emphasis here: beauty is greater than the good, and adds to the good. Norton's own critical comments on art, however, do not follow this emphasis, as we shall see presently. Norton's "aesthetic," in barest outline, then, was essentially a concept of the imagination after the "romantics," and a pseudo-Platonic view of the nature of beauty. Significantly, he left out the troublesome matter of "the true" in the Platonic scheme. The passage just cited from Norton's notebook contained an additional notation which he had blotted out: *"Rien de beau que le vrai.* Veracity." Why this discomfort with "truth"? The answer would require a complete history of Norton's religious conflicts from the tender years when his father was fighting the transcendentalists and writing tomes on *The Evidence of Christianity.* It is interesting that Emerson's Divinity School Address, which the elder Norton had termed "the latest form of infidelity," remained for Charles Norton Emerson's "beautiful discourse." [67] Norton's early attraction to the Pre-Raphaelite school of art, which celebrated beauty and morality outside any limiting religious context, marked the clear beginnings of his agnosticism. In the 1860's, the only remaining appeal of Unitarianism for Norton was the emphasis on morality — on the "good" life and the brotherhood of man. Though Darwin became his close friend in 1869, Norton could not embrace the scientific version of "truth" nor its amorality. Art rather than science became a substitute religion for Norton, but only art which combined beauty with high moral instruction.

He criticized the modern concern with mere craftsmanship just as he had denounced Renaissance cleverness in execution, with its accompanying disregard for morality. In an address at Norwich, Massachusetts, in 1888, Norton commented on this attitude toward technique and morality in the James-Flaubert school of fiction:

> It is the creed of a powerful school of artists, perhaps the predominant school at the present day, that art and morality are absolutely independent, that the relation between the Beautiful and the Good is purely external, and that it is an impertinence to ask for anything in a work of art more than that it should be well executed.[68]

Norton's insistence on the moral and didactic function of art led to certain deficiencies in critical judgment. He was incapable of fully understanding the position of the "formalist" — that the artist can be moral without carving cruciforms for a Gothic cathedral; that in his very striving for perfection of technique, the artist consecrates that world which his experience has revealed to him. Norton, further, was reluctant to admit that art could contribute to the civilization of the race when it dwelt on the ugliness and desperation of human life as well as its refinement and grandeur. "There are poems in the body of English poetry which are full of merit in their mere form," he told his classes at Harvard, "but so foul that one regrets to have come across them." [69] And he advanced one step further by declaring that the choice of ignoble subject matter in art vitiated the artist's craftsmanship and corrupted his sense of beauty:

> The preference of the base subject corrupts, with slow but sure determination, the sense of beauty of form, clouds the eyes of the imagination, and at length makes the hand incapable.[70]

Following Ruskin's logic in *Modern Painters,* Norton criticized many writers by the dubious "badman" theory of literature: men of bad character write bad books. Beginning with the previous century and the English Augustans, Pope was a "liar," Swift a "cynic," Gay a "vulgarian," Young a "sychophant," and Sterne a "mocker." [71] Many of the English Romantics fared no better: "Shelley seems to me to show that he was deficient in the feelings and instincts of a gentleman. — Bryon, Hunt, Trelawny they were none of them gentlemen; as for Hogg — well, his name befits him." [72] Wordsworth, Keats, Tennyson, Arnold, Dickens, Clough, Browning, and above all, "the great and gallant Scott" passed Norton's character test. Kipling, living with his American wife in Vermont during the early 1890's, became Norton's friend. Despite Norton's misgivings about the tone of the "Barrack Room Ballads," he considered Kipling personally a charming friend. Writing in the *Atlantic Monthly* (January, 1897), Norton praised Kipling as a poet in the great English tradition. But Landor, Trollope, and Swinburne were not gentlemen, and neither was Oscar Wilde. Wilde carried two letters of introduction to Norton during the famous American tour in 1882. But Norton had left Boston to deliver a series of lectures at Princeton, thereby escaping an unpleasant experience with what he called Wilde's "affectations and maudlin sensualisms." [73] In America, Norton considered Whitman's behavior objectionable, and refused to give money to a subscription fund to preserve Poe's cottage at Fordham, suggesting that the cottage might better be burned to the ground and bury in its ashes the memory of Poe's final years.

Norton, then, valued literature primarily as a means to promote a moral civilization. The calling of the writer was to guide his readers along the paths which lead to higher aspirations and purer lives. He should avoid incidents involving guilty passion (the case of Edith Wharton) and excessive violence (Henry B. Fuller). Norton wanted characters in our native fiction who would act out the type of life which Americans should try to live, though he never quite seemed to know where American models for these characters could be found. The coarse frontiersman, the lower-class immigrant, and the grasping businessman were all unsuitable for a noble literature, and Norton took some pains to tell Howells and Fuller of their error. The influence of contemporary poets was equally bad. The frank expressions of passion in modern verse only fed the appetite for scandal among the mass of readers who should be elevated above the newspaper level.

What is Norton's significance, then, as a literary critic? His editors have obviously overstated the matter by commending his "openness to the modern appeal in literature." [74] It is true that he welcomed the early work of Kipling, Fuller, Woodberry, and William Vaughn Moody (all cited as evidence by the editors). He was momentarily hopeful whenever he saw new signs of life on the literary scene. He was also prone to reverse his excited first impressions, as he soon did in the case of Kipling and ultimately with other writers whom he at first had greeted. I have already noted his moral reservations on various writers, including the mature Fuller of *The Cliff-Dwellers* and *With the Procession*. His interest in the early development of his former students, Woodberry and William Vaughn Moody, was natural. But while he praised some of Woodberry's early poetry (including the "North Shore Watch"), he found the later poetry occasionally obscure. "Clearness, simplicity, freedom from involved utterance, are among the tests of the excellence and permanence of poetry," he instructed Woodberry.[75] Similarly, he praised Moody's first poems, and liked especially the anti-imperialist ode "On a Soldier Fallen in the Philippines." When Bliss Perry sent Norton a group of Moody's poems in 1901, however, Norton returned them with the criticism that they were too frequently "enigmatic." [76] (For the same reason, he objected to the later novels of Henry James.) He was insensitive not only to the diction of modern poetry, but to the form as well. His definition of proper form in poetry had changed since his twenties when he was reading Horatio Greenough and Emerson, and writing his own verses in imitation of Whitman. He had grown more reluctant to accept "organic form" in a poem, and in later years criticized Emerson as a poet for his "indifference to form," by which Norton meant "verses that have no proper rhythm and . . . rhymes that set one's teeth on edge." [77] Perhaps most damaging of all are the omissions in his criticism (not, of course, to be taken in every case as omissions in his reading). Melville is conspicuously absent. Norton may have been the author of one short, unenthusiastic review of Melville's poetry, which carried a tantalizing reference to "the abilities which he has shown in some of his other works . . ." [78] One searches in vain through Norton's reviews and extensive correspondence for a reference to the work of Mark Twain, Hamlin Garland, Edward Eggleston, Stephen Crane, Harold Frederic, and Frank Norris. Emily Dickinson never appears, even though Norton's friend Thomas Wentworth Higginson edited separate volumes of her work in 1890 and 1891.

Norton's service as a literary critic was corrective rather than creative, and usually monitory rather than inspiriting. He saw in the manner and content of modern literature a decline which he found again in modern scholarship. Both marked a failing interest in the human spirit and its ripest achievements in the past. Like Dryden, Norton believed the writer should himself be something of a scholar and have a thorough classical training — a "well-stocked mind" for the fancy to roam through. He once said of Howells: "Neither he nor Henry James has been as good as they would have been if they had been trained with some acquaintance in childhood with Homer and Vergil and the historical stream of imagination in literature." [79] But instead of such training, the modern writer and scholar were being schooled in the dispassionate accumulation of data and surface detail, in the manner of the scientist. Norton did not disparage exacting scholarship. With President Eliot, he worked to establish the graduate school at Harvard. But he warned against the rise of pedantry and the abuses of the scientific method in the fields of humane learning. The evil genius corrupting American colleges in the later nineteenth century he traced to German scholarship.

In his earlier travels through Europe, Norton had expressed a distaste for the society and learning of Germany. He cared little that George Ticknor, Longfellow, Everett, Motley, Bancroft, and even his friend Lowell had gone there to study. Contrasting German civilization with Italian in 1857, he had written, "It is the brewery against the vineyard." [80] In the winter of 1871, while he lived in Germany, Norton again felt the contrast with Italy. The tempo of society in Italy was leisurely. Enjoyment of art and life was more important than erudition. But in Germany Norton heard the busy hum of men in the libraries, and felt "the impropriety of enjoyment unless the pleasure is united with instruction." The same spirit had spread to the worship of Wagner, and in turn, to a patronizing attitude toward Italian music:

> Passions as expressed in melody, — all the music of Italy, — is good perhaps for baby lovers like Romeo and Juliet, — but for grown men something deeper is needed, something in which the mind shall rise superior to the feelings, in which melody shall be suppressed, and intricate harmonies, puzzling to the most trained ear, shall instruct and elevate if not delight the soul.[81]

The brutal, acquisitive instincts of modern society were present in Germany, and even exaggerated there. "Today it is given up to brutality, — preparing for war, and stockjobbing," he recorded in his notebook. "It is as mercenary as New York, — and as vulgar."

On his return to America, therefore, Norton labored to re-establish the arts in modern life and scholarship. His lecture notebooks in the fine arts contain phrases alive with meaning:

> The humanities and the sciences. Both needed for knowledge of oneself. Evil of "specialization" . . . Exactness and thoroughness of learning. Danger of pedantry; of vague knowledge. Discipline of mind.

The end of education, he wrote in *Harper's,* should be "the development of the breadth, serenity, and solidity of mind, and in the attainment of that complete self-possession which finds expression in character." [82] During this effort to keep the humanities alive, he watched Germany's fatal attraction for American graduate students, who came back to this country "Germanized pedants . . . ill-taught in Germany by the masters of the art of useless learning." [83] As the years passed, he became more irritable. Weir Mitchell, the physician-novelist with whom Norton corresponded late in life, chided Norton for calling football "the chief industry of the University of Pennsylvania." Norton apologized for overlooking the current research at Mitchell's college. He understood that it was pushing back the horizons of humane knowledge, "that it has been compiling references to seasickness in Greek and Latin authors, that it is preparing an edition of the critical works of Dennis and of one or two writers of equal importance, [and] that it is continuing its investigation of the knee-jerk . . ." Norton promised, "I shall henceforth be as little likely to speak disrespectfully of your University as of the Equator." [84]

Norton's fame as a scholar grew during his lifetime from the cumulative weight of his contributions in many fields rather than from the success of any single work. The academic reception of his books, in fact, is hard to describe accurately since his own friends usually wrote the reviews. Lowell reviewed the *Notes of Travel and Study in Italy,*

Howells the *Vita Nuova*, Joseph T. Clarke the *Church-Building in the Middle Ages,* and Norton's ex-student William R. Thayer the *Divine Comedy.* A single work like the literal, repetitious *Church-Building* suffers when placed against the more exciting interpretation of the period in Henry Adams' *Mont St. Michel and Chartres.* But when we comprehend the massive scope of Norton's entire work, we begin to see why Higginson called Norton America's foremost scholar, and we cannot but place him among the select few of our really first-rank scholars — alongside men like Child and Kittredge. One associates the name Klaeber with Beowulf, or Stoll with Shakespeare, but Norton came to personify Scholarship itself, both at Harvard and in the rest of the academic world. During his lifetime, he was accorded the highest academic honors from Cambridge (Litt. D., 1884), Columbia (L.H.D., 1885), Harvard (LL.D., 1887), Oxford (D.C.L., 1900), and Yale (LL.D., 1901).

Norton's extensive labors as a scholar had a unity of idea and purpose. His pioneer efforts in archeology and foreign studies, his criticism of literature as a mirror of American life in the late years of the century, his studies in Dante and Donne, all were aimed at saving America from her own folly. A reckless, shallow, acquisitive, boastful nation, America lacked, Norton felt, the sense of continuity with the great epochs of the past — the golden ages of Athens, Florence, and Venice. Through the Archaeological Institute of America, which he helped to found, he hoped that his country eventually would discharge her debt to the Old World by helping to write the history of the human spirit. For in that history Americans could discover the origin of their habits and thoughts and feelings. He resisted the trend of a new age in America — an age which he thought was losing its native roots and sense of the past. The new generation had begun to look for its standards of value from the philosophers of pragmatism, its literary method from Zola, its scholarship from the University of Gottingen, and its world view from William Randolph Hearst. Norton's work in opposing this trend helped to prepare the ground for the "New Humanists," Irving Babbitt and Paul Elmer More, whose early writing he heralded in the years just before his death. As a last survivor of an earlier society in New England, Norton thus provides the continuity between Emerson's America and a revitalized humanism in the twentieth century.

VII

THE INTELLECTUAL AS CITIZEN

We are just entering on a Presidential campaign — not a very good time for an optimist. Human nature is not at its best in a democracy at these periods. I wish I were not to see a newspaper for six months; and yet such inconsistency is mine that I shall read one every day, with ever increasing dislike of my fellow countrymen. Like Horace Walpole, I should love my country exceedingly if it were not for my countrymen.

(Norton to Leslie Stephen, June 3, 1892)

It is after all for Chicago that we are all working, — Chicago, or New York, or Denver City, however our democracy may call its palace-hovels.

(Norton to Henry B. Fuller, May 30, 1895)

CONCEPT OF SERVICE — THE MORAL BASIS

I<small>N</small> perspective, Norton's activities as a journalist, teacher, and scholar seem to have formed merely a part of a larger life devoted, in the Ciceronian tradition, to the service of society. Like Hawthorne, Howells, Lowell, Curtis, and others, Norton set an example of the nineteenth-century man of letters who left the privacy of his study to engage in an active life of public service.

The idea of duty was part of Norton's Puritan heritage, and it reappeared in the altruism of the Unitarians. His religious background influenced Norton as a young man when he pioneered in improving the education and housing of the industrial worker. The concept of service provided the moral basis for his first book of social criticism and for his articles, newspaper letters, and public lectures to encourage programs of charity and public welfare in the early 1850's. His social philosophy lacked precision, however, until 1856. At the archives in Orvieto, Norton discovered the correlative he was looking for. In the cathedral towns, the Catholic Church in the Middle Ages had established the traditions of benevolence and charity which gave a moral unity to the religious and civic life of the people. Returning to America, Norton again wrote and lectured, this time drawing upon the medieval parallel. As late as 1867, he was instructing a popular audience on the thirteenth-century resolution passed by Florentine citizens to build a cathedral which would surpass all others "because composed of the spirit of many citizens united together in one single will." [1]

Without the authoritarianism of the medieval Church, religion in America (Norton hoped) could unite in a similar spirit of charity and civic duty, with a new "social gospel" of humanity and brotherhood. In an address to the annual convention of Unitarians during the 1860's, he outlined the modern function of the church. Religion should become as liberal as American politics by teaching the "moral unity of the human race . . . In our religion this law is expressed in the commandment of love to man, in our politics in the principle of the equality of rights of men." Influenced by the mutual sacrifice and shared sorrows of the war months, older religious creeds already were being replaced by a "religion that binds all men together." [2]

Writing in the *North American Review* shortly after the War, Norton called the church an anachronism, and encouraged Americans to become freethinkers, united only by the Christian bond of brotherly love. He predicted that the new church would teach a religion based not on dogma and ceremony, but inspired by a concept of service to the community. This spirit of brotherhood, he wrote, "exists wherever the individual has learned that he has no private ends, — that for all he is, and all he desires, and all he does, he is responsible to the community of which he forms a part, and which endows him with its united powers, — . . . and that the true worship of God consists in the service of His children, and devotion to the common interests of men." [3]

During his five years of travel and residence abroad, Norton was strongly tempted to submerge himself in his medievalism and leave behind the acquisitive society of America. He rationalized to Lowell in 1870:

> I am sometimes inclined to think that simply to cultivate one's-self, is perhaps the best service an American can render in these days, when men are so ready to desert the highest paths, and to devote themselves body and soul to "getting on" in lower ways.[4]

Such feelings were encouraged further by the teasing letters of men like Ruskin. "Suppose we both give up our confounded countries?" he wrote Norton. "Let them go their own way in peace, and we will travel together, and abide where we will, and live B. C. — or in the thirteenth century." [5] In the months after his wife's death in 1872, Norton sank perilously close to complete despair. He had come to loathe the sight of Americans in Europe and any reminder of the commercial spirit of America in Europe — whether in hotel architecture or in an image of the railroad or steamboat on the horizon. In these fits of depression, Norton drifted into morbid exaggerations about America. In 1873, he recorded in his notebook that from the beginning, America with her gold had been a "malign influence" on Europe, and had "corrupted the best blood of Spain." America, then must have been one of the causes for Italy's moral decline in the late Renaissance! "The evil influence spread from Spain to Italy; America was in part the cause of the decline of Italy in the sixteenth and seventeenth centuries."

An ingrained sense of duty remained. Norton returned to America in 1873, and prepared to wage the "fight with the devils of prosperity and ease," first as a teacher and scholar, and pre-eminently as a citizen. In his critical writing and public addresses, Norton returned time and again to the barrenness of American life and the "vulgarity" of the people. And yet, he never fully lost hope in the people or the future progress of America. In countless ways, he continued to serve the society which at times he so bitterly rebuked. These acts of service help to show that, then as now, the intellectual who criticizes America most severely may be one of her most valuable citizens.

SAVING NIAGARA AND THE ADIRONDACKS

One of Norton's chief concerns for many years was the callous attitude of Americans toward preservation of the national landscape. Norton himself had been a lover of the out-of-doors from his earliest years. During his student years at Harvard, he had made two horseback and mountain-climbing expeditions into Northern New England. He traveled to see Niagara Falls for the first time in 1848. In the 1850's, Norton had become a member of the Adirondack Club, a small group which included Emerson, Agassiz, Lowell, Longfellow, and others. The men bought a tract of wild nature in the Vermont hills and made excursions into this wilderness. Norton's health had grown delicate by this time and prevented him from actively roughing it with the other members. But the experience with these New England "pioneers" helped him to admire one of the region's famous sons, John Brown, and his later short-lived interest in Thoreau may have been inspired by the spirit of the Adirondack Club.[6] The Club also may have prompted his decision in 1864 to give up the fashionable summer home at Newport in favor of a new residence among the hills of Ashfield in western Massachusetts.

Norton's mature ideas about natural landscape as a formative influence on the imagination and character of a nation began to develop in the years after his return from Europe in

1873. He grew increasingly alarmed by the forces of late nineteenth-century industrialism which not only were ravaging the land but also drawing human society away from the soil and into the streets and factories. In 1879, he prepared to oppose these forces by immediate action. With Frederick Law Olmsted, whose landscape architecture in Central Park during the previous decade had drawn Norton's praise, he inaugurated a campaign to preserve Niagara Falls and the surrounding land as a state park. The natural beauty of the rapids above the Falls was being marred by shanties and mills, and by small shops which were reaping tourist profits by selling American Indian products (frequently manufactured in Ireland). Industrial exploiters, on their part, were fixing greedy eyes on the Falls themselves. As a first step in their campaign, Norton and Olmsted secured signatures to a petition describing the crusade. In the succeeding months, Norton obtained such signers as Carlyle and (through the help of Grant-Duff) some of the most powerful figures in Parliament, as well as American writers, senators, and Supreme Court justices.

After this beginning, Norton and Olmsted in June, 1880, gathered certain men of wealth and influence in New York to organize a campaign which would overcome public apathy and save the Falls. They secured funds to pay J. B. Harrison and Henry Norman for writing articles on Niagara. Though Norton did not write any articles himself, he helped to indoctrinate their authors. In the summer of 1881, he told Harrison to

write something to indicate to the mass of unreflecting, uneducated Americans what the value of noble scenery may be in its influence upon life and character . . . . Very few of them recognize in [Niagara] one of those works of Nature which is fitted to elevate and refine the character, and to quicken the true sense of the relations of man with that nature of which he is a part, to the beauty of which he should be sensitive, and of whose noble works he should feel himself to be the guardian.[7]

The words recall Norton's lectures to his classes at Harvard on the Athenian landscape as a shaper of national character.

Several months later, Norton received the discouraging news from Agassiz that an English firm was bargaining for Niagara ($800,000) as a site for an electric power plant. The writing of pamphlets and letters, mainly by Harrison, continued under Norton's direction in 1882. But Norton had begun to despair that their efforts were having any success in "quickening the dull imaginations and for raising the sordid conceptions of this happy-go-lucky democracy." [8] By July of 1882, he was ready to concede failure. Civic pride and community spirit were rapidly disappearing in America; men growing fat on industrial speculation and individual enterprise could not afford to spend time on such impractical concerns as the beauty of national landscape. Norton wrote to Harrison:

> The growth of wealth and of the selfish individualism which accompanies it (and corrupts many who are not rich) seems to weaken all properly social motives and efforts. Men in cities and towns feel much less relation with their neighbors than of old; there is less civic patriotism; less sense of a spiritual and moral community. This is due in part to other causes, but mainly to the selfishness of the individualism in a well-to-do democracy.

He admitted that their attempt to bring the mass of Americans to feel responsibility for saving the Falls had failed. Any further effort would be a token effort "not so much to save the Falls, as to save our own souls. Were we to see the Falls destroyed without making an effort to save them, — the sin would be ours." [9]

With most of the work completed and the chance of its success in the New York Assembly doubtful, Norton's health was undermined once again, this time by a long siege of insomnia. On the advice of his doctor, he returned to Europe in 1883. But even there he found a society rapidly succumbing to the impulses of materialism and the "progress of democracy." During this summer in Europe, he was oppressed as never before by modern American excrescences on the ancient landscape. American tourists with their newly-gotten wealth produced in Norton the same old feelings of revulsion. At Dijon the picturesque charm of the ancient provincial inns remained. But their existence was threatened by the invasion of American architecture. "A great new modern Americanized hotel with all the improvements is building," he sadly noted, and then added with melancholy irony: "[It is] as much superior to the old as Aladdin's bright new lamp was to the dull and battered lamp by which he could find his way through the magician's caves . . ." [10]

In Italy, too, the imagination labored in vain to dwell in the past. The poetic associations connected with Lake Como were shattered for Norton by the intrusion of industry and "the vulgar democracy":

As in Venice so here . . . The little smoky steamers are puffing about with bustling speed too constantly, there are too many second-class travellers with their second-class style, the vulgar democracy invades the sacred retreats of the Muses, and here at Bellagio the hotels and the shops for travellers give to the edge of the lake the air of a cheap modern watering-place, a place of trivialities and trinkets and dust and fashion . . . [11]

He wished that a "barrier" might be built around Lake Como which could be penetrated only by "those who could prove their right as lovers or as poets, or as lovers of lovers and poets . . ." The "horde of barbaric travellers, these glaring democratic palaces called hotels" filled him with loathing. Their appearance in his beloved Italy was "incongruous and intolerable." [12]

In September, Norton sailed to America never again to return to Italy. This last European experience had been disheartening in many ways. He had relied on the natural and man-made glories of the Old World to provide a corrective example to economic man in America, and a refuge from the low ambition and vulgar pretentiousness he found in American life. He wrote back to a Paris acquaintance: "In Europe I could not but feel with pain the ill wrought by the progress of democracy, — the destruction of old shrines, the disregard of beauty, the decline in personal distinction, the falling off in manners." [13]

What could America any longer hold for an idealist? Norton looked through the gloom and tried to reaffirm his hope in the future. The widespread abundance and material comfort of American life compensated "in a certain measure for the absence of high culture, of generous ideals and of imaginative life . . ." [14] Moreover, the election of the reform candidate, Grover Cleveland, in 1884, gave Norton new encouragement, and after the Inaugural Address in March of the next year, he wrote to Olmsted in guarded praise of the new President: "Lincoln and Cleveland (if he prove what he seems) correct one's disposition to doubt as to the quality of character in the average citizen, — but the character is mostly latent and inoperative." [15] In the same month, he witnessed the final success of the long years of effort to save Niagara. The bill to preserve the Falls had passed in the New York Assembly. Elated by their victory, he wrote to Olmsted: "I congratulate you, — prime mover! I hail you as the Savior of Niagara!" [16] The praise was generous, for men who had been closest to the campaign well knew the part Norton himself had played in saving Niagara. The instant Henry Norman learned that the Niagara Falls Appropriation Bill had been voted, he went to the telegraph office and wired a message of congratulations to Norton.

The success at Niagara gave Olmsted and Norton encouragement to continue the campaign against plunderers of the American landscape. Within a few months, they had begun a new program, this time to save the forests of the Adirondacks from the lumbering interests. Norton did not discount the magnitude of this new struggle against public apathy. He

Professor Norton, probably in the 1880's

Ashfield, 29 August, 1903.

My dear Howells : —

Such a letter as you sent to me the other day is worth living for, even (perhaps all the more) if one feel that it in part gives evidence of the illusions of affection, and even if it bring home to one the saying of the Preacher, "The words of the wise are as goads." In the lack of any satisfaction in the course or promise of public affairs, one falls back for

Facsimile page from a letter to William Dean Howells

had tried earlier in the *Nation* to warn Americans that lumber tycoons were depleting the national forests. Now he encouraged J. B. Harrison once more to write articles which might bring the citizens of New York to an understanding that "the question of the proper use, maintenance and protection of the forests of the United States, is not less important from the point of view of national morality and the character of our people, than from that of their material prosperity." [17]

The crusade progressed fitfully. Norton advised Olmsted to try to organize an association of citizens, as they had done in the case of Niagara, in order to gain united support for the program. Their work seems to have met with small success. Norton sent checks to Harrison, enabling him to continue writing articles, and in 1880 (and again in 1893) tried without luck to find a publisher for Harrison's collected writings. The publishers' attitude only reflected the popular indifference and private self-interest which Norton had reckoned with from the outset of the Adirondacks project:

The indifference of the people of New York, of all classes, to this great public interest is striking, and would be discouraging were it not that the condition of character in which it has its root is so general that it must be taken into account in every effort for the common good, by which no special individual interest is promoted.[18]

Norton's apprehensions were shared by other writers. One of them predicted that the destruction of the Adirondacks would eventually create Pontine marshes in the State of New York:

Unless the existing campaign of destruction is arrested the valley of the lower Hudson will become a desert and the site of New York City a bed of malaria upon which human life cannot exist . . .[19]

An apathetic public eventually was alerted. Norton's successors in later years accomplished the work he and others had begun. If these voices sound strident to modern ears, it is because our age has easily forgotten the discouraging early days of a long campaign which has saved the Adirondacks and other forests from destruction.

AN AMERICAN ARCADIA — LIFE AT ASHFIELD

The theme of Nature versus Industrialism in Norton's ideas and work dominated his description of life at Ashfield in western Massachusetts. During his summers at Ashfield, Norton lived the part of his ideal citizen in a rural village, which, through the final decades of the nineteenth century, was making a last stand against the disrupting forces of modern industrial society. Norton there put into practice his belief that the hope of America rested finally in the intimate social ties and civic spirit of the local community.

The decision to move his summer home from Newport to rustic Ashfield in 1864 had strong Jeffersonian overtones. This homogeneous rural community, he discovered, had been able to escape the urban problems created by the machine and the immigrant industrial worker. There were only three town poor, and these had grown too old to work. He remarked approvingly that, except for one Irish family, the township contained no mixture with the old Anglo-Saxon stock. (Norton was beginning to share the alarm of other old-guard Bostonians over the number of Irish and Jewish immigrants in Boston.) "One could write Massachusetts idylls or a New England 'Arcadia' in this happy tranquil region of the world," he wrote glowingly to George Curtis. "Ashfield has neither telegraph nor railroad, and but one mail a day . . . The scenery all around is delightful, with the mingled charms of fresh wild nature and the cultivation of cheerful farms." [20] And to Lowell, after the War, Norton painted a seductive picture of retirement at Ashfield in the Horatian manner, and urged Lowell to join him in the frugal life of the farmer: "here we would welcome the tax-gatherer as a messenger from our dear country, — we would not dread our annual bills; but we would live in content and in peace and grow old, loving each other . . ." [21] Lowell resisted Norton's salesmanship, but Curtis succumbed and bought a summer home in 1872, separated by one field from Norton's.

When Norton returned to Ashfield in 1873, after five years in Europe, the older generations of cheerful, hard-working farmers were still drawn together by common labor and suffering, and the community retained its tranquil charm and Arcadian freshness, free as yet from the smoke and noise of railroad and factory. But while the machine itself had not yet invaded Ashfield, Norton discovered that the effects of the machine elsewhere had begun to threaten the life of the community. The small yield of the thin New England soil and the rocky hills could not compete with the richer harvests of mechanized farming in the West. Among some of the younger men, "the temptations of Western prairies" was proving stronger than "love of birthplace and home." Others had learned of the economic opportunity in the city, and had packed their suitcases and departed, "attracted by the activity, the promise, the wider variety, the glare of Boston and New York." [22] Even the girls of the village, their curiosity awakened by a common-school education and the weekly newspaper, had grown restless to leave the dull isolation of the farm and seek the novelty and excitement of life in the city.

In some of the other New England towns, the past was giving way to the future more directly. Visible signs of change were appearing which no eye could miss. Cambridge was being transformed and modernized. At Norton's own home, the trees were being felled and the land graded in preparation for the new streets which would presently cut through Shady Hill. At Northampton, where Norton stopped overnight, the quiet grace and "the old sense of common interests and relations," seemed all but to have vanished among the people with whom he talked. He sensed a new restlessness among the townspeople, a change in civic spirit which was accompanying the physical changes of the buildings and streets. Northampton was taking on "the showy looks and pert airs of a chromo-civilized country town." [23]

With change and novelty the rule wherever he traveled, Norton came to cherish the leisure and tranquility of his summers at Ashfield. He chided Curtis in 1877 for receiving publicity in New York (probably for his activities in civil service reform), since these notices from the newspaper carried references to Ashfield and aroused the public's curiosity over their summer retreat:

> Every time that "Ashfield," "Summer Home of . . ." [sic] etc., "Pretty Village," "Wooded Hills," etc., are seen in a New York paper, a bit of our wall of defence against the public is thrown down, and I see summer visitors climbing in through the breach to break up the precious seclusion and leisure of our summer days.[24]

Two summers later, however, it was Norton who broke down the walls of their seclusion and began to attract public attention in regions far beyond Ashfield. In 1879, he inaugurated a local harvest festival called the "Academy Dinner." The Academy was the local school, founded in 1817, and badly in need of funds. Norton hoped that through an annual feast, sponsored and served by the villagers (at one dollar a ticket), the town could renovate the school, hire good teachers, and prevent further emigration by providing a good secondary education for the children of Ashfield. Norton presided at these dinners and through the years invited prominent men to come to Ashfield and speak to the townspeople on topics of national interest. The list of speakers was impressive. It included Curtis, Lowell, Howells, William James, Josiah Royce, Dana, Warner, Hamilton W. Mabie, George W. Cable, Booker T. Washington, and many others. These men spoke on such subjects as political corruption, civil-service reform, Negro education, and anti-imperialism. Such an array of speakers naturally attracted the attention of the newspapers, and notices of the annual celebration were even distributed by the Associated Press. In later years, the guests from outside Ashfield grew in number until at times they matched the attendance of the native villagers. The dinners became a success financially, and in 1889, the townspeople held dedication ceremonies for the newly constructed Ashfield Academy.

Norton's other services to the Ashfield community included delivering public lectures on literature and community affairs; helping to provide the town with a library; serving on various citizens' committees; and cooperating in any number of minor civic events. One of these was an Ashfield children's prize exhibit of handiwork, instituted by Norton and held each Labor Day beginning in 1896. Years before, he had entered a notation in his diary regarding the "evil influence of machinery on handicraft," and later had preached the superiority of the handmade article, first to his classes at Harvard, and then to the audiences at his public lectures. His "Ashfield Children's Labor and Prize Day" became one more individual protest against the industrial civilization outside Ashfield. He hoped to encourage in the village's new generation a habit of developing the manual skills by making products with only the most elementary tools. Prizes went to the children displaying the best needlework, carving, baking, broom-making, and basket-weaving. Recognition also was given to the best essays in citizenship (sample titles: "How to Improve Sanderson Academy," "How to Improve the Town and Village of Ashfield," "The Wood and Lumber of Ashfield," and "The History of Traditions of Ashfield"), as well as rewards for the best nature studies recorded during the year.[25] The entire array of prizes added up to an indictment of technology in American life. Norton's leadership in the encouragement of handicrafts, here and elsewhere, slowly became known in America. When the Society of Arts and Crafts organized in 1897, it chose Norton to act as the Society's first president.

An atmosphere of sweet melancholy lingers over the Ashfield story. John Jay Chapman aptly described Norton's life there as "that rarest of all phenomena in America, the relation of the man of intellect to the soil." [26] Time and again, Norton left his writing or his studies behind to spend his summer afternoons amid the fields and hills of Ashfield. "The longest summer days are too short, and too full of temptations," he told Leslie Stephen. "The garden, and the hills, and the woods, solicit one to leave books and desk, — and I often yield." [27] Another year, he wrote, "We . . . have been haying and finding it one of the chief pleasures of the summer. I am a farmer up here and like it better than being a professor." [28]

The happiest circumstances led Norton to choose Ashfield as a summer residence. The sharp economic and political grievances of the laborer and the farmer elsewhere in America were not felt in this quiet little agrarian community. They were grievances, moreover, which Norton could not fully understand. In public lectures he urged manufacturers to improve the beauty of their product, as well as the physical atmosphere of the factory. But he did not recognize the modern industrial worker's need to form his own pressure group — the labor union — as a recourse against exploitation by management. When he expounded on the "rights of labor" and in Europe predicted a Marxian revolution, he was speaking not to the laborer but to the irresponsible upper classes and captains of industry. Neither did the rights of labor include the right to strike. He favored the use of state militia to break industrial strikes in the East. In 1894, he considered the Pullman Strike as the most "wrongheaded wrongdoing since the world began" and called Eugene Debs "the democratic analogue of the mediaeval baron who levied war on the roads." [29] Norton would probably have understood the plight of the exploited farmer little better than he did that of the laborer. But at Ashfield, he could meditate on an earlier era, on a time when Jefferson had found in the farmer a model of self-reliance and good citizenship. Isolated from the railroad and telegraph, the farmers of Ashfield had retained these earlier virtues (Norton wrote to Charles Darwin), "the simplicity of manners, the vigor of character, and the general intelligence which were characteristic of early New England, before the flood of Irish immigration set in, and before the gold in California and Australia had begun to corrupt and vulgarize the world." [30] At Ashfield, Norton's view was backward into the past, and his modest achievements as a citizen of that village resulted from this nostalgic yearning for an earlier America which he could recall each summer as he boarded the stagecoach and rode those last few miles through the hills toward Ashfield.

THE FUTURE OF AMERICA — CHICAGO, 1893

Near the end of the century, Norton's protest against industrialism seemed more and more the hopeless yearning for a lost Arcadia. Yet, at the very moment when his attitudes appear to fall into a neatly consistent pattern, Norton's nervous antennae had a way of picking up new impulses on the horizon. So it was that in late summer of 1893, he set out on the longest trip he was ever to make in America — to witness personally the Chicago Exposition of that year.

What possessed Norton to leave the serenity of Ashfield and buy a railroad ticket to the Middle West? Impulsive as the act may have seemed even to some of his closest friends, in reality the trip culminated his many years of watchful interest in the westward movement in America. This interest had begun early in life, and came largely from the secondhand reports of his friends. The first of these friends was Francis Parkman, whose *Oregon Trail* Norton had helped to revise during the evenings in 1848 after the day's work at the countinghouse. Also, in his earliest reviews, Norton had described the archeological findings of E. G. Squier in the Mississippi Valley. The slavery problem in the South, which he followed carefully, had become in the fifties a western problem also, creating serious disturbances in Missouri, Kansas, and Nebraska. During the war years, Norton corresponded with western newspaper editors, J. B. Harrison in particular, and became the close friend of other men who had lived in the West, notably Frederick Law Olmsted and William Dean Howells. In postwar years, he continued to be curious and fascinated by the new society mushrooming in the western states. When his former student, George Woodberry, moaned about the dismal life of an English professor at the University of Nebraska ("Oh, the desolate dreariness of this landscape"), Norton replied with corrective enthusiasm:

> What a chance it affords to study Primitive Institutions! I wish I had as clear a concept as you are getting of the first rough stage of a modern civic community. It is all elucidation of history.[31]

Several years later as Harvard's representative at the Tercentenary Celebration at Emmanuel College, Cambridge, Norton told Englishmen about "the Great West peopled by the children of New England, — that Great West which seems, more than any other region of the world, to hold the future in its hand." [32] The interesting hint here that the settling of the "Great West" was essentially an Anglo-Saxon phenomenon shows Norton again as a professional New Englander.

In one of his most incisive essays in social criticism (1888), Norton described western society as he had come to know it from its newspapers, poets, and political orators: "The prevailing spirit of the West . . . is not promising. It is not modest; it is not serious; it is not large-minded. In a word, it exaggerates the defects in the spirit and temper of the country at large." The effects on the West of rapid expansion and commercial prosperity did not mean, however, that its society should remain forever disjointed and barbarous. Norton remembered that the thriving trade and commercial energies of medieval Florence and Venice had achieved a strong bond of civic pride and the wealth and leisure necessary for a cultivation of the arts. Characteristically, his gloomier fears were accompanied by a glimmer of hope: "The very energy displayed in the attainment of material things, may, indeed, now that the means of culture have been so abundantly secured, exhibit itself in acquiring the culture itself." [33] This promise seemed closer to fulfillment several years later when Norton on March 25, 1893, was invited to attend the dinner in New York celebrating the completion of the work for the Chicago Exposition which would open in May. The dinner was given by the architect Daniel H. Burnham, who was director of works at the Fair. Norton sat at the main table amid a large gathering of America's leading architects, citizens and men of letters. He had been asked to talk on behalf of the fine arts at the Fair (which obviously he had then seen from plans or photographs). Norton praised the work at Chicago, calling it the highest art achievement in America's history. He singled out for special recognition Olmsted's design of the grounds and arrangement of the buildings, Burnham's work as chief of construction, and Charles B. Atwood's Palace of the Fine Arts and Peristyle.

Impelled by optimism and curiosity, Norton risked the long trip to Chicago in 1893 to confirm his praise of the Fair and test at first hand his earlier generalizations about life in the West. He apparently kept no journal of his trip to the Columbian Exposition. We know that he stayed at Chicago in Franklin MacVeagh's home (designed by Richardson in the 1880's). We can only imagine his immediate reactions as he walked around the Court of Honor and gazed at the work of painters led by Francis D. Millet and the sculpture inspired by Augustus Saint-Gaudens, both united by and contributing to the architectural performance of Atwood (Palace of Fine Arts); Richard M. Hunt (Administration Building); McKim, Mead, and White (Agricultural Building); Peabody and Stearns (Machinery Hall); and Adler and Sullivan (Transportation Building). From his later account of the Fair, we know that Norton responded with at least some of the wonder which other visitors felt at the Exposition. One spectator compared the overwhelming brilliance of the "White City" to the splendor of ancient Rome:

> The Exposition as completed, with its banners fluttering in the breeze, its fountains splashing in the sunshine, its lagoons troubled by the course of the launches and gondolas which crashed into a million fragments the fairy visions reflected on their breasts, its emerald lawns jewelled with flowers and birds, and its tremendous and many palaces with their regal equipment of terraces, bridges and esplanades all bathed in sunshine against the azure setting of the lake, furnished a spectacle unequalled in the history of the world for the magnificence of its beauty. Imperial Rome in the third century might have approached but surely did not surpass it.[34]

Henry Adams, who had visited the Fair in May, came west in September to study again the baffling spectacle at Chicago:

> The Exposition itself defied philosophy. One might find fault till the last gate closed, one could still explain nothing that needed explanation. As a scenic display, Paris had never approached it, but the inconceivable scenic display consisted in its being there at all — more surprising, as it was, than anything else on the continent, Niagara Falls, the Yellowstone Geysers, and the whole railway system thrown in, since these were all natural products in their place; while, since Noah's Ark, no such Babel of loose and ill-joined, such vague and ill-defined and unrelated thoughts and half-thoughts and experimental outcries as the Exposition, had ever ruffled the surface of the Lakes.[35]

Norton returned to Boston in October. The strenuous exertion of the trip had badly weakened him, and for several days he placed himself under a doctor's care. But his spirits remained high. Though he badgered Howells (whom he had seen at the Fair) about the uninteresting midwestern landscape, with its isolated farmsteads amid lonely stretches of flat prairie, his memories of Chicago were far from disappointing. In a letter to Woodberry, he exulted: "The Fair and Chicago interested me greatly. The spirit of the city is better than that of any of our Eastern cities. I should like to live where there is so strong and wholesome a communal feeling." [36] In the same buoyant mood, he wrote to Henry B. Fuller and mildly reprimanded him for the one-sided portrait of Chicago which Fuller recently had drawn in *The Cliff-Dwellers*:

> I do not wonder that you detest the Chicago you have drawn, but I think you should have sympathetic admiration, nay, even affection, for the ideal Chicago which exists not only in the brain, but in the heart of some of her citizens. I have never seen Americans from whom one could draw happier auguries for the future of America, than some of the men I saw at Chicago. The Fair, in spite of its amazing incongruities, and its immense "border" of vulgarities, was on the whole a great promise, even a great pledge. It, at least, forbids despair.[37]

The favorable impressions left by Chicagoans who, to Norton's astonishment, had shown a surprising degree of refinement and intelligence, began to disintegrate almost as rapidly as they had formed. After several months of settled reflection, Norton reconsidered his sanguine predictions about life in the West. These second thoughts centered primarily on the architectural expression of America embodied in the buildings at the Fair. Olmsted's landscape planning now became the only achievement Norton could wholeheartedly praise at Chicago. The other architects betrayed a defect both in education and imagination; but then, Norton averred, there was little in the experience of the respective states which could inspire the highest poetic expression of the artist. The buildings mirrored in their confusing variety of forms and dazzling exteriors, in their decorativeness and "degrading accessories," both the ingenuity and the uncultivated tastes of a wealthy, immature people. The Columbian Exposition was "full of material promise. Was it full also of spiritual promise?" [38] Or as Henry Adams put it, "Chicago asked in 1893 for the first time the question whether the American people knew where they were driving. Adams . . . decided that the American people probably knew no more than he did; that they might still be driving or drifting towards some point in space; and that, possibly, if relations enough could be observed, this point might be fixed." [39] In 1898, Norton also looked hopefully to the future for the answer. He returned to the popular lecture platform, repeating the mood and even the phrasing and imagery of thirty years before:

> We are on the top of Pisgah; the promised land lies before us, but we shall not go over thither; we life up our eyes westward and north-ward and southward and eastward, and behold it with our eyes, but we shall not go over this Jordan; we can only charge our children, and encourage them, and strengthen them, that they may go over and inherit the good land which we see beyond.[40]

AMERICAN ARCHITECTURE AND THE NATIONAL CHARACTER — LAST REFLECTIONS

In criticizing the buildings at the Chicago Fair, Norton continued his habit of viewing art as the moral expression of an age. In architecture as in other art forms, he had little use for the finer aspects of execution. Like his studies of the medieval church, Norton's criticism of the Fair ignored the important technical problems which men like Atwood, Hunt, and McKim had tried to solve. The decision by architects at Chicago to build in the Classic rather than the current Romanesque style caused a major shift in American architecture. But Norton was concerned with a different problem, and despite the pleadings of Henry Van Brunt for exact technical criticism "instead of Rhadamanthine judgments which condemn or approve and give no reason," Norton continued to apply his subjective moral standards to American architecture.[41] Like all the arts, architecture should express the national *Zeitgeist* rather than the technical virtuosity of the

artist. Norton had preached this nebulous doctrine for thirty-
five years, and never grew tired of repeating himself. In 1867,
he had told a popular audience:

> In their highest achievements the arts are not so much the instru-
> ments and expression of the solitary individual artist, as the means
> which the nation adopts, creates, inspires for the expression of its faith,
> its loftiness of spirit. They are the embodiment of its ideals; the perma-
> nent form of its poetic moods. When the nation is great enough to re-
> quire great art there will be artists ready for its need.[42]

Again, in an address at Hingham in 1881, Norton judged the
Puritan church and meetinghouse not on the principles of
fitness for function or the relation of style to the materials of
construction. Rather, he regretted the absence of the Gothic
spirit. He conceded that in Puritan architecture he could
discern "the expression of the moral convictions and material
convictions of the men who built it," but in judging its quality, Norton returned to the Gothic parallel: "The fancy can
hardly . . . recognize, in the builders with plank and shingle,
a community of spirit with those who wrought miracles of
stone in mediaeval church and cathedral." [43] Similarly, when
he viewed American architecture of the nineteenth century,
he was forced to make the same judgment. For if architecture
was to reflect the spirit of an age so tainted by popular ignorance, superficial taste, and moral turpitude as the late nineteenth century in America, how could the same architecture
express the good and the beautiful? Norton finally turned
from his criticism of contemporary architecture to the condition requisite for communal art forms of the future: the
creation of a civilization in America which could inspire
noble monuments of architecture. Like his friends Ruskin
and Morris in England, he came more and more to consider
art criticism ancillary to social criticism.

In the years just preceding the Chicago Exposition, and
again after his return from the West, Norton published a
number of articles expressing his mature opinions on Ameri-

can life. He had seen all his editions of Carlyle through the press, and was pausing, as it were, for one long final view of the American scene as the century drew toward an end. Lowell a few years before had spoken his piece in the address on "Democracy" (a bit too optimistically, Norton thought) and Godkin had been editorializing in *Nation* about the undesirable tendencies of life in America. Matthew Arnold had made two visits to America in the eighties — he had been a guest of Norton's — and had also passed judgment on American civilization. Now Norton was to have his say. In the first of his articles, he proposed to examine "the effect of our material prosperity, our democratic institutions, and other national conditions, upon the character and development of the intellectual life of America." [44] Near the beginning of his analysis, Norton conceded that American institutions had produced a mass society with a certain minimum education, a society which enjoyed more of the material comforts and personal freedoms than any people in history. America was a nation of "fifty millions well housed, well fed, well protected in their rights." Apart from these admirable gains in comfort and human rights, what had the American experiment accomplished in the non-material aspects of civilization? The world awaited an answer to the question

whether the highest results attained by the civilization of the past, and hitherto confined to a select and comparatively small body, can be preserved, diffused, and made the foundation of a social order in which all advantages shall be more equally shared; or whether the establishment of more democratic forms of society will involve a loss which such gains in human conditions as may result from the new system cannot make good, however much they may outweigh it in their sum. The indications at present are doubtful, and admit of widely differing interpretations.

Thus far in America, economic opportunity and easy wealth had crowded out the older ideals of honor, learning, and obligation to posterity. America's failure in the arts reflected the spiritual barrenness in which her people lived. (The lack of an elevating "passion" in the American character, which was essentially Arnold's recent criticism, also, had been Norton's theme both before and since the Civil War.) "In the length and breadth of the United States," said Norton, "what have we to show in which the spirit of a great nation is revealed through the beauty and dignity of the works of its creative imagination?" Apart from its inventive cleverness, the American mind had produced little, had been, in fact, remarkably jejune. In the ironic mood and rhetoric which Thorstein Veblen soon would adopt, Norton observed that "were the product of pure thought in America to be subtracted from the sum of the world's wisdom, it may be questioned if the diminution would be felt as a serious loss."

Norton summed up all the achievements of America in the nineteenth century — the supposed two-party system, the common school, the railroad, the steamboat, the telegraph, the newspaper — and found only a pattern of widespread uniformity throughout the States, a "similarity of standards in habit and thought," rather than the elevated peaks of individual excellence. The predominance of one language, the absence of mountain and sea to divide social groups, the advances in communication — all these were preventing "the growth of strongly marked distinctions of national type." The immigrant was quickly assimilated, since he had come "from the lower and least intelligent classes, destitute of ideas of the power of initiative action." This lack of diversification in American life had brought a stultifying conformity and the loss of moral and intellectual courage. Echoing Tocqueville, Norton wrote, "In such a society, public opinion exercises a tyrannical authority. Suspicious of independence and originality, it establishes a despotism of custom, encourages moral timidity, and promotes an essentially servile habit of mind."

The article pivoted on this criticism of "the ascendant power of mediocrity" which Norton fearfully predicted was bringing "an increase of vulgarity, by which I mean a pre-dominance of the taste and standards of judgment of the uneducated and unrefined masses, over those of the more enlightened and better-instructed few." At this point, his discussion moved from a diagnosis of the American character to the remedy. The masses, he declared, were not to be blamed for the dead level of mediocrity in American life. The fault lay with the few who "having better opportunities for self-culture than the great body of their countrymen, receiving better education, understanding better the meaning of things, accept with indifference the conditions of inferiority, and make no effort to raise the general standards of character and of conduct." How could this elite raise the standards of American intellectual and moral life? Norton concluded by offering his cure — in the "wider diffusion of the higher education":

> If our civilization is to be prevented from degenerating into a glit-tering barbarism of immeasurable vulgarity and essential feebleness; if our material prosperity is to become but the symbol and source of mental energy and moral excellence, — it is by the support, the increase, the steady improvement of the institutions devoted to the highest educa-tion of youth.[45]

These themes — the vulgar tastes, shallow minds, acquisi-tive instincts, and dull uniformity of the lives in America — were repeated in Norton's articles published in the next few years. In "The Lack of Old Homes in America," he studied the massive effects of the migration from the closely-knit village community into the industrial centers of America. This aimless quest for excitement and wealth had destroyed traditional sentiment toward one's place of birth and, in some cases, the old home itself. This callous destruction of sentimental ties with the past was particularly regrettable in a country where life was already impersonal and prosaic to an extreme:

> In our country, barren as it is of historic objects that appeal to the

imagination and arouse the poetic associations that give depth and charm to life, such a home is even more precious than in lands where works abound that recall the past by transmitting its image to our eyes.

What Americans had finally gained, in the name of economic efficiency, was the standardized matchbox style in modern urban housing, a style of architecture which found an appropriate parallel in the correspondingly uninteresting and skimpy dimensions of the mass intellect. Returning to a favorite image of his, that of Aladdin, Norton wrote:

> If the genius of the lamp were employed in transporting in a night twenty houses from twenty cities, east and west . . . they would offer a dull level of uniformity, and the dwellers within them would be as indistinguishable as the dwellings themselves.[46]

Possibly as a protest against this "dull level of uniformity," Norton never adopted gas or electricity at Shady Hill. Lighting came from student (oil) lamps and candles. He installed a furnace, but the rooms were more often warmed by their own fireplaces.

The following year Norton wrote a pessimistic article on the "Prospects of Architecture as a Fine Art" in America. What hope remained for architecture in America? Norton now toyed with the inevitable alternative to his communal theory of architecture. Perhaps the architect should work uncorrupted by contact with the masses in America, Norton now suggested, for "there is little in the condition of public sentiment from which he may draw inspiration or encouragement." [47] Was the answer, after all, an architectural elite who would instruct and guide popular taste and moral sentiments? To embody the national character as it presently displayed itself, architecture would remain doomed as a fine art. But the old theory died slowly, and after the Chicago Exposition of 1893, when Norton tried to explain his dissatisfaction with the architecture of the World's Fair, he found himself once more entangled in his paradoxical concept of architecture. He complained of the lack of skill and education in the individual architect at Chicago. But he also blamed the national character for the inferior architecture at the Fair. For to abandon the communal theory of inspiration, Norton would also have been forced to reject his views on the mutual relationship between artist and audience and therefore the humanely moral basis of all art.

In the decisive political year of 1896, Norton wrote an article in *Forum* magazine ("Some Aspects of Civilization in America") which brought to a focus his recurring gloom in the years after Chicago. Most of the old guard by then had vanished from the scene: Asa Gray in 1888, Lowell in 1891, Whittier and Curtis in 1892, Parkman in 1893, and Holmes in 1894. The Boston of Norton's youth had disappeared. The "old traditions and inherited culture," he wrote in 1896, were being endangered by the new West, grown "ignorant, rude, careless of social obligations, lawless in disposition, and of dull moral sense." Free education had not stemmed the tide of ignorance, for mechanical methods of popular instruction had failed "to train the judgment, to quicken the imagination, to refine and elevate the moral intelligence of the pupils." Newspapers throughout the country had lost their sense of responsibility as shapers of opinion and character. They now pandered to the popular will and merely reflected "an image of a people with few mental interests, of uncultivated tastes, of shallow disposition, of dull lives, and devoid of intellectual or moral education of a high order." [48]

In one of his blackest moods, Norton wrote this last public essay in social criticism. In England, the article was praised as a valuable and provocative analysis of American civilization. But hearing such reports only added to Norton's discouragement — "It brings home the contrast which the manners and temper of our government and people exhibit to it." [49] He doubted that America would profit by any further criticism, and planned to write no more.

THE SPANISH-AMERICAN WAR — FIN DE SIÈCLE

By 1896, the pressures mounting in Norton's mind were reflected in his final essays in social criticism, but even more sharply in his correspondence. Each month brought some new turn in public affairs to deepen his gloom. His earlier resilience of mind — the ironic humor and willingness to concede certain humane results of the American experiment — is harder to find in his letters of 1896 and after. The beginning of the end came in December of 1895, when Cleveland delivered his Venezuelan message with its hint of possible war with England. In Cleveland's person, Norton previously had seen the finest image of the country since Lincoln. But in his war message, Cleveland had roused the basest passions of an already arrogant nation "by the evoking of the war-spirit." Norton wrote to Godkin,

> It will be a very long time before America can recover from the blow which he has dealt her. The worst of all is the injury to the national character, far-reaching in its effect, by the evoking of the war-spirit. It makes a miserable end for this century.[50]

A few weeks later to Leslie Stephen, Norton called "the rise of the democracy to power" equivalent to "the rise of the uncivilized, whom no school education can suffice to provide with intelligence and reason." With a heavy heart, he predicted that the world was "entering on a new stage of experience, unlike anything heretofore, in which there must be a new discipline of suffering to fit men for the new conditions." [51] In March, Norton still felt the "barbaric spirit of arrogance" asserting itself in America. More disheartened than before, he wrote again to Leslie Stephen:

> Public affairs are depressing. I am not cynic enough not to feel sorry, disappointed, and at times disheartened. It is hard to have the whole background of life grow darker as one grows old. I can understand the feeling of a Roman as he saw the Empire breaking down, and civilization dying out. It will take much longer than we once hoped, for the

world to reorganize itself upon a democratic basis, and for a new and desirable social order to come into existence.[52]

He had been unable to foresee "the inevitable slowness of the process of civilization to the masses of men who were rising to power," he now confessed. "The Democracy has been a disappointment in its incapacity to rise morally in proportion to its rise in material welfare and in power." [53]

Norton continued to believe that signs of hope still lay ahead. But the country first needed some "discipline of calamity to bring it to a sense of responsibility and duty." [54] Redemption would come only after the country's reckless folly had produced some national tragedy which would enable "better dispositions and better conditions . . . [to] be slowly beaten out on the anvils of time." [55] And to Godkin late in the year, he wrote, "Nothing short of seven lean years, or the plagues of Egypt will make this nation serious, honest, full-grown, and civilized." [56] The weakened fiber of the national character showed itself in the widespread absence of moral and intellectual courage. America had become the land of timid conformity rather than the protector of free opinions, Norton wrote to Stephen. And to another fellow agnostic, Goldwin Smith, he wrote, "Timidity which seems to be one of the intellectual conditions of the present stage of democracy, prevents [agnostics] from giving expression to their convictions. In my own circle I find myself almost solitary in my open profession of freethinking." [57]

Norton waited for the calamity which he felt inevitably must come. Nor did he need to wait long. In the summer of 1897 — an Indian summer for Norton — he longed for the simple sweetness and charm of early New England "before the coming in of Jacksonian Democracy, and the invasion of the Irish," the age which continued to live only in the verses of Longfellow, Emerson, and Lowell.[58] These nostalgic reveries were cut short abruptly when, several months later, the revolution in Cuba reawakened the "war-spirit" in

America. President McKinley, egged on by the country's newspapers, soon declared war on Spain. Norton returned from his musings about the past to the realities of the present and performed one of his last acts of moral courage as a citizen and idealist.

The incident for which Norton was to suffer nationwide insult and even threats of personal injury occurred immediately after the declaration of war with Spain in late April, 1898 (see p. 141). He told his class at Harvard, then grown accustomed to his open criticism of public men and national affairs, that they should not enlist in the "criminal war" against Spain. As educated young men, their responsibilities lay in the civilizing work of peace rather than in fighting a weak country in an unnecessary war. The students responded favorably to these words, Norton felt, but his remarks were reported inaccurately, and widespread repercussions followed at once. A local political orator proposed a lynching party for Norton. Other personal threats arrived in the mail at Norton's home. One of these letters informed him that "there are stray bullets somewhere that are liable to hit our country's enemies." Another read briefly,

> You had better pull out
> Yours with contempt —
> A white man [59]

The role of the yellow press in agitating the public during the hostilities against Spain is strikingly revealed in the newspapers' treatment of Norton. He had received in the mail a card from a Massachusetts soldier, announcing with some patriotic fervor that "Proff Norton is a unamircan ass." Norton laughed and showed the illiterate message to newspaper reporters. One paper, the *Los Angeles Times* (then thriving under the rule of the infamous General Harrison Gray Otis) gave the following interpretation of the incident:

Prof. Charles Elliott Norton of Harvard University, whom some astute American calls "an un-American ass" because of a lecture to his students counseling them not to enlist in the nation's defense, has been interviewed instead of being ducked into a swill barrel, as he deserves.

The Chicago Tribune, not to be outdone when an eastern professor was involved, accused Norton of trying to "kill the generous impulses of patriotism and to besmirch the noble cause of humanity upon which the war against Spain is based . . ."

Norton's personal statements to friends show that the entire incident brought him deep personal injury. But he refused to waver from his original stand on the war, and on June 7, delivered an address on "True Patriotism" at Cambridge. The speech, which appeared in the *Boston Transcript* the following morning, clarified his position and corrected statements which earlier had been misquoted. He reviewed the bullying tactics which America had used in forcing the issue of war and compelling "a weak and unwilling nation to a fight, rejecting without due consideration her earnest and repeated offers to meet every legitimate demand of the United States." He restated his views on the citizen's duty to his country. When the press, the pulpit, the masses, and the military all are trapped in a web of thought control and irrational patriotic sentiment, "then, more than ever, it is the duty of the good citizen not to be silent, and spite of obloquy, misrepresentation and abuse, to insist on being heard, and with sober counsel to maintain the everlasting validity of the principles of the moral law." Norton agreed that since the nation had declared war, it was the citizen's legal duty to give financial support to the army, but he chose to let the unthinking "patriot" march off to the fighting. "Better the paying of bounties to such men to fill the ranks than that they should be filled by those whose higher duty is to fit themselves for the service of their country in the patriotic labours of peace." The willful aggression in Cuba and the conduct of the people had been "a bitter disappointment to the lover of his country; it is a turning-back from the path of civilization to that of barbarism."

Norton by then had retired from the Harvard faculty, and within a few days, arrived at Ashfield. He prepared to let the tranquil skies of Ashfield restore his spirit, and wrote to his friends that the storm was apparently subsiding. Rest and retirement, however, did not come so easily. In July, his long-time acquaintance and former classmate, Senator George Hoar, publicly assailed Norton for urging Harvard students not to fight in Cuba. Hoar quoted remarks made by Norton on the arrogant tactics of the military and the "trifling" character of American people. Hoar's speech, delivered at the Clark University Summer School, was partly instigated by a grief-stricken mother whose son had died in battle in Cuba. After reading Norton's condemnation of the war, she had written to Hoar, asking him if her son had lost his life fighting a "criminal war." In his public reply, Hoar attacked Norton personally:

> The trouble with Professor Norton, who thinks his countrymen are lacking in a sense of honour, is that there are two things he cannot in the least comprehend — he cannot comprehend his countrymen, and he cannot comprehend honour.[60]

When Norton learned of these remarks, he wrote to Hoar and rebuked him for breaking fifty years of friendship by quoting "garbled sentences from an account in a Western newspaper of an interview with me, dishonourably obtained and incorrectly reported." But Norton stood fast on his earlier assertion that the war was "inglorious, . . . needless and consequently criminal." [61] Hoar's reply to Norton included a final judgment on Norton's entire career as a teacher and citizen:

> All lovers of Harvard, and all lovers of the country, have felt for a long time that your relation to the University made your influence bad for the college and bad for the youth of the country . . . I am afraid that the habit of bitter and sneering speech about persons and public affairs has so grown upon you that you do not yourself know, always, what you say . . .[62]

The summer of 1898 was a bitter trial for Norton. At the Ashfield summer festival that year, he spoke out as an anti-imperialist. A guest speaker, whom he had invited, presented the viewpoint of those who supported the war with Spain. The Ashfield citizens by then had also turned against Norton. They did not applaud his speech, but they applauded his opponent's. Many said they would not attend the celebration again.

VIII

RETIREMENT

I reach one conclusion — that I have been too much of an idealist about America, had set my hopes too high, had formed too fair an image of what she might become. Never had nation such an opportunity; she was the hope of the world. Never again will any nation have her chance to raise the standard of civilization.

(Norton to S. G. Ward, March 13, 1901)

Surely it is interesting to hear the questions of the generation that succeeds our own.

(Norton to Howells, December 20, 1905)

AFTER his retirement, Norton continued at Harvard for several years as Professor Emeritus, teaching a small class in Dante. He was elected to the Board of Overseers in 1899 and issued one final blast against the architectural design and incongruity of the buildings erected at the University during his professorship, as well as two more built since his retirement — the Harvard Union and Robinson Hall (McKim, Mead and White, architects). He advised such young scholars as Paul Elmer More and Irving Babbitt, and aided older ones like the Reverend Charles A. Dinsmore in Dante, and Furness in Shakespeare, by reading proofs of their publications. He encouraged and helped to guide the early writing efforts of Edith Wharton, his summertime visitor from nearby Lenox. And he continued until 1903 to preside at the Ashfield celebrations each summer, and to criticize America's later "bastard imperialism" in the guerrilla warfare in the Philippines. A good part of the old toughness remained during the final ten years of his life. These were also years of reminiscence and regret over the vanishing traditions of the past, and of anxiety and hope for the social order of the future.

THE PAST — NOSTALGIA AND REGRET

The years had taken from Norton all but a handful of his old friends. To those who had weathered the century and remained — Godkin, Ward, Howells, and some few others — Norton wrote his final impressions of the country which he had loved and quarreled with for more than half a century. It had been a long fight against overwhelming numbers in the enemy camp, an attempt to build — or rebuild — a moral civilization in America. In late 1898, Norton felt "worn and tired" as he wrote to S. G. Ward:

> It is easy enough to see that we have all (or shall I say except you?) expected too happy a result from the fortunate conditions of America; that we looked for too great an effect upon human nature itself, and were too confident that in the long run the good would prevail over the evil element in society . . . The future for America looks to me very threatening. But calamity may do more for our improvement than prosperity has done.[1]

Other letters in these last years re-echoed these tones of disillusionment and despair. "The heaviest burden of old age," Norton wrote to Goldwin Smith, was that all "hopes for the advance of civilized man" had been shattered by the late jingoism of the American people during the war in Cuba and the Philippines.[2] He rebuked himself repeatedly for his earlier optimism:

> I am fully aware that I made a mistake early in life in holding to the hope that the marvelous opportunities of the American People would have such effect upon their disposition that better conditions for the world would follow. I had not rightly considered the lessons of history. If I had done so, I should feel less disappointment now. Man changes slowly from age to age.[3]

And again, after his seventy-seventh birthday, he wrote to

S. G. Ward, "Length of life has brought me bitter disappointment in regard to the country that I have loved and hoped for. I admit that had I been wiser I should have expected less and been less disappointed." [4]

The last years passed with returning melancholy and regret. He railed against "the spirit of this football generation! of this generation without a poet!" and qualified his judgment of Kipling, whom he had praised before the Cuban War, for his "passionate, moral, imperial patriotism." [5] When the twentieth century became too painful to contemplate, he returned in memory to old Cambridge with its "pure New England type" in the days when "the progress of democracy had not swept away the natural distinctions of good breeding and superior culture." [6] Norton had gradually come to realize that the old type of society, and the dominance of the intellectual class which he had known as a boy no longer remained in New England. "There is no good talk now-a-days," he complained to Ward, "as there used to be at [George Ticknor's] table, with Frank Gray and Prescott and Allston, and Everett and my father taking part in it." [7] New Cambridge had adopted new rulers. Earlier he had written with undisguised fear of the Irish, whose personal ties with the Boston community were helping them to dethrone from power the old-guard Anglo-Saxons. And similarly, he feared the rising population of Jews in America and at Harvard. He believed that the illiterate newly rich were crowding out the old ruling classes in the East. In a letter to Lowell, Norton had described the amusing malapropisms of a "Mrs. Leiter, the wife of a Chicago grocer or dry-goods man who has made a great fortune":

They live now in Washington and Newport, and have bought their place in fashionable society. They give great and costly parties, and Mrs. L declares that society in Washington has become so overgrown that she is "really obliged to confine her invitations to the *demi-monde.*" She wanted her daughter's portrait painted as she said not with any splendid ornaments and dress "but entirely au naturel." She was speaking one day of Baillie Loring's daughter, who is marvellously stout, — "a charming girl, full of talent, but what a pity that she's so obscene"! [8]

The years had passed and Norton occasionally found himself more and more isolated from both the past and the present. The old traditions of learning and manners had been obliterated, and the new era seemed to have no common traditions which could make "society" and even conversation possible. "Not even in Cambridge can I now get together half a dozen men or women round a table, who have a large common background for their thoughts, their wit, their humour," he told Godkin. "Literature in the best sense used to supply a good deal of it, but does so no longer. My fair neighbour asks, 'What are Pericles?' " [9] In a commencement address to the graduating class of Radcliffe College in 1900, he warned that "with the rapid rise in the social order of great masses of men and women who till very lately have had little share of civility . . . it is for you, the gentle and well-bred, to conform in nothing to the vulgar standard, and, in the crowd, to set the example of refinement, elegance, and propriety." [10] Harvard itself was "given over to science and athletics," and Norton could not find at the College "one literary man *par excellence* . . . with a social tradition, with acquaintance with the polite world and with the means and the disposition to make his house a center of hospitality and the expression of a gracious culture." [11] His estrangement from the College was increased further when it honored McKinley with a Doctor of Laws Degree in 1901. Norton protested that the President deserved no more than an M.A. — "as a Master in all the Arts of political corruption." [12] With the same disgust he wrote in 1905 of Harvard's plan to honor the hero of San Juan Hill ("a semicivilized festival to celebrate the good cowboy become President"). Norton vowed, "I shall not go to Cambridge to hurrah for him. The cheers for him remind me of the 'Hurrah for Jackson' of my early boyhood, — for which there was a better excuse." [13]

THE FUTURE — COMPENSATION AND HOPE

At the very moment he was condemning bourgeois America most severely, Norton stopped short and re-examined his feelings. He was by nature a skeptic, and despite his impulsive outbursts, his complex outlook was essentially humane. He could still feel a return of compassion for the downtrodden classes who had come to America to find a release from physical suffering and material want. He encouraged Harvard to admit students of all social levels and of all races (provided that the "Christian boys" would remain in the majority) and to assist the promising, needy student. In 1903, and during the years until his death, he wrote to Mackenzie King, the Canadian Labor Minister, for information on the progress of collective bargaining in Canada. Although the old aristocracy had given way to a new "commercial aristocracy," Norton wrote to King, the gains for the many made up in large part for the losses in "the higher regions of civilization":

> If vulgarity is taking the place of refinement among the upper classes, yet we may be content in reflecting that these upper classes are but few compared with the multitude of the lower class that are rising from degradation into comparative civilization and comfort.[14]

Norton's humane sympathies appeared again during these last years in his Sunday afternoon visits to the local Catholic hospital for incurables. There he read aloud to the patients, and admired the charity and sacrifice of the Grey Nuns, who had abandoned the quest for earthly goods and were relieving the suffering of these patients who were received into the Hospital without consideration of creed or color.

Other problems of the twentieth century excited his curiosity: the role of Japan in world politics (after the outbreak of hostilities with Russia in 1904), the dangers of British imperialism and its caste system, the signs of leadership and public spirit in the West, and the higher education of the

Negro in the South. To his friend Booker T. Washington, who had been a guest speaker at Ashfield, Norton sent several money contributions to help Washington's Tuskegee Institute. Some years earlier, Norton had agreed to serve as president of the Tavern Club, a group of young professional men of Boston interested in the arts. He still confessed an interest in the rising generation of scholars and writers. While he could not recognize one commanding voice among contemporary poets, he anticipated a rebirth of the poetic spirit soon in America. In 1905, sensing that the end of his life was near, Norton regretted that so little time was left to follow America's future course in the twentieth century. "We have seen only the beginning of the mightiest revolution of human affairs," he wrote to Goldwin Smith, "and we shall have to quit the stage in the very middle of a most entertaining scene." [15]

RECOGNITION

Norton continued to live until his very durability seemed to argue the permanence of an older civilization in America. On his eightieth birthday, the symbolic force of his life and presence began to be realized. Harvard printed a sheaf of letters written by faculty and friends in a belated attempt to express publicly the meaning of Norton's life and his contribution to America. President Charles W. Eliot, George H. Palmer, Horace Howard Furness, and Richard Watson Gilder praised him as a teacher whose influence had shaped the lives of thousands of Harvard students. Excerpts from these public statements included the following tributes:

Thousands of Harvard students attribute to his influence lasting improvements in their modes of thought, their intellectual and moral interests, and their ideas of genuine success and true happiness.
(President Eliot)

Who may compute his influence as a Teacher? When, from the echoes of his voice, through these many years, young men, in annual waves,

are gone forth into the world, imbued with a devotion to whatever is pure and refined in art, broadened in culture, and gentled in condition.
(H. H. Furness)

The methods of Mr. Norton were superbly out of date in our specialistic time. He saw in the Fine Arts the embodiment of man's deepest and most durable ideals, and with almost a religious fervor he brought these to bear on every aspect of the petty and careless life around him. He has been a preacher of reverence to a headlong age. And if sometimes a despairing note has been heard in his voice, it has been perhaps a necessary corrective of overconfident America.
(George H. Palmer)

He stands for all that [students] hoped to acquire at Harvard — in a word, for Culture.
(Richard W. Gilder)

Bliss Perry celebrated Norton's civic leadership in the community at Ashfield:

The Franklin County farmers who used to drive to Ashfield, year after year, to hear Mr. Norton speak at the Academy dinners, knew very little about his special claims upon the gratitude of artists, critics, and scholars. But they were prompt to recognize beauty and dignity of character, in exquisite feeling for the claims of communal life, and novel views of public service.

And William Dean Howells saw in Norton the last trace of a golden age which had all but vanished in America, and perhaps never was to return:

For me he is of that Golden prime which we Americans shall not see renewed in the course of many centuries. While he lives, Emerson and Hawthorne, Longfellow and Lowell, Whittier and Holmes, are not lost to the consciousness of any who knew them; the Cambridge, the Boston, the New England, the America which lived in them, has not yet passed away.[16]

THE LAST YEAR

Norton expressed his thanks for the birthday statements of affection and praise, but did not quite comprehend the fuss that had taken place. "It has seemed to me as if it was the birthday of some unknown person in the celebration of which I had only the concern of an interested spectator," he told Thomas Wentworth Higginson.[17] He could feel the rapid advance of age in recent months, and the dwindling reserve of physical strength from a supply which had never been abundant. The winter of 1907 passed quietly. In January, despite his objections to publishing private memoirs, he dictated an autobiographical paper to his daughter Sara. His mind retained its vigor and he continued to follow new contributions to Dante scholarship in America, to aid Furness in Shakespeare studies, and to dictate letters to his few remaining friends. He enjoyed the approach of spring with more awareness of its beauty than ever before. But as warm weather arrived, he obeyed his doctor's orders not to travel to Ashfield for the summer months. He followed public affairs from his home at Shady Hill with as keen an interest as before, but his energy was failing and he could no longer trace the tangled pattern of national events or attempt even to predict their outcome. "Forecasts of the future seem to me more difficult than they used to be, for the forces exhibited by a democratic community such as ours, are a new thing in history," he wrote to Howells in July, 1908.[18] Several weeks afterward, his strength declined sharply, and he was confined to his room, never again to leave. In letters dictated to Furness in September, he regretted that he could no longer read as before. What he did read was significant — the daily newspaper and then Shakespeare.

In the final weeks, his children, then full grown, returned to Shady Hill, to the home filled with memories of earlier years when their father had read aloud to them at bedtime from Scott, Dickens, and Howells with the energy he had managed to save by the end of a day. There on the morning of October 21, 1908, with his six children near him, Norton lost consciousness and, within a few hours, died. A life of suffering and courage had come to an end.

Conclusion:
NORTON'S REPUTATION IN THE
TWENTIETH CENTURY

Since Norton's death, several writers have tried to interpret the meaning of his life and work. One group has seen Norton as a "gentleman of culture," a determined missionary of the arts, but, somewhat like Miniver Cheevy, an anachronism in modern society. Another group has vaguely hinted that Norton's response to his age may have been a bit more complex — and possibly more sympathetic. No critic has established Norton's place in the main stream of twentieth-century American thought.

In the months immediately following Norton's death, tributes and resolutions came from friends, students, academic societies, and the townspeople of Cambridge and Ashfield. But Sara Norton and Mark Howe provided the first chance to obtain some perspective of her father's life, when they edited his letters in 1913. The following year, Henry James published his perceptive essay on Norton. He recalled that Norton, as editor of the *North American Review*, had accepted James's earliest critical essays and had set an example of consecration to the life of art and letters. Though their literary relationship afterwards had never been close — Norton's dislike of the later novels, for example, has already been noted — yet James's letters to Norton reveal an influence that is unmistakable and enduring. Primarily through Norton, it will be remembered, James had gained a close acquaintance with English society, the experience out of which he would conceive the international themes of his best work. Writing to Norton later from Italy, James confessed that many of his responses were being shaped by Norton's writings on Italy. Having identified the quality of his European experience with Norton's, James went further and, in the essay of 1914, concluded that the problems of his own alienation from America were Norton's also. Norton's determination to stay and work in America was to James a supreme gesture of renunciation. He called Norton a "representative of culture" with a "civilizing mission" and underlined the frustrations of Norton's "extremely individual character and career." James's sympathetic portrait made Norton into an isolated figure who could not actively share the eager hopefulness of the century. In James's memory, Shady Hill became the home of a charming antiquarian; it was a museum where one could make a "pilgrimage among pictures and books, drawings and medals, memories and relics and anecdotes, things of a remote but charming reference, [with] very much the effect of a sudden rise into a fine and clearer air and of a stopgap against one's own coveted renewal of the more direct experience." [1]

Without James's sympathy, John Jay Chapman wrote in the next year a maliciously clever essay describing Norton as "nothing else than a darling old saint with a few sophistical hobbies which, when you went to see him, he drew from his cabinet and showed you with glee — old philosophical gimcracks." Chapman had attended Harvard in the 1880's and remembered Norton's "enormous influence over the youth who sat under him," but Chapman had apparently been personally offended by what he took to be Norton's "polite, sardonic, patronizing smile." This personal dislike colored Chapman's judgment of Norton's ideas. As a critic of his time, Norton (said Chapman) merely "loved to tease . . . [with] old-maidish whimsicalities of opinion." In later years, Norton "must have found out that his earlier exclusiveness and pose of cultivation were not worth keeping up, for they dropped from off him, and left him rosy. He was a beaming little old gentleman with a note as sweet as an eighteenth-century organ . . ." [2]

The stereotype of Norton as a reactionary and rather snob-bish "representative of culture" continued into the 1920's. Kate Stephens, who had been Norton's junior editor for a set of children's readers, *The Heart of Oak Books* (1894–1895, 6 volumes), published a history of their relations. She alleged that Norton, motivated by selfish ambition, allowed D. C. Heath and Company to remove her name from the second edition (for incompetent proofreading). With all the wrath of a woman scorned, she selected passages from Norton's published *Letters* for an impassioned epilogue which showed him to be a social snob and a spiteful critic of his country. Effects of this sketch were partly offset two years later by Rollo W. Brown's more favorable essay on Norton. Selecting colorful anecdotes about Norton, Brown pictured him as a courageous, lonely individualist, though not a domi-nant force in later American thought.

The most influential portrait of Norton has been the one by Van Wyck Brooks, which I have mentioned previously. Norton's criticism of America sounded a sour note in Mr. Brooks's rhapsodic New England histories. Borrowing from writers cited here, and others who in their lives had both praised and ridiculed Norton, Mr. Brooks pieced together anecdotes and judgments unfavorable to Norton. Chiefly from Mr. Brooks's omissions, Norton has suffered the reputa-tion of a somewhat plodding, sanctimonious, eccentric, fastid-ious old Bostonian.

Several critics in the twentieth century have touched on Norton's deeper significance. Santayana spoke of the "Polite America" and the "crude but vital America" of the last cen-tury, and found both in Norton, so that Norton's countrymen could call him "un-American" at the same time that a French friend (talking to Santayana) labeled him "a terrible Yankee." [3] Kenneth Murdock, on the centenary of Norton's birth, published the discovery that Norton had written the *Leaves of Grass* review in *Putnam's* magazine, though Mr.

Murdock rather too easily concluded that Norton never returned to the mood of 1855.

Norton's contribution to modern literary criticism was briefly recognized both by F. O. Matthiessen in 1941, and a year later by Alfred Kazin. Matthiessen called attention to Norton's role in the Dante and Donne traditions in American literature, and described Norton as a "perturbed spirit" whose acute sense of suffering anticipated the mood of twentieth-century writers like T. S. Eliot.[4] Mr. Kazin, in his *On Native Grounds,* noted in passing that the "New Humanist" criticism in the late 1920's owed something to the earlier work of Norton, though Mr. Kazin felt the continuity to have been somewhat tenuous.

Many critics, then, even the well-intentioned ones, have seen Norton as a misfit, yearning for the age of Dante, on the one hand, or looking ahead to the disillusioned 1920's on the other. Either view has a sentimental attractiveness and one can find evidence to support both interpretations. But it happens that Norton was also very much a part of his own time. He shared some of its most extravagant hopes as well as its gloomier forebodings. The striking pattern of disenchantment recurred throughout his life. His impulsive enthusiasms — Chartism, European revolutions, popular education, model lodginghouses, *Leaves of Grass,* the public-lecture platform, Civil War patriotism, the teachings and spirit of Emerson, the writing of Howells and Fuller, the Chicago Exposition — these and other signs of the "progress of democracy" he first welcomed and later questioned. The tenacity with which he stayed in America and continued to serve the country and criticize its foibles suggests an ultimate faith in popular intelligence. So, too, does his "democratic" interpretation of the great cathedrals of the Middle Ages. During the 1890's when that faith was tested most severely, he could still praise the New World with its "larger, more generous, modern spirit of democratic society, in which each man has the opportunity and is consequently under the responsibility to make the best of himself for the service of his fellowmen." [5] In 1893, he eagerly traveled west to attend the Chicago World's Fair, and in 1896, he still believed that leadership might come to any man "by virtue of the right use of faculties which are a common inheritance, and of qualities which every youth . . . may hope to attain." [6] Nor should one forget that despite Norton's friendship with virtually all of the eminent men of letters in America and England of the later nineteenth century, the portraits of two American "commoners," John Brown and Abraham Lincoln, shared the mantelpiece in his home at Ashfield.

The age of Emerson lived on in Norton, though in his mature period he soberly reappraised the values Emerson had handed on to a "less childlike" generation of Americans. In this disillusionment, Norton becomes an important transitional figure between that earlier period in America and the less optimistic twentieth century. The main continuity flows from Norton through the work of men like Irving Babbitt (and in lesser degree, Paul Elmer More) to T. S. Eliot.

The debt of More and Babbitt is clear in their writings. Norton was More's critic and adviser as early as 1898. In subsequent years More wrote to Norton for comments on "where and how far you disagree with my judgment or with my tone," and he thanked Norton for giving valuable criticism of his articles in the *Nation*.[7] More reviewed Norton's posthumous *Letters* in 1913, and praised "the traditional New England conscience and sense of evil" in Norton, traits of character which had helped to restrain the followers of Emerson who had broken from their New England bondage.[8]

Irving Babbitt came under Norton's spell at Harvard in the 1890's. "Norton's name was daily on his lips with a vivid reverence," Frank Jewett Mather remembered.[9] Babbitt visited frequently at Shady Hill, and a portrait of Norton hung on the wall of Babbitt's study. He wrote to Norton in

1907: "I note signs of late of a reaction against certain excesses of the scientific spirit in literary study. Your own work will have helped largely to bring this reaction about." [10] The next year in his *Literature and the American College,* Babbitt publicly acknowledged his debt to Norton with a prefatory note:

> Those who during the past generation have felt the need of a more humane scholarship are indebted to him, many for direct aid and encouragement, and all for an example.[11]

When Babbitt wrote these words, his most famous pupil, T. S. Eliot, was in his second year at Harvard. Babbitt's influence on Eliot is well known and needs no comment. Accordingly, one can infer Norton's indirect influence on Eliot. But Eliot's obligation is more explicit. In 1932, as Charles Eliot Norton Professor of Poetry at Harvard, he introduced his lectures by paying tribute to his relative (Norton was second cousin of Eliot's grandfather, the Reverend William Greenleaf Eliot). Significantly, Eliot presented Norton as a twentieth-century man. Quoting from the period of Norton's most complete disillusionment (December, 1869), Eliot commented: "He was able, even at an early age, to look upon the passing order without regret, and the coming order without hope." The statement, of course, exaggerates Norton's pessimism. What is important is that Eliot recognized the strain of Norton's thought which today is the most congenial. Though by 1932 Eliot had embraced the Christian — Anglo-Catholic — tradition, yet he could sympathize with Norton's naturalistic humanism and the modernity of Norton's problem:

> Charles Eliot Norton had the moral and spiritual qualities, of a stoic kind, which are possible without the benefits of revealed religion . . . And living as he did in a non-Christian society, and in a world which, as he saw it on both sides of the Atlantic, showed signs of decay, he maintained the standards of the humanity and humanism that he knew.[12]

To Eliot, Norton's thought warned a later age of certain

perils of an egalitarian society. The twentieth-century humanism we associate with taste, tradition, learning, status, will, and restraint (particularly in the opposition to Romantic poets), has its native origins in the work of Norton, continued through Babbitt and More to Eliot, and radiating outward from Eliot to such diverse figures as Allen Tate and Robert Penn Warren, on one hand; and to the "new conservatives," Russell Kirk and Peter Viereck, on another.

Norton saw in his lifetime many of the shortcomings of American society which we recognize so painfully today: the anemic intellectual life of a literate nation at large; the death-struggle of humanistic learning in our "practical" schools and colleges; the gradual leveling of regional, ethnic, and class distinctions; the lack of training in manners among our youth; the stultifying pressures of mass opinion upon freedom of thought and action; the surrender by the agencies of mass communication to the adolescent tastes of a happy-go-lucky people. Against these pitfalls of "democracy" Norton gave early warning. He maintained a sense of continuity with his Puritan ancestry and the European past as he lived through the revolutionary changes in American life during the last century. In appraising his country, Norton censured, deplored, reviled, and ridiculed. But his response was never simple. He was also a Yankee and could praise, exult, and boast. He confessed his attraction to the vibrant optimism of a young nation that was ambitious, inventive, and secure in its belief in the rights of the individual and the destiny of free men. In short, Norton never lost that youthful vision of America which for shorthand purposes he labelled "Emersonian." In May, 1903, he accepted an invitation to speak at the Concord centenary of Emerson's birth. In his speech, Norton repeated his earlier criticism of Emerson's thought ("He would not entertain for a moment the evidence of ruthlessness and disorder in nature, of perversion of the moral nature in men"), but he praised Emerson's idealism and its enduring influence on the American spirit. "Emerson's fame is secure," he avowed. "The years will sift his work, but his true message and services were not for his own generation alone." [13]

Norton's attempt, though largely unconscious and unsystematic, to envision an American humanism without denying the spirit and teachings of Emerson makes him a key figure in American intellectual history. Had he brought together into a volume his scattered essays and pronouncements on the American scene during the later nineteenth century, his influence would have been felt far more widely than it has been. But he did not choose to publish more in what he termed "these days of cheap and easy printing." Even with his collected essays and addresses bequeathed to posterity, however, he would hold no great claim as a consistent or an original thinker; indeed, the historian of ideas will find Norton's opinions on art and society shared by widely differing writers of the age. The nature of his influence, rather, can be found in his own tribute to Emerson:

> It is not the founders of schools whose influence is the strongest and most lasting in the world, but rather that of teachers who lift and invigorate the souls of men by sentiment and habitual loftiness of view.[14]

Norton was one of these "teachers" of the spirit. As a magazine editor, scholar, teacher, and social critic, he tried to rediscover "the best" in our native and European heritage and make it an important part of the consciousness of his students and countrymen. The main purpose of this teaching becomes clear in his final words to his students: "Be a good man!" Not pleasure in artistic form and method, but the sterner lesson of character was what Norton stressed in his art history classes. The emphasis, of course, betrays his Puritan origins as well as his utilitarian leanings, both of which conspired to weaken his aesthetic sense. Though he often talked about the concepts of beauty and imagination, Norton appears seldom to have released his "inner check" and responded deeply to the sensuous aspect of the arts. As he grew older, he became increasingly suspicious of stylistic innovation and any display of technical virtuosity. (The French schools of painting in the last century, as well as contemporary American painters, suffer nearly total neglect in his art criticism.) More than once, he correlated an artist's integrity with his adherence to tradition. On the other hand, the "sincerity" and moral temper which characterized the "democratic" community of artists and citizens during the great periods of Greek and Italian art history was his favorite and most inspired subject. And as he tirelessly preached this lesson of individual and communal greatness in the ages of Phidias and Dante, Norton remembered that the same message appeared, somewhat oversimplified, in Emerson's doctrine of the "Oversoul."

Undoubtedly in Norton's later criticism of America one finds, along with some remarkable insights, some rather severe limitations — his moral strictures on American architecture and literary "realism," for example, and his futile protests against labor strikes, mass production, the "new" immigration, and other forces which were shaping modern industrialism. But again, these limitations reveal the central conflict of his career and help to explain his significance. The tensions and contradictions of "culture" in a "democracy" appear throughout his life and writings as in no other member of his circle. Norton's ideal America would have been a harmonious fusion of Lincoln and Pericles, John Brown and Sir Philip Sidney, Tuskegee Institute and Oxford University, Whitman and Dante, Longfellow and John Donne, of Chicago and Ashfield and medieval Florence. More aware of our shortcomings than Emerson, Norton was, at the same time, more optimistic about them than are many of the writers who have followed him in the twentieth century. He came to maturity in the post-Civil War age of technology, at a time when the alternative to Emerson's overly romantic view of man was the equally unsatisfactory argument of scientific naturalism. Norton's difficult task, we can now see, was to preach the values of tradition and order to new generations who were becoming rootless in an era of advancing materialism and social leveling (the "progress" which, because of his own utilitarian sympathies, brought him so much conflict). He tried to add a necessary dimension to the Emersonian man by teaching the lessons of the past — the discipline and achievement, but also the disillusionment, corruption, suffering, and tragedy — and thereby promote a richer ideal of American individualism, a saner view of the human spirit than Emerson had conceived. Through the many roles that he played during a long life, Norton became an important civilizing influence on his time. He also becomes a significant transitional figure in America. In his thought and work, we discover the links between the age of Emerson and the age of Eliot.

APPENDIX

NORTON'S POETRY

APPENDIX

NORTON'S POETRY

A Leaf of Grass

I will pluck a leaf of grass & give it to you to look at.
It is made of sunshine & rain, of the dew of the evening and
    of the cool air of the still starlighted night,
It springs from the earth fresh as the first blade that
    tinged the brown soil with green
When the world was young, and each day a new miracle to
    eyes not blinded with the dust of accustomedness.

In it is the order of all things, in the narrow stem is
    enclosed the mystery of life & of death.
Its slender flag is the banner on which the names of God
    are inscribed.

Here is a leaf dry & dead as we call it; brown, wasted &
    rattling against its dry next neighbour in the wind,
This is the valley of dry bones, and here all the dead lie
    in order.

But who knows what it is to die, and he who dies does he
    know what it is to be dead?
Even now the life which ran through this dry spire of grass
    is not dead but has only hidden itself & retreated,
Retreated to burst into fuller existence somewhere else in
    the boundless Creation.

I walk in the wood, underneath my feet are the crackling
    curiously decaying limbs soft with gray mould, &
    slimy with dampness.
I step secure and mind not the snake that lies sunning
    himself hidden under a log.
He hears me coming, and with red eye sees that he cannot
    escape.
I feel a sharp prick in my foot.
There is a small red dot, a pin's point would make a larger,
But in at that hole, that little insignificant hole comes
    death,
And out of it passes my soul. My soul needs no large door
    to escape from the grip of death.

Death has a poor worthless thing, the burden & waste of
    my soul
And I rejoice in the freedom from life in which men fear
    death.
For now look at the boy in the mine, cold, dirty, hardworked,
    low browed, cruel & mean.
He strikes one false blow, the mine caves, he is dead, and
    do you think he is sorry?
I go to a factory; the whirling wheels, the noise and jar
    of the spindles, the rush of the steam make me
    proud of myself
And I think all this I have made with my head & my hands.
A band that I see not catches the skirt of my coat,
The cloth will not yield, and I am pulled in between rollers
    & come out flat & what is called dead,
But I look down with disdain on the poor flattened carcass
And laugh for death did not flatten my soul.

              (1855)

Palace of the Caesars

Once more the spring doth hang these palace walls
With a fresh tapestry of leaves and flowers;
The rich mosaic pavement of these halls
Grows in her sunshine, quickens 'neath her showers.

No Tyrian purples had so deep a dye
As these dark weeds that in this crevice grow;
No cloth of gold e'er dazzled in the eye
Like these gold wall flowers in their noonday show.

On this cracked pier that once held up a roof
Gleaming with marbles, quarried far away,
Now the sad cypress stands, and, winter proof,
The ivy clings and hides the slow decay.

Where once the noisy riot of the crowd
Round Rome's base emperors broke the sacred air,
Where drunken shouts and screams of fright rose loud,
Now the lark sings his sweet and joyful prayer.

Where crazy, coward Nero staggered wild
Where Messalman flamed with cruel lust,
Now plays the little dark-eyed Roman child,
And builds his houses out of palace dust.

Here once were pride, and splendor, and gay charms,
Here too were treachery and cold deceit.
The secret stroke of hate, the clash of arms,
The hurrying to and fro of enemy feet.

Now all is still, and these huge broken piers
Rise like a monument o'er the rifled tomb,
In which lay sepulchred the wrongs of years,
Wrongs followed surely by avenging doom.

Old Rome has perished, new Rome has its day; —
The warm air trembles to the convent bell; —
And when this second Rome shall pass away,
What story will its awful ruins tell?

(1857)

* * * *

From this old city seated on a hill
Pietro Perigino took his name
And many of the works are shown here still
By which he gained his pure and lofty fame.

Here too young Raphael studied and here learned
The deepest lessons of . . . .*
For here his youth with holy fires burned
Nor worldly lusts had yet defiled his heart.

A strange old city gray-grown with the moss
Of lengthened centuries of change and war
Its annals tell the tale of many a loss
Its walls are marked with many a dented scar.

Nor is its present better than its past;
For the worst government is that of priests
And poverty and discontent grow fast,
Where superstition chains men down like beasts.

(1857?)

To R. W. Emerson

May 25, 1873

Blest of the highest gods are they who die
    Ere youth is fled. For them their Mother Fate
Clasping from happy earth to happier sky,
    Frees life and joy and love from dread of date.

---

* Words omitted by Sara Norton in her copy of the poem.

But thee, revered of men, the gods have blest,
    With fruitful years. And yet for thee, in sooth,
They have reserved of all their gifts the best, —
    For thou, though full of days, shall die in youth.

(1873)

BIBLIOGRAPHY
NOTES
INDEX

BIBLIOGRAPHY

IN his notebooks from 1864 to 1868, Norton recorded his contributions to the *North American Review* (abbreviated *NAR* below). His articles in the *Atlantic Monthly* (abbreviated *At. Mo.* below) and a large number of reviews which have been verified as his in the *Nation* are listed respectively in two valuable indexes:

The Atlantic Index, 1857–88. Boston: Houghton Mifflin Co., 1889.
The Nation, Volumes 1–105 . . . Compiled by Daniel C. Haskell. New York: New York Public Library, 1953. 2 vols.

See also my prefatory comment to the Notes regarding the materials in the Norton collection in the Houghton Library at Harvard University.

I. NORTON'S PUBLISHED WORKS

(These are listed by year of publication. Unless I have noted otherwise, the articles and reviews are unsigned until after 1870, and most of the *Nation* contributions thereafter continue to be unsigned. The titles that appear in brackets have been supplied.)

1840's

"The Life of William Tyndale," *NAR,* LXVII (Oct., 1848), 322–353.
"Ancient Monuments in America," *NAR,* LXVIII (April, 1849), 466–496.

1850's

BOOKS

Five Christmas Hymns. (Ed. by Norton) Cambridge, Mass.: privately printed, 1852.
Considerations on Some Recent Social Theories. Boston: Little, Brown, & Co., 1853. (Published anonymously)
A Book of Hymns for Young Persons. (Ed. by Norton) Cambridge, Mass.: John Bartlett, 1854.
The New Life of Dante, An Essay with Translations. Cambridge, Mass.: privately printed, 1859. Enlarged from " 'The New Life' of Dante," *At. Mo.,* III (January, 1859), 62–69; (Feb.), 202–212; (March), 330–339. Later revisions appeared in 1867 and 1892 (Boston: Houghton Mifflin Co.); and in 1906 (Cambridge, Mass.: privately printed).
Notes of Travel and Study in Italy. Boston: Houghton Mifflin Co., 1859. Portions of the book were printed earlier in *The Crayon,* III (March, 1856), 85–87; (April), 118–120; (May), 151–155; (June),

179–181; (July), 206–209; (Aug.), 246–247; (Sept.), 274–276; (Oct.), 306–309; (Nov.), 338–340; (Dec.), 371–372.

ARTICLES AND REVIEWS

"Sir Jamsetjee Jeejeebhoy: A Parsee Merchant," *NAR,* LXXIII (July, 1851), 135–152.
"Dwellings and Schools for the Poor," *NAR,* LXXV (April, 1852), 464–489.
"The St. Nicholas and Five Points," *Putnam's,* I (May, 1853), 509–512.
"Canals of Irrigation in India," *NAR,* LXXVII (Oct., 1853), 439–466.
"The Palankeen," *Putnam's,* III (June, 1854), 654–660.
"Sketches of India," *Crayon,* II (Aug. 29, 1855), 127–128; (Sept. 5), 143–144; (Sept. 12), 160–162; (Sept. 26), 192–193; (Oct. 10), 223–224; (Oct. 17), 239–240.
"Whitman's Leaves of Grass," *Putnam's,* VI (Sept., 1855), 321–323.
"The Opening of the Ganges Canal," *NAR,* LXXXI (Oct., 1855), 531–543.
"The Manchester Exhibition," *At. Mo.,* I (Nov., 1857), 33–46.
"The Indian Revolt," *At. Mo.,* I (Dec., 1857), 217–222.
[*The Life of Michael Angelo Buonarotti* . . . , by John S. Hanford], *At. Mo.,* I (Feb., 1858), 510–512.
"The Catacombs of Rome," *At. Mo.,* I (March, 1858), 513–522; (April), 674–685; (May), 813–821; II (June), 48–58; (July), 129–139.
"Despotism in India," *NAR,* LXXXVIII (April, 1859), 289–312.
"The Oxford Museum," *At. Mo.,* IV (Dec., 1859), 767–770.

1860's

PAMPHLET

The Soldier of the Good Cause. Boston: American Unitarian Assoc., Army Series, No. 2, 1861.

ARTICLES AND REVIEWS

[*Plutarch's Lives,* by A. H. Clough], *At. Mo.,* V (Jan., 1860), 110–119.
[*Friends in Council*], *At. Mo.,* V (Jan., 1860), 125–126.
[*The West Indies & the Spanish Main* by Anthony Trollope], *At. Mo.,* V (March, 1860), 375–378.
[*The Public Life of Captain John Brown,* by James Redpath], *At. Mo.,* V (March, 1860), 378–381.
[*Le Prime Quattro Edizione della Divina Commedia,* by G. G. Warren Lord Vernon], *At. Mo.,* V (May, 1860), 622–629.
"Model Lodging-Houses in Boston," *At. Mo.,* V (June, 1860), 673–680.
"Pasquin & Pasquinades," *At. Mo.,* VI (Oct., 1860), 395–405.
[*Essays & Reviews,* London, 1860], *At. Mo.,* VI (Nov., 1860), 633–635.
[*Fr. Rogeri Bacon Opera,* ed. by J. S. Brewer], *At. Mo.,* VI (Dec., 1860), 746–759.

[*The Laws of Race, as Connected with Slavery*], *At. Mo.*, VII (Feb., 1861), 252–254.

[*Il Politecnico*], *At. Mo.*, VII (April, 1861), 508–509.

"Original Memorials of Mrs. Piozzi," *At. Mo.*, VII (May, 1861), 614–623.

[Tambarini's Translation of the Commentary by Benvenuto da Imola on the *Divina Commedia*], *At. Mo.*, VII (May, 1861), 629–637.

"The Advantages of Defeat," *At. Mo.*, VIII (Sept., 1861), 360–365.

"Journal of a Privateersman," *At. Mo.*, VIII (Sept., 1861), 353–359; (Oct., 1861), 417–424.

"Alexis de Tocqueville," *At. Mo.*, VIII (Nov., 1861), 551–557.

"Arthur Hugh Clough," *At. Mo.*, IX (April, 1862), 462–469.

"Gillett's Life and Times of John Huss," *NAR*, XCVIII (Jan., 1864), 282–285.

"Immorality in Politics," *NAR*, XCVIII (Jan., 1864), 105–127.

"St. Louis & Joinville," *NAR*, XCVIII (April, 1864), 419–460.

[*Hints to Riflemen*, by H. W. S. Cleveland], *NAR*, XCIX (July, 1864), 310.

"Notices of Gillett's Huss," *NAR*, XCIX (July, 1864), 269–274.

"Our Soldiers," *NAR*, XCIX (July, 1864), 172–204.

"Parton's Life and Times of Benjamin Franklin," *NAR*, XCIX (July, 1864), 302–303.

"Goldwin Smith," *NAR*, XCIX (Oct., 1864), 523–539.

"Abraham Lincoln," *NAR*, C (Jan., 1865), 1–21.

"America and England," *NAR*, C (April, 1865), 331–346.

"White's Shakespeare," *Nation*, I (July 6, 1865), 23–24.

"The Paradise of Mediocrities," *Nation*, I (July 13, 1865), 43–44.

"Education at the Great English Public Schools," *Nation*, I (Aug. 3, 1865), 149–150.

"Draper's Civil Policy of America," *Nation*, I (Sept. 28, 1865), 407–409.

"American Political Ideas," *NAR*, CI (Oct., 1865), 550–566.

"Burke's Works," *NAR*, CI (Oct., 1865), 624–625.

"Atalanta in Calydon," *Nation*, I (Nov. 9, 1865), 590–591.

"The President's Message," *NAR*, CII (Jan., 1866), 250–260.

"Tuscan Sculptors," *Nation*, II (Jan. 25, 1866), 116–117.

"Waste," *Nation*, II (March 8, 1866), 301–302.

"Dante and His Latest English Translators," *NAR*, CII (April, 1866), 509–529.

"The American Lectureship at Cambridge, England," *Nation*, II (April 12, 1866), 457–459.

"Good Manners," *Nation*, II (May 4, 1866), 571.

"Sir Alexander Grant's Ethics of Aristotle," *Nation*, III (Aug. 9, 1866), 106–107.

"Venetian Life," *Nation*, III (Sept. 6, 1866), 189.

"Harvard Memorial Biographies," *NAR*, CIII (Oct., 1866), 498–509.

"Wight's National Academy of Design," *NAR*, CIII (Oct., 1866), 586–589.

"The Work of the Sanitary Commission," *NAR*, CIV (Jan., 1867), 142–155.

"Religious Liberty," *NAR*, CIV (April, 1867), 586–597.

"Mr. Longfellow's Translation of the Divine Comedy," *Nation*, IV (May 9, 1867), 369–370.

"Mr. Emerson's Poems," *Nation*, IV (May 30, 1867), 430–431.

"Female Suffrage and Education," *Nation*, V (Aug. 22, 1867), 152.

"The Life and Death of Jason," *Nation*, V (Aug. 22, 1867), 146–147.

"Compulsory Education," *Nation*, V (Sept. 5, 1867), 191–192.

"Mr. Longfellow and His Critics," *Nation*, V (Sept. 19, 1867), 226–228.

"Arthur Hugh Clough," *NAR*, CV (Oct., 1867), 434–477.

"Dr. Parsons's Translation of the Inferno of Dante," *Nation*, V (Oct. 3, 1867), 269–271.

"Biddle's Musical Scale," *NAR*, CVI (April, 1868), 734–736.

"The Church and Religion," *NAR*, CVI (April, 1868), 373–396. (Signed article)

"Charles Dickens," *NAR*, CVI (April, 1868), 671–672.

"John Hookham Frere," *NAR*, CVII (July, 1868), 136–166. (Signed article)

"The Autotype or Carbon Process in Photography," *Nation*, VIII (Jan. 21, 1869), 47.

"The Poverty of England," *NAR*, CIX (July, 1869), 122–154. (Signed article)

"The International Congress of Peace and Liberty," *Nation*, IX (Sept. 17, 1869), 313–315.

"Nicolas's Quatrains de Khèyam," *NAR*, CIX (Oct., 1869), 565–584. Includes first quotations from Fitzgerald's *Rubaiyat* to appear in America.

"The Congress of Peace and Liberty at Lausanne," *Nation*, IX (Oct. 21, 1869), 336–337.

1870's

BOOKS

Philosophical Discussions by Chauncey Wright. With a biographical sketch of the author, by Charles Eliot Norton. New York: Henry Holt and Company, 1878.

ARTICLES AND REVIEWS

"The Crisis at Rome," *Nation*, X (June 2, 1870), 350–351.

"The Cesnola Collection of Antiquities from Cyprus," *Nation*, XVI (Jan. 23, 1873), 62–63.

[The Literary Work of the Late King of Saxony], *Nation*, XVII (Nov. 6, 1873), 306–307.

"Sara Coleridge," *Nation,* XVII (Dec. 25, 1873), 425–426.

"Laugel's England," *Nation,* XVIII (Dec. 25, 1873), 425–426.

"Rossetti's Translations from the Early Italian Poets," *Nation,* XVIII (March 5, 1874), 159–160.

"Popularizing Art in America," *Nation,* XVIII (March 12, 1874), 170–171. (Signed letter)

[Samuel Rogers], *Nation,* XIX (July 2, 1874), 8.

"Brigham's Cast Catalogue of Antique Sculpture," *Nation,* XIX (July 9, 1874), 28.

"The Montpensier Gallery," *Nation,* XIX (Oct. 15, 1874), 255–256.

"John Hookham Frere," *Nation,* XIX (Oct. 22, 1874), 270–271.

[*Elementary History of Art,* by N. D'Anvers], *Nation,* XIX (Nov. 5, 1874), 307.

[Michael Angelo], *Nation,* XIX (Nov. 12, 1874), 319.

[*The Hanging of the Crane,* by H. W. Longfellow], *Nation,* XIX (Dec. 17, 1874), 402–403.

[The Illustrations to Ruskin's Works], *Nation,* XIX (Dec. 31, 1874), 439.

[Morris Moore's Alleged Raphael Painting], *Nation,* XIX (Dec. 31, 1874), 439–440.

[*Singers and Songs of the Liberal Faith,* by A. P. Putnam], *Nation,* XIX (Dec. 31, 1874), 443.

"Records of the Past — Assyria and Egypt," *Nation,* XX (March 11, 1875), 176–177.

[Sir Arthur Helps], *Nation,* XX (March 18, 1875), 191.

[The Third Volume of *Records of the Past*], *Nation,* XX (March 18, 1875), 192.

[*Architecture for General Students,* by C. W. Horton], *Nation,* XX (March 18, 1875), 194.

[H. A. Bright's *Some Account of the Glenriddell MSS. of Burns's Poems*], *Nation,* XX (March 25, 1875), 208.

[*An Essay on the Madonna in Christian Art,* by H. M. Ladd], *Nation,* XX (April 29, 1875), 300–301.

[The Poetry in the Current Magazines], *Nation,* XX (May 27, 1875), 362.

[Sir Henry Maine's Rede Lecture], *Nation,* XX (June 17, 1875), 411.

[Rajon's Etching of Watts' Portrait of Mill], *Nation,* XX (June 17, 1875), 411.

[Sir Henry Maine], *Nation,* XXI (July 1, 1875), 9.

[The Proposed Beatification of Columbus], *Nation,* XXI (July 1, 1875), 42.

"Recent Poetry," *Nation,* XXI (July 15, 1875), 44.

[*William Sharp, Engraver,* by W. S. Baker], *Nation,* XXI (July 15, 1875), 46.

"Tennyson's Queen Mary," *Nation,* XXI (July 22, 1875), 60–61.

[*Representative Names in the History of English Literature*, by H. H. Morgan], *Nation*, XXI (July 22, 1875), 61–62.

"Some Recent Volumes of Poetry," *Nation*, XXII (Jan. 6, 1876), 14–15.

[Editorial answer to communication "Art-Instruction in Massachusetts"], *Nation*, XXII (Jan. 27, 1876), 62.

[John Forster], *Nation*, XXII (Feb. 10, 1876), 97.

[*American Engravers and Their Works*, by W. S. Baker], *Nation*, XXII (Feb. 10, 1876), 104.

[*The Early Coins of America*, by S. S. Crosby], *Nation*, XXII (Feb. 10, 1876), 104.

[Hogarth], *Nation*, XXII (Feb. 17, 1876), 114.

"Stedman's Victorian Poets," *Nation*, XXII (Feb. 17, 1876), 117–118.

"Feminine Poetry," *Nation*, XXII (Feb. 24, 1876), 132–134.

"The Life of George Ticknor," *Nation*, XXII (March 2, 1876), 148–149.

"The Massachusetts System of Instruction in Drawing," *Nation*, XXII (April 13, 1876), 252–253.

[Editorial comment on the communication "General art instruction"], *Nation*, XXII (May 11, 1876), 306–307.

[Sidney Lanier], *Nation*, XXII (May 25, 1876), 336.

"A Flock of Songsters," *Nation*, XXII (June 1, 1876), 353–355.

"O'Hara and His Elegies," *Nation*, XXII (June 29, 1876), 417–418.

[*Verses from the Harvard Advocate*], *Nation*, XXIII (Aug. 31, 1876), 139–140.

"The Dimensions and Proportions of the Temple of Zeus at Olympia," *Proceedings of the American Academy of Arts and Sciences*, XIII (May–Nov., 1877), 145–170.

[William Cullen Bryant], *Nation*, XXVI (June 20, 1878), 404–405.

[*Turner's Liber Studiorum*, by W. G. Rawlinson], *Nation*, XXVIII (March 6, 1879), 169–170.

[*Tanagra Figurines*], *Nation*, XXIX (Oct. 9, 1879), 248.

"List of the Principal Books Relating to the Life of Michelangelo, with Notes," *Bibliographical Contributions, Harvard College Library*, ed. by Justin Winsor, Cambridge, Mass.: John Wilson and Son, 1879.

1880's

BOOKS

Historical Studies of Church Building in the Middle Ages: Venice, Siena, Florence. New York: Harper & Bros., 1880. The chapters on Venice and Florence appeared earlier in "Venice and St. Marks," *At. Mo.*, XLI (Feb., 1878), 202–217; "Florence, and St. Mary of the Flower," *At. Mo.*, XLII (Nov., 1878), 564–575, and (Dec., 1878), 657–669.

The Correspondence of Thomas Carlyle and Ralph Waldo Emerson, 1834–72. (Ed. by Norton) Boston: James R. Osgood & Co., 1883,

2 vols. Norton edited seventeen supplementary letters in 1886 (Boston: Ticknor and Co.).

Early Letters of Thomas Carlyle. (Ed. by Norton) London: Macmillan Co., 1886. 2 vols.

Correspondence Between Goethe and Carlyle (Ed. by Norton) London: Macmillan Co., 1887.

Reminiscences by Thomas Carlyle. (Ed. by Norton) London: Macmillan Co., 1887. 2 vols.

Letters of Thomas Carlyle, 1826–1836. (Ed. by Norton) London: Macmillan Co., 1888. 2 vols.

ARTICLES AND REVIEWS

"Painting and Sculpture in their Relation to Architecture," *American Art Review,* I (1880), 192–195, 249–253.

[Restoration of St. Mark's, Venice], *Nation,* XXX (Jan. 1, 1880), 13.

[A New Edition of Ruskin's *Stones of Venice*], *Nation,* XXX (Jan. 29, 1880), 75–76.

[*The Early Teutonic, Italian, and French Masters* by A. H. Keane], *Nation,* XXX (Feb. 12, 1880), 124.

[C. H. Moore's Mezzotints], *Nation,* XXX (June 3, 1880), 418–419.

"Butler's Translation of Dante's Purgatory," *Nation,* XXXI (Dec. 2, 1880), 397–398.

"Newton's Essays on Art and Archaeology," *Nation,* XXXI (Dec. 23, 1880), 449–450.

"Turner's Drawings for the Liber Studiorum," *Nation,* XXXII (Jan. 6, 1881), 8. (Signed letter)

"Muntz's Life of Raphael," *Nation,* XXXII (March 24, 1881), 208–209.

"Remarks of Mr. Norton at the Annual Meeting of the Dante Society," *First Annual Report of the Dante Society* (May 16, 1882), pp. 17–25.

"Murray's History of Greek Sculpture," *Nation,* XXXII (June 23, 1881), 444–445.

"The Greek Play at Harvard," *At. Mo.,* XLVIII (July, 1881), 106–110.

"Perry's History of Greek and Roman Sculpture," *Nation,* XXXIV (June 29, 1882), 547–548.

"Early Mention of Assos," *Nation,* XXXV (July 6, 1882), 11. (Signed letter)

[G. G. Hardingham's edition of *The Republic of Cicero*], *Nation,* XXXV (Aug. 10, 1882), 113.

"Major di Cesnola's Salaminia," *Nation,* XXXV (Aug. 17, 1882), 138.

"Clough," *Nation,* XXXVI (March 22, 1883), 259–260.

"The First American Classical Archaeologist," *American Journal of Archaeology,* I (Jan., 1885), 39.

"Two Recent Translations of the Divine Comedy," *Nation,* XL (June 25, 1885), 524–525.

"Recollections of Carlyle, with Notes Concerning the Reminiscences," *New Princeton Review,* II (July, 1886), 1–19.

"Omissions by Mr. Froude in Carlyle's 'Reminiscences,' " *Nation,* XLIII (July 22, 1886), 74.

"A Gift of Dante," *Nation,* XLIII (Sept. 23, 1886), 251. (Signed letter)

"Dean Plumptre's Translation of the Divine Comedy," *Nation,* XLIV (Feb. 3, 1887), 102–104.

"Time References in the Divina Commedia," *Nation,* XLIV (April 14, 1887), 322–324.

"The Excavations at Crotona," *Nation,* XLIV (May 5, 1887), 386. (Signed letter)

"Matthew Arnold," *Proceedings of the American Academy of Arts and Sciences,* New Series, XV (1888), 349–353.

"The Intellectual Life of America," *New Princeton Review,* VI (Nov., 1888), 312–324.

"A Definition of the Fine Arts," *Forum,* VII (March, 1889), 30–40.

"Mr. Cole's Woodcuts in the *Century,*" *Nation,* XLVIII (March 28, 1889), 267. (Signed letter)

"The Lack of Old Homes in America," *Scribner's Magazine,* V (May, 1889), 636–640.

"Rawdon Brown and the Gravestone of 'Banished Norfolk,' " *At. Mo.,* LXIII (June, 1889), 740–745.

"The Prospects of Architecture as a Fine Art in the United States," *Technology Architectural Review,* II (Aug. 3, 1889), 19.

"A Last Word on the Excavations at Delphi," *Nation,* XLIX (Aug. 29, 1889), 169–170. (Signed letter)

"The Building of the Church of St.-Denis," *Harper's Magazine,* LXXIX (Oct., 1889), 766–776.

"The Building of the Cathedral at Chartres," *Harper's Magazine,* LXXIX (Nov., 1889), 944–955.

1890's

BOOKS

Latest Literary Essays and Addresses of James Russell Lowell. Cambridge, Mass.: Riverside Press, 1891.

The Divine Comedy of Dante Alighieri. (Trans. by Norton) Boston: Houghton Mifflin Co., 1891–92, 3 vols. Rev. ed., 1902, 3 vols.

Letters of James Russell Lowell. (Ed. by Norton) New York: Harper & Bros., 1893. 2 vols.

Orations and Addresses of George W. Curtis. (Ed. by Norton) New York: Harper & Bros., 1894. 3 vols.

The Heart of Oak Books. (Ed. by Norton) Boston: D. C. Heath & Co., 1894–95. 6 vols.

Four American Universities: Harvard, Yale, Princeton, Columbia. New York: Harper & Bros., 1895. "Harvard" is by Norton, reprinted from "Harvard University in 1890," *Harper's New Monthly Magazine,* LXXXI (Sept., 1890), 581–592.

Last Poems of James Russell Lowell. (Ed. with a Prefatory Note by Norton) Boston: Houghton Mifflin Co., 1895.

The Poems of John Donne, from the Text of the Edition of 1633 revised by J. R. Lowell. With the various readings of the other editions of the seventeenth century, and with a preface, an introduction, and notes by Norton. New York: The Grolier Club, 1895. 2 vols.

The Poems of Mrs. Anne Bradstreet (1612–1672); Together with Her Prose Remains. (With an introduction by Norton) New York: The Duodecimos, 1897.

Two Note-Books of Thomas Carlyle . . . (Ed. by Norton) New York: The Grolier Club, 1898.

[Kipling, Rudyard] *Plain Tales from the Hills.* (With a biographical sketch by Norton) New York: Doubleday & McClure Co., 1899.

ARTICLES AND REVIEWS

[*An Introduction to the Study of Dante,* by J. A. Symonds], *Nation,* LI (Oct. 2, 1890), 271–272.

"The Early Biographers of Dante," *Nation,* LI (Oct. 16, 1890), 307–309.

"James Russell Lowell," *Harper's Magazine,* LXXXVI (May, 1893), 846–857.

"The Letters of James Russell Lowell," *Harper's Magazine,* LXXXVII (Sept., 1893), 553–560.

"Sambo and Sancho," *Nation,* LVIII (May 31, 1894), 407. (Signed letter)

"The Educational Value of the History of the Fine Arts," *Educational Review,* IX (April, 1895), 343–348.

"Some Aspects of Civilization in America," *Forum,* XX (Feb., 1896), 641–651.

"The Public Life and Services of William Eustis Russell," *Harvard Graduate's Magazine,* V (Dec., 1896), 177–194.

"The Text of Donne's Poems," *Studies and Notes in Philology and Literature,* V (1896, issued 1897), 1–19.

"The Poetry of Rudyard Kipling," *At. Mo.,* LXXIX (Jan., 1897), 111–115.

"Francis James Child," *Proceedings of the American Academy of Arts and Sciences,* XXXII (July, 1897), 333–339. This article was reprinted, with some additions, in *Harvard Graduate's Magazine,* VI (Dec., 1897), 161–169.

"Recent Works on Dante," *Nation,* LXIX (Sept. 7, 1899), 191–192; (Sept. 14, 1899), 210–212.

" 'Letters of Emerson to a Friend,' " *Nation,* LXIX (Nov. 9, 1899), 351; (Nov. 23, 1899), 391. (Signed letters)

1900–08

BOOKS

Comments of John Ruskin on the Divina Commedia. (Compiled by George P. Huntington, with an introduction by Norton) Boston: Houghton Mifflin Co., 1903.

The Poet Gray as a Naturalist . . . Boston: Charles E. Goodspeed, 1903.

Letters of John Ruskin to Charles Eliot Norton. Boston: Houghton Mifflin Co., 1904. 2 vols. Some of these letters were first published in the *At. Mo.,* XCIII (May, 1904), 577–588; (June), 797–806; XCIV (July), 8–19; (Aug.), 161–170; (Sept.), 378–388.

The Love Poems of John Donne. (Selected and ed. by Norton) Boston: Houghton Mifflin Co., 1905.

Henry Wadsworth Longfellow; A Sketch of His Life by Charles Eliot Norton, Together with Longfellow's Chief Biographical Poems. Boston: Houghton Mifflin Co., 1907.

ARTICLES AND REVIEWS

"The Work of the Archaeological Institute of America . . . ," *American Journal of Archaeology,* IV (Jan.–March, 1900), 1–16.

[Temple edition of Dante's *Paradiso*], *Nation,* LXX (Feb. 1, 1900), 91.

"Gosse's Life of Donne," *Nation,* LXX (Feb. 8, 1900), 111–113; (Feb. 15, 1900), 133–135.

[Edmund Gardner's *Dante*], *Nation,* LXX (May 17, 1900), 377.

[P. H. Wicksteed's translation of Dante's *Paradiso*], *Nation,* LXX (May 17, 1900), 377.

[*Amyntas,* by Torquato Tasso, tr. by Frederic Whitmore], *Nation,* LXIII (Sept. 19, 1901), 232.

[*An English Comment on Dante's Divina Commedia,* by H. F. Tozer], *Nation,* LXXIII (Oct. 17, 1901), 307–308.

"Tribute to William Wetmore Story," *Proceedings of the Massachusetts Historical Society,* XV (1902), 368–371.

"Address of Charles Eliot Norton," in *The Centenary of the Birth of Ralph Waldo Emerson.* Concord: The Riverside Press, June, 1903, pp. 45–58.

"The Founding of the School at Athens," *American Journal of Archaeology,* VII (1903), 351–356.

"A Criticism of Harvard Architecture Made to the Board of Overseers," *Harvard Graduate's Magazine,* XII (March, 1904), 359–362.

"Reminiscences of Old Cambridge," *Cambridge Historical Society Publications,* I (Oct., 1905), 11–23.

"The New Humanistic Type," *The Printing Art,* VI (Jan., 1906), 273–283.

"The Launching of the Magazine," *At. Mo.,* C (Nov., 1907), 579–581.

"A Note on 'The Pleasant Art of Reading Aloud,'" *Nation,* LXXXVI (Jan. 9, 1908), 32. (Letter signed "C. E. N.")
"The Japanese Point of View," *Nation,* LXXXVI (March 19, 1908), 257. (Signed letter)

II. BACKGROUND SOURCES

(For reasons of space, I have omitted most of the standard biographies and editions of the correspondence of major figures in the period unless such works have been cited in the Notes.)

BOOKS

Adams, Henry. *The Education of Henry Adams.* Boston: Houghton Mifflin Co., 1918.
—— *Letters of Henry Adams.* Ed. by Worthington C. Ford. Boston: Houghton Mifflin Co., 1930. 2 vols.
Arnold, Matthew. *Culture and Anarchy.* New York: Macmillan Co., 1875.
Arvin, Newton. *Whitman.* New York: Macmillan Co., 1938.
Austin, James C. *Fields of the Atlantic Monthly: Letters to an Editor, 1861–1870.* San Marino, California: Huntington Library, 1953.
[Babbit, Irving] *Irving Babbitt: Man and Teacher.* Ed. by Frederick Manchester and Odell Shepard. New York: G. P. Putnam's Sons, 1941.
Babbitt, Irving. *Literature and the American College.* Boston: Houghton Mifflin Co., 1908.
Brooks, Van Wyck. *The Flowering of New England, 1815–1865.* New York: E. P. Dutton & Co., 1936.
—— *New England: Indian Summer 1865–1915.* New York: E. P. Dutton & Co., 1940.
Brown, Rollo W. *Harvard Yard in the Golden Age.* New York: Current Books, Inc., A. A. Wyn Publisher, 1948.
—— *Lonely Americans.* New York: Coward-McCann, Inc., 1929.
Cady, Edwin H. *The Road to Realism . . .* Syracuse: Syracuse University Press, 1956.
[Carlyle, Thomas] *New Letters of Thomas Carlyle.* Ed. by Alexander Carlyle. London: John Lane, 1904. 2 vols.
Cary, Edward. *George William Curtis.* Boston: Houghton Mifflin Co., 1894.
Chapman, John Jay. *Memories and Milestones.* New York: Moffat, Yard & Co., 1915.
Chittenden, L(ucius) E. *Personal Reminiscences.* New York: Richmond, Croscup & Co., 1893.
[Clough, Arthur Hugh] *The Correspondence of Arthur Hugh Clough.* Ed. by Frederick L. Mulhauser. Oxford: The Clarendon Press, 1957. 2 vols.

Cram, Ralph A. *My Life in Architecture.* Boston: Little, Brown, & Co., 1936.

The Critique of Humanism: A Symposium. Ed. by C. Hartley Grattan. New York: Brewer & Warren, 1930.

The Development of Harvard . . . 1869–1929. Ed. by Samuel E. Morison. Cambridge, Mass.: Harvard University Press, 1930.

Dunn, Waldo H. *Froude and Carlyle.* London: Longmans, Green & Co., 1930.

Eaton, Allen H. *Handicrafts of New England.* New York: Harper & Bros., 1949.

Eliot, T. S. *Notes Towards the Definition of Culture.* New York: Harcourt, Brace & Co., 1949.

—— *Selected Essays, 1917–32.* London: Faber & Faber Ltd., 1932.

—— *The Use of Poetry and the Use of Criticism.* London: Faber & Faber, Ltd., 1933.

Emerson, Edward W., and William F. Harris. *Charles Eliot Norton: Two Addresses.* Boston: Houghton Mifflin Co., 1912.

[Gaskell, Elizabeth C.] *Letters of Mrs. Gaskell and Charles Eliot Norton, 1855–1865.* Ed. with an introduction by Jane Whitehall. Oxford University Press, 1932.

[Godkin, Edwin L.] *Life and Letters of Edwin Lawrence Godkin.* Ed. by Rollo Ogden. New York: The Macmillan Co., 1907. 2 vols.

Godkin, Edwin L. *Reflections and Comments, 1865–95.* New York: Charles Scribner's Sons, 1895.

Harrison, Frederic. *Autobiographic Memoirs.* London: Macmillan Co., 1911. Vol. II.

—— *Among My Books.* London: Macmillan Co., 1912.

Hawthorne, Nathaniel. *Our Old Home, and English Note-Books.* Boston: Houghton Mifflin Co., 1902. 2 vols.

Higginson, Thomas W. *Carlyle's Laugh and Other Surprises.* Boston: Houghton Mifflin Co., 1909.

Howe, Mark A. DeWolfe. *The Atlantic Monthly and its Makers.* Boston: Atlantic Monthly Press, Inc., 1919.

—— *John Jay Chapman and His Letters.* Boston: Houghton Mifflin Co., 1937.

[Howells, William D.] *Life in Letters of William Dean Howells.* Ed. by Mildred Howells. Garden City, New York: Doubleday, Doran & Co., 1928. 2 vols.

Howells, William D. *Literary Friends and Acquaintances.* New York: Harper & Bros., 1902.

Humanism and America . . . Ed. by Norman Foerster. New York: Farrar & Rinehart, 1931.

James, Henry. *Note of a Son & Brother.* New York: Charles Scribner's Sons, 1914.

—— *Notes on Novelists, with Some Other Notes.* New York: Charles Scribner's Sons, 1914.

—— *William Wetmore Story and His Friends.* Boston: Houghton Mifflin Co., 1903. 2 vols.

Kazin, Alfred. *On Native Grounds.* New York: Reynal & Hitchcock, 1942.

Kirk, Russell. *The Conservative Mind from Burke to Santayana.* Chicago: Henry Regnery Co., 1953.

LaPiana, Angelina. *Dante's American Pilgrimage* . . . New Haven: Yale University Press, 1948.

Lippincott, Benjamin E. *Victorian Critics of Democracy: Carlyle, Ruskin, Arnold, Stephen, Maine, Lecky.* Minneapolis: University of Minnesota Press, 1938.

[Lowell, James R.] *New Letters of James Russell Lowell.* Ed. by Mark A. DeWolfe Howe. New York: Harper & Bros., 1932.

Maitland, Frederic W. *The Life and Letters of Leslie Stephen.* London: Duckworth & Co., 1910.

Matthiessen, F. O. *American Renaissance.* London: Oxford University Press, 1941.

Miller, Perry. *The New England Mind.* New York: Macmillan Co., 1939.

—— *The Transcendentalists: An Anthology.* Cambridge, Mass.: Harvard University Press, 1950.

Miller, Perry, and Thomas H. Johnson. *The Puritans.* New York: American Book Co., 1938.

Milne, Gordon. *George William Curtis and the Genteel Tradition.* Bloomington: Indiana University Press, 1956.

Moore, Charles. *Daniel H. Burnham.* Boston: Houghton Mifflin Co., 1921. 2 vols.

—— *Personalities in Washington Architecture.* Washington, D. C.: Reprinted from the Records of the Columbia Historical Society, 1937.

Morison, Samuel Eliot. *The Puritan Pronaos: Studies in the Intellectual Life of New England in the Seventeenth Century.* New York: New York University Press, 1936.

—— *Three Centuries of Harvard.* Cambridge, Mass.: Harvard University Press, 1936.

Mott, Frank L. *American Journalism.* New York: Macmillan Co., 1950.

—— *A History of American Magazines* . . . Cambridge, Mass.: Harvard University Press, 1938. 3 vols.

Murdock, Kenneth B. *A Leaf of Grass from Shady Hill.* Cambridge, Mass.: Harvard University Press, 1928.

Orcutt, William D. *Celebrities off Parade.* Chicago: Willet, Clark & Co., 1935.

——*From My Library Walls.* New York: Longmans, Green & Co., 1945.

[Peabody, Josephine P.] *Diary and Letters of Josephine Preston Peabody.* Selected and ed. by Christina H. Baker. Boston: Houghton Mifflin Co., 1925.

Perry, Bliss. *Walt Whitman.* Boston: Houghton Mifflin Co., 1906.

Perry, Ralph Barton. *Puritanism & Democracy.* New York: Vanguard Press, 1944.

Rossetti Papers, 1862 to 1870. A compilation by William M. Rossetti. London: Sands & Co., 1903.

Ruskin, John. *Praeterita.* London: George Allen, 1907.

Ruskin: Rossetti: PreRaphaelitism. Ed. by William M. Rossetti. London: George Allen, 1899.

Santayana, George. *Character & Opinion in the United States.* New York: Charles Scribner's Sons, 1920.

——*The Genteel Tradition at Bay.* New York: Charles Scribner's Sons, 1931.

——*Winds of Doctrine.* New York: Charles Scribner's Sons, 1926.

Spiller, Robert E., *et al. Literary History of the United States.* New York: Macmillan Co., 1948. 3 vols.

Stephens, Kate. *A Curious History in Book Editing.* New York: Antigone Press, 1927.

Stillman, William J. *The Autobiography of a Journalist.* Boston: Houghton Mifflin Co., 1901. 2 vols.

Tallmadge, Thomas E. *The Story of Architecture in America.* New York: W. W. Norton & Co., 1927.

Villard, Oswald G. *Fighting Years: Memoirs of a Liberal Editor.* New York: Harcourt, Brace & Co., 1939.

Warren, Austin. *New England Saints.* Ann Arbor: University of Michigan Press, 1956.

Wilbur, Earl M. *A History of Unitarianism.* Cambridge, Mass.: Harvard University Press, 1952.

ARTICLES

"The Athletic Commitee," *Harvard Alumni Bulletin,* XIV (Jan. 3, 1912), 196–198.

"C. E. Norton on Dime Issues," *Massachusetts Historical Society Proceedings,* L (Feb., 1917), 196–199.

"Charles Eliot Norton," *Nation,* XCII (May 11, 1911), 471–472. Unsigned tribute from a former student.

"Charles Eliot Norton," *Time and the Hour,* VII (April 2, 1898), 6–8.

"For Professor Norton's Eightieth Birthday," *Harvard Graduates Magazine,* XVI (Dec., 1907), 217–230.

Hall, Chadwick. "America's Conservative Revolution," *Antioch Review,* XV (Summer, 1955), 204–216.

Howe, Mark A. DeWolfe, and Charles Adams. "Memoir of Charles Eliot Norton," *Proceedings of the Massachusetts Historical Society,* XLVIII (Oct., 1914), 57–68.

Howells, William D. "Charles Eliot Norton: A Reminiscence," *NAR,* CXCVIII (Dec., 1913), 836–838.

—— "Part of Which I Was," *NAR,* CCI (Jan., 1915), 135–141.

—— "Recollections of an Atlantic Editorship," *At. Mo.,* C (Nov., 1907), 594–606.

Jones, Howard M. "The Recovery of New England," *At. Mo.,* CLXXXV (April, 1950), 521.

Madden, Edward H. "Charles Eliot Norton on Art and Morals," *Journal of the History of Ideas,* XVIII (June, 1957), 430–438.

Mason, Daniel G. "At Harvard in the Nineties," *New England Quarterly,* IX (March, 1936), 43–70.

[Mill, John S.] "Letters of John Stuart Mill to Charles Eliot Norton," *Proceedings of the Massachusetts Historical Society,* L (Oct., 1916), 11–25.

Moore, Charles. "Standards of Taste," *American Magazine of Art,* XXI (July, 1930), 365–367.

More, Paul Elmer. "Charles Eliot Norton," *Nation,* XCVII (Dec. 4, 1913), 529–532.

Norman, Henry. "The Preservation of Niagara," *Nation,* XXXIII (Sept. 1, 1881), 170–171.

Shaffer, Robert B. "Ruskin, Norton, and Memorial Hall," *Harvard Library Bulletin,* IX (Spring, 1949), 213–231.

Smith, Henry Nash. " 'That Hideous Mistake of Poor Clemens's,' " *Harvard Library Bulletin,* IX (Spring, 1955), 145–180.

Thayer, William R. "Charles Eliot Norton," *Nation,* LXXXVII (Oct. 29, 1908), 403–406.

—— "Professor Charles Eliot Norton," *28th Annual Report of the Dante Society,* 1909 (Boston: Ginn & Co., 1910), pp. 1–6.

—— "The Sage of Shady Hill," *The Unpartizen Review,* XV (Jan.–March, 1921), 76–90.

"Two Notable Letter-Writers," *The Athenaeum,* No. 4492 (Nov. 29, 1913), 615–616.

Wendell, Barrett. "Charles Eliot Norton," *At. Mo.,* CIII (Jan., 1909), 82–83.

Wolff, Samuel L. "Scholars," *Cambridge History of American Literature,* IV (New York, 1921), 489.

NOTES

I have abbreviated the following sources in the notes:

At. Mo. = *Atlantic Monthly*
NAR = *North American Review*
Letters = *Letters of Charles Eliot Norton.* Ed. by Sara Norton
and Mark A. DeWolfe Howe. Boston: Houghton Mifflin
Co., 1913. 2 vols.
Mass. Hist. Soc. Proc. = *Massachusetts Historical Society Proceedings*
Norton Papers = The extensive collection of Norton materials
in the Houghton Library, Harvard University. In addition to Norton's correspondence, a generous portion of
which is published in the *Letters,* the collection includes
his journals, poems, scrapbooks, business account-books,
manuscript copies of his public addresses, passports, newspaper clippings, and miscellaneous other papers. Letters
and other biographical materials in this book are drawn
from the Norton Papers unless indicated otherwise.

INTRODUCTION

1. Whitman almost certainly was directing certain passages of *Democratic Vistas* at Norton and the other distinguished Bostonians who had established the *Atlantic Monthly* in 1857. Whitman's essay was based on articles he had written in 1867 and 1868 for the *Galaxy,* a New York monthly founded during the late sixties as an opponent of the *Atlantic.* The *Galaxy*'s crusade for a wider nationalism in American letters appears to have been somewhat futile. Upon its demise in 1878, in fact, the *Galaxy* sold its subscription list to the *Atlantic.* For the genesis of Whitman's criticism of "democracy" and his relation to the *Galaxy,* see Edward F. Grier, "Walt Whitman, the *Galaxy,* and *Democratic Vistas,*" *American Literature,* XXIII (Nov., 1951), 332–350.

Chapter I. New England Heritage

1. *Letters,* I, 82.
2. *Memories and Milestones* (New York, 1915), p. 133.
3. These and succeeding quotations from the *Magnalia* are from Vol. I of the 1853–55 ed. (Hartford: Silas Andrus and Son).
4. From Charles Eliot Norton's "Address at the Celebration of the Two-Hundredth Anniversary of the Old Meeting-House at Hingham," (1882), manuscript in Norton Papers.
Charles Norton himself later edited *The Poems of Mrs. Anne Brad-*

street (New York, 1897), partly out of reverence for his ancestor's memory.

5. Norton, "Address at . . . Hingham."

6. *Diary of Samuel Sewall,* reprinted in *Collections of the Massachusetts Historical Society,* 5th Ser., V (Boston, 1878), 417–418.

7. Perry Miller and Thomas H. Johnson (eds.), *The Puritans* (New York, 1938), p. 18.

8. Earl M. Wilbur, *A History of Unitarianism* (Cambridge, Mass., 1952), pp. 385–386.

9. Frank L. Mott, *A History of American Magazines* (Cambridge, Mass., 1939), II, 278.

10. *The Boston Daily Advertiser,* August 27, 1838. Reprinted in Perry Miller, *The Transcendentalists: An Anthology* (Cambridge, Mass., 1950), p. 193. For Charles Eliot Norton's friendship with Carlyle, see Chapters IV and VI below.

11. In the *Boston Quarterly Review,* October, 1838, reprinted in Miller, *The Transcendentalists,* pp. 189–190. Mr. Miller points out the intentional thrust of the word "standard" in Ripley's title.

12. The *Boston Quarterly Review,* January, 1839, reprinted in Miller, *The Transcendentalists,* p. 208.

13. Quoted in Miller, *The Transcendentalists,* p. 213.

14. Quotations are in Miller, *The Transcendentalists,* pp. 313, 489, and 159. See also *The Collected Works of Theodore Parker,* ed. by Francis P. Cobbe (London, 1865), XII, 280; and the *Memorial History of Boston,* ed. by Justin Winsor (Boston, 1881), IV, 299.

15. July 6, 1840.

16. Sept. 17, 1853.

17. Letter to his mother, April 20, 1845.

18. *Mass. Hist. Soc. Proc.,* 2nd Ser. (Boston, 1890), V, 249.

Chapter II. From Business to Scholarship

1. Letter to George Woodberry, Oct. 11, 1877.

2. In an autobiographical paper dictated by Norton in 1908, *Letters,* I, 27–28.

3. *Ibid.,* I, 28.

4. Aug. 26, 1849.

5. Letter to William S. Bullard, Sept. 14, 1849.

6. Letter to Charles Mills, Oct. 4, 1849.

7. Sept. 26, 1850.

8. *NAR,* LXXIII, 139, 150, 151.

9. *NAR,* LXXV, 482.

10. *Ibid.,* pp. 465, 467.

11. "The St. Nicholas and Five Points," *Putnam's,* I (May, 1853), 510, 511.

12. "Model Lodging-Houses in Boston," *At. Mo.,* V (June, 1860), 673.

13. *Ibid.,* p. 678.

14. *Considerations on Some Recent Social Theories* (Boston, 1853), pp. 7, 13, 15, 19–20, 53–54, 69, 145. Stress of the word "authority" is mine.

15. *Ibid.,* pp. 38, 158.

16. Van Wyck Brooks devotes a paragraph to the book in his *Flowering of New England* (New York, 1936), p. 455. Russell Kirk, *The Conservative Mind* (Chicago, 1953), makes no mention of Norton's *Considerations.*

17. Jan. 25, 1855.

18. Letter to Child, March 15, 1855.

19. "The Opening of the Ganges Canal," *NAR,* LXXXI (Oct., 1855), 542.

20. Letter to Lowell, April 6, 1855.

21. Letter to Appleton, May 7, 1855.

22. To Miss Smith, Dec. 26, 1852, *The Correspondence of Arthur Hugh Clough,* ed. by Frederick L. Mulhauser (Oxford, 1957), II, 318. "Miss Smith" (Blanche) became Mrs. Clough in 1854.

23. The Norton Papers contain a scrapbook to 1864 with a short story and two poems by Thoreau, and a clipping which lists the titles of Thoreau's works. Norton read *The Maine Woods* after its publication in 1864 and disliked the style though he praised it as a "good study of nature" (Letter to Lowell, July 16, 1864). He wrote to the publishers Ticknor and Fields the next year, asking for a copy of *Walden* and *A Week on the Concord and Merrimack Rivers* (August 21, 1865).

24. "Whitman's Leaves of Grass," *Putnam's* VI (Sept., 1855), 321. Norton's authorship was established by Kenneth B. Murdock, *A Leaf of Grass from Shady Hill* (Cambridge, Mass., 1928).

25. Jan. 23, 1854.

26. Sept. 23, 1855.

27. Lowell to Norton, Oct. 12, 1855, in *Letters of James Russell Lowell,* ed. by Norton (New York, 1893), I, 242.

28. Sept. 18, 1856.

29. *Notes of Travel and Study in Italy* (Boston, 1859) pp. 1–2. The stress is mine. In 1856, Norton allowed portions of these notes to be published in *The Crayon,* an unsuccessful art magazine edited by his friend William J. Stillman. Norton had hoped to see the magazine thrive and refused to accept payment for the articles.

30. *Ibid.,* pp. 12, 18–19.

31. *Ibid.,* pp. 52, 62–63.

32. *Ibid.,* pp. 3–4, and letter to Lowell, Jan. 13, 1856.

33. *Ibid.,* pp. 163–164.

34. *Ibid.,* pp. 105–106. The stress is mine.

35. *Ibid.,* pp. 119, 124, 130, 143.

36. *Ibid.*, pp. 106, 117, 119, 128. Implications which his theory might have held for the American scene did not directly concern Norton during this period, though he did feel a need to explain why the combination of religious enthusiasm and self-government in America had not produced significant church architecture. America had lacked inspired leaders in religion and art who could direct the energies set loose by revivalism into "great and noble" channels. "It is a difference exhibited in the contrast between the bare boards of a Methodist meeting-house and the carved walls of a Catholic cathedral." *Ibid.*, pp. 125–126.

37. *Praeterita* (London, 1907), III, 76, 77, 78, 79. Dr. John Brown (1810–82) was also a close friend of Lord Jeffrey, Thackeray, and other prominent Englishmen. He was the author of *Horae Subsecivae*, a three-volume collection of essays on medicine, poetry, painting, dogs, and human nature, in the manner of Montaigne.

38. Nov. 9, 1856.

39. Aug. 31, 1856.

40. *Notes*, pp. 293–294, 303–306.

41. *Ibid.*, pp. 299, 315, 316, 317.

42. July 8, 1856, in *Letters of James Russell Lowell*, I, 260.

43. *Praeterita*, III, 80.

44. *Letters of John Ruskin to Charles Eliot Norton* (Boston, 1904), I, 8, 116, 171.

45. *Letters*, I, 156; *Letters of Mrs. Gaskell and Charles Eliot Norton*, ed. by Jane Whitehill (London, 1932), p. 108.

Chapter III. *The Journalist and Civil War Optimism*

1. June 20, 1857.

2. April 19, 1850.

3. Nov. 22, 1855.

4. *Notes*, pp. 178, 180.

5. Fragment of a page dated Jan. 1857, in Norton Papers.

6. Aug. 17, 1857.

7. "The Manchester Exhibition," *At. Mo.*, I (Nov., 1857), 45. Hawthorne, whose pragmatic approach to painting and sculpture struck Norton as untrained and arrogantly Yankee, described the Exhibition in his *English Note-Books* (Boston, 1902, II, 517–545). The two discussions contrast sharply — Norton's being comprehensive and pontifical, Hawthorne's offhand and mildly irreverent.

8. Review of *"The Life of Michael Angelo Buonarotti . . .* , by John S. Hanford," *At. Mo.*, I (Feb., 1858), 510–511.

9. " 'The New Life' of Dante," *At. Mo.*, III (Jan., 1859), 64–65, and (February, 1859) 202.

10. "The Oxford Museum," *At. Mo.*, IV (Dec., 1859), 770.

11. Review of *Le Prime Quattro Edizione della Divina Commedia* by G. G. Warren Lord Vernon, *At. Mo.*, V (May, 1860), 628.

12. Review of *"Essays and Reviews* . . . , London, 1860," *At. Mo.*, VI (Nov., 1860), 634–635.

13. Review of *Le Prime Quattro Edizione della Divina Commedia* by G. G. Warren Lord Vernon, *At. Mo.*, V (May, 1860), 623.

14. Letter to Child, March 15, 1855.

15. *The Education of Henry Adams* (Boston, 1918), p. 44.

16. *At. Mo.*, VII (Feb., 1861), 252–254. In September, Norton wrote a paper, "Emancipation and the Constitution," denouncing slavery on still a third ground: that it ran contrary to the United States Constitution by affecting the "general welfare" of the nation. Slavery figured in such matters as federal representation and taxes, Norton argued. Hence the institution made its influence felt beyond the boundaries of the individual slave states. Norton did not publish the argument in pamphlet form until 1863, after Lincoln had issued his Emancipation Proclamation. "I was doubtful as to the correctness of the 'general welfare' argument," Norton explained. "I did not wish to publish anything which, not being incontrovertible, might hurt the cause of liberty." (Norton's manuscript note on the title page, dated 1863.)

17. *At. Mo.*, V (March, 1860), 380.

18. *Notes*, p. 300.

19. Letters to Clough: Oct. 25, 1857; Dec. 11, 1860; and April 10. 1861.

20. May 27, 1861.

21. Letter to Curtis, Aug. 24, 1861; letter to Mrs. Gaskell, Aug. 12, 1861, *Letters of Mrs. Gaskell and Charles Eliot Norton*, pp. 90–91.

22. Letter to Aubrey de Vere, Oct. 2, 1861.

23. May 11, 1862.

24. *New Letters of James Russell Lowell*, ed. by M. A. DeWolfe Howe (New York, 1932), p. 99. The bracketed insertion is the editor's.

25. Letter to Norton, Dec. 31, 1861, *Letters of Mrs. Gaskell and Charles Eliot Norton*, p. 95.

26. Letter to Lowell, Dec. 19, 1861.

27. Feb. 26, 1863.

28. *Letters of Mrs. Gaskell and Charles Eliot Norton*, p. 100. The correspondence between Norton and Forbes from 1863 to 1866 (Norton Papers) contains much information on the Society. Norton later gave his own copies of the broadsides to the Boston Public Library.

29. Aug. 14, 1863, and Oct. 2, 1863.

30. July 16, 1864.

31. Oct. 10, 1864.

32. Dec. 27, 1864.

33. Nov. 2, 1865, *Letters of James Russell Lowell*, I, 351.

34. July 7, 1864.

35. Jan. 24, 1864.

36. Letter to de Vere, Dec. 27, 1864.

37. Letter to James Parton, May 23, 1866.

38. James, *Notes on Novelists* (New York, 1914), p. 413.

39. Norton at this time was a member of a committee trying to decide on the architectural plans for Harvard's projected Memorial Hall. He unsuccessfully urged the adoption of Sturgis' Gothic design instead of that of Ware and Van Brunt's.

40. "Notices of Gillett's Huss," *NAR*, XCIX (July, 1864), 270–272. Norton's review appeared in *NAR*, XCVIII (Jan., 1864), 282–285.

41. April 9, 1864, in "C. E. Norton on Dime Issues," *Mass. Hist. Soc. Proc.*, L (Feb., 1917), 196.

42. Oct. 2, 1863.

43. *Mass. Hist. Soc. Proc.*, L (Feb., 1917), 197–198.

44. "Beadle's Dime Books," *NAR*, XCIX (July, 1864), 308–309.

45. July 5, 1864, in *Mass. Hist. Soc. Proc.*, L (Feb., 1917), 198–199.

46. "Our Soldiers," *NAR*, XLIX (July, 1864), 173, 174.

47. "Goldwin Smith," *NAR*, XCIX (Oct., 1864), 526.

48. Dec. 27, 1864.

49. "Abraham Lincoln," *NAR*, C (Jan., 1865), 4, 6, 20, 21.

50. *Ibid.*, p. 8.

51. "American Political Ideas," *NAR*, CI (Oct., 1865), 551.

52. "The President's Message," *NAR*, CII (Jan., 1866), 255.

53. Letter to Meta Gaskell, Oct. 2, 1865.

54. Letter to Olmsted, Sept. 16, 1866.

55. Sept. 23, 1867.

56. Curtis to Norton, April 26, 1865, in Edward Cary, *George William Curtis* (Boston, 1894), pp. 189–192.

57. Quoted and paraphrased from *Life and Letters of Edwin Lawrence Godkin,* ed. by Rollo Ogden (New York, 1907), I, 235–240.

58. July 18, 1865, *ibid.*, I, 245.

59. January 15, 1866, *ibid.*, I, 244; *ibid.*, I, 250.

60. Letters of Jan. 31, 1868, and May 11, 1868.

61. *Reflections and Comments, 1865–95* (New York, 1895).

62. "The Paradise of Mediocrities," *Nation,* I (July 13, 1865), 44.

63. "Good Manners," *Nation,* II (May 4, 1866), 571.

64. Letter to Aubrey de Vere, March 25, 1867. The stress is mine.

Norton's use of the term "culture" here is characteristically imprecise. In a lecture entitled "American Culture," which he delivered at the Parker Institute on October 29, 1867, Norton stressed again certain Old-World views of "culture." Early in the lecture, his definition of "culture" was simply "whatever discipline or training fits a man to make the best use of all his faculties." Later, however, "culture" became more specifically the discipline or training achieved by the well-educated few. Heavily indebted to the great minds of the European past, these attainments by the few would filter down among the masses of people so that all might share the benefits: "Culture is like a river which flows downward from the heights, still widening as it flows, — till, from this far, exhaustless source, it spreads its fertilizing waters over a continent, and the whole nation drinks of its refreshing stream" (Manuscript, Norton Papers). For Arnold's similar discussion in *Culture and Anarchy* (1869), see my Introduction above.

65. Oct. 9, 1865.
66. "Part of Which I Was," *NAR,* CCI (Jan., 1915), 136.
67. July 3, 1868.
68. Letter to Ticknor and Fields, in Horace E. Scudder, *James Russell Lowell* (Boston, 1901), II, 123.

Chapter IV. European Interlude: Disillusionment

1. The speech was given on April 18, 1868. The manuscript is in the Norton Papers. Norton also celebrated Dickens' American visit with an article, "Charles Dickens," *NAR,* CVI (April, 1868), 671–672.
2. Aug. 30, 1868.
3. Sept. 4, 1868.
4. *Ibid.*
5. Norton's reply (undated) to Mill's letter of Sept. 26, 1868.
6. Jan. 1, 1869.
7. Jan. 29, 1869.
8. Letter to Chauncey Wright, May 1, 1869.
9. Letters to Curtis, Jan. 29, 1869, and July 22, 1869.
10. "The Congress of Peace and Liberty at Lausanne," *Nation,* IX (Oct. 21, 1869), 336.
11. July 17, 1869.
12. Letter to Wright, Dec. 5, 1869.
13. *Ibid.*
14. Letter to Meta Gaskell, Dec. 21, 1869.
15. Letter to Ruskin, May, 1870.
16. Godkin, "The Prospects of the Political Art," *NAR,* CX (April, 1870), 419.
17. July 12, 1870.
18. Sept. 13, 1870.
19. Letter to Ruskin, June 15, 1870.
20. Letter to Wright, Dec. 13, 1870.
21. Letter to Curtis, Dec. 25, 1870; and to Meta Gaskell, Jan. 2, 1871.
22. Letter to Curtis, Nov. 17, 1871.
23. April 1, 1872.
24. Letter to his brother, May 10, 1873, *New Letters of Thomas Carlyle,* ed. by Alexander Carlyle (London, 1904), II, 298.
25. Letter to Lowell, July 20, 1867. See Norton's article, "Mr. Emerson's Poems," *Nation,* IV (May 30, 1867), 430–431.
26. Norton Papers. See Appendix for verses in ambiguous praise of Emerson which Norton entered in his Journal on May 25, 1873, and gave to his friend as a birthday gift.

Chapter V.   *Teacher of the Fine Arts at Harvard*

1. May 30, 1873.
2. July 9, 1873.
3. Nov. 16, 1873.
4. Undated, but written some time before the death of Norton's mother on Sept. 24, 1879.
5. July 20, 1873.
6. May 26, 1875, *Letters of Henry Adams,* ed. by W. C. Ford (Boston, 1930), I, 267.
7. Letters to Ruskin, Jan. 10, 1874, and Feb. 10, 1874.
8. Norton had taught at Harvard very briefly on two previous occasions. On November 8, 1851, after an unexpected death on the faculty, President Jared Sparks had secured Norton as a temporary instructor in French. Since the position included such extra duties as the reading of junior class prize-dissertations, Norton probably returned to the business world with a sense of relief. He held a lectureship late in 1863, possibly in the medieval studies on which he had lectured at Lowell Institute during the previous winter.
9. Quoted in Charles Moore, "Standards of Taste," *American Magazine of Art,* XXI (July, 1930), 367. The author is the architect Charles A. Moore, not to be confused with the teacher Charles H. Moore.
10. Letter to Curtis, June 20, 1869.
11. March 18, 1874. Norton was strongly obsessed by a desire to discover the origins of Greek architectural genius, and apparently infected his student, George Woodberry, with the same curiosity. In 1877, Norton read a paper to the American Academy of Arts and Sciences on "The Dimensions and Proportions of the Temple of Zeus at Olympia," concluding that the mathematical ratio contained in the musical scale had been adopted by the architects of the temple. See Academy *Proceedings,* XIII (May–Nov., 1877), 145–170.
12. "History of Ancient Art," 1881, Lecture Notebook. Until otherwise indicated, quotations are taken from this notebook.
13. "Lectures on the History of Ancient Art," 1888–89, I, 5, taken and compiled by Harry F. Brown, Archives, Harvard University Library. The stress is mine.
14. I am indebted here to the notebook of William R. Thayer on Norton's course in Florentine and Venetian Art (Archives, Harvard Library). Thayer, who went on to become a scholar in his own right, noted the close similarity between the *Historical Studies of Church Building* and Norton's lectures. See Thayer's article, "Charles Eliot Norton," *Nation,* LXXXVII (Oct. 29, 1908), 405. The articles on Chartres and St. Denis appeared in *Harper's Magazine* in 1889. Norton's study of the church at Cluny was never published. Manuscript notes remain in the Norton Papers.

14. Lecture notebooks, Norton Papers.

15. *Hist. Studies*, pp. 12, 21, 27n, 30–31, 90, 187.

16. "The Building of the Cathedral at Chartres," *Harper's Magazine*, LXXIX (Nov., 1889), 955. See also Norton's "Painting and Sculpture in their Relation to Architecture," *American Art Review*, I (Boston, 1880), 192–195, 249–253.

17. Lecture Notebook, Fine Arts 2, Feb. 1, 1875.

18. *Hist. Studies*, pp. 62, 177.

19. Lecture Notebook, Fine Arts 2, Feb. 1, 1875. A full discussion of Norton's ambivalent opinions of the Renaissance would go beyond the scope of this study. His failure to come to terms with the period may account for his including it merely as an appendix to his survey of art history. He was attracted by the powerful individuality of the gentlemen and ladies in the Renaissance portraits, and once asked Howells to write a book on "Portraits of Women in the Italian Renaissance" (Letter of Jan. 10, 1869). He admired the genius of a Michelangelo or a Tintoretto, but their noble work in a corrupt age disturbed his notion that the genesis of an artist's inspiration derived from the nature of his audience. In Norton's private correspondence, for example, he wrote of Tintoretto: "The more I studied him, the more wonderful, the more original, the more complete his genius seemed to me" (Letter to Lowell, Dec. 4, (1873). But in his class in Venetian Art, the question on the final examinations asked for "Illustrations of [Venice's] decline in the character of the work of Titian and Tintoretto." (William R. Thayer, "Notes in Fine Arts 5, 1885–6.")

20. William D. Orcutt, *From My Library Walls* (New York, 1945), p. 174.

21. *Fighting Years* (New York, 1939), p. 82.

22. Oct., 1895, in *Diary and Letters of Josephine Preston Peabody*, ed. by Christina H. Baker (Boston, 1925), p. 73. More pejorative criticism follows in the diary passage and is used by Van Wyck Brooks in his unsympathetic portrait of Norton (*New England: Indian Summer*, New York, 1940, p. 421n). Mr. Brooks quotes the entire passage — with the significant omission of the "unwilling affection" clause.

23. "Harvard University in 1890," *Harper's New Monthly Magazine*, LXXXI (Sept., 1890), 591. Arthur R. Wendell records similar criticism in his student notebook for Norton's Fine Arts 4, 1894–95 (Archives, Harvard Library).

24. XXXII (Jan. 15, 1897), 152.

25. Rollo W. Brown, *Lonely Americans* (New York, 1929), pp. 176–177.

26. "Harvard University in 1890," pp. 586–587; and "Some Aspects of Civilization in America," *Forum*, XX (Feb., 1896), 645–646.

27. Letter to Sir Mountstuart E. Grant-Duff, Nov. 8, 1895. Norton had

met Grant-Duff, M.P. and literary essayist, in England during the late sixties.

28. Daniel G. Mason, "At Harvard in the Nineties," *New England Quarterly*, IX (March, 1936), 64.

29. Letter from Arthur Sedgwick to Sara Norton, *Letters*, II, 438.

30. Brown, *Lonely Americans*, p. 186.

31. *Ibid.*

32. Orcutt, *From My Library Walls*, p. 174.

33. Mason, "At Harvard in the Nineties," p. 43.

34. Letter to Norton, Nov. 30, 1883.

35. *John Jay Chapman and his Letters*, ed. by M. A. Howe (Boston, 1937), p. 191.

36. Orcutt, *Celebrities off Parade* (Chicago, 1935), p. 41.

37. Letter to Simon, May 15, 1875.

38. Mason, "At Harvard in the Nineties," p. 64.

39. Feb. 22, 1879.

40. Anonymous letter, 1912, *Letters*, II, 10–11.

Chapter VI. The American Scholar in the "Gilded Age"

1. "For Professor Norton's Eightieth Birthday," *Harvard Graduates Magazine*, XVI (December, 1907), 219.

2. Letter to Carlyle, May 7, 1874.

3. "The Work of the Archaeological Institute of America," *American Journal of Archaeology*, IV (Jan.–Mar., 1900), 2.

4. Feb. 24, 1870, and Jan. 19, 1874.

5. "The Life of George Ticknor," *Nation*, XXII (March 2, 1876), 149.

6. Oct. 13, 1879.

7. "The Work of the Archaeological Institute," p. 8.

8. "Newton's Essays on Art and Archaeology," *Nation*, XXXI (Dec. 23, 1880), 450.

9. "Perry's History of Greek and Roman Sculpture," *Nation*, XXXIV (June 29, 1882), 548.

10. Letters to Woodberry, Jan. 31, 1881, and May 22, 1881.

11. "The Greek Play at Harvard," *At. Mo.*, XLVIII (July, 1881), 109.

12. "The Work of the Archaeological Institute," p. 9.

13. Letter to Carlyle, Nov. 16, 1873.

14. Feb. 6, 1874.

15. Letters to Lowell, Feb. 23, 1874, and March 15, 1874.

16. *Life in Letters of William Dean Howells*, ed. by Mildred Howells (Garden City, 1928), I, 9.

17. The quotation is in Henry N. Smith, " 'That Hideous Mistake of Poor Clemens's,' " *Harvard Library Bulletin*, IX (Spring, 1955), 151. Mr. Smith describes the *Atlantic* dinner in full detail, and interprets the event and its aftermath.

18. *Ibid.*, pp. 155, 156.
19. Howells to Norton, Dec. 19, 1877, *Life in Letters*, I, 243.
20. Oct. 4, 1903.
21. Aug. 29, 1903.
22. July 1, 1897.
23. Dec. 12, 1891, and July 21, 1895, *Life in Letters*, II, 19, 62–63.
24. April 12, 1907.
25. Letters to Lowell, June 27, 1880; to Curtis, Dec. 29, 1889; and to Howells, April 13, 1896, and May 2, 1902.
26. May 27, 1902.
27. Letter to Howells, Dec. 13, 1902.
28. "Recollections of an Atlantic Editorship," *At. Mo.*, C (Nov., 1907), 604.
29. "Charles Eliot Norton: A Reminiscence," *NAR*, CXCVIII (Dec., 1913), 845.
30. Dec. 3, 1890, and Dec. 26, 1890, quoted in Bernard R. Bowron, "Henry Blake Fuller: A Critical Study," unpublished dissertation, Archives, Harvard University Library, pp. 202, 204.
31. Nov. 9, 1892.
32. Oct. 30, 1893.
33. May 6, 1895.
34. May 30, 1895.
35. March 19, 1898.
36. April 6, 1898.
37. "Feminine Poetry," *Nation, XXII* (Feb. 24, 1876), 133–134.
38. "O'Hara and his Elegies," *Nation*, XXII (July 29, 1876), 418; my italics.
39. "Some Recent Volumes of Poetry," *Nation, XXII* (Jan. 6, 1876), 15.
40. Nov. 4, 1902.
41. Van Wyck Brooks notes that Mark Twain was the favorite bedside reading of Charles Darwin. Darwin was a friend of Norton's and was an eminent Englishman. (His son married Mrs. Norton's sister.) So, Mr. Brooks reasons, Norton would conform to English taste and like Mark Twain, too (*New England: Indian Summer*, p. 209n).
42. Howells to Norton, Dec. 19, 1877, and Howells to Mark Twain, Dec. 25, 1877, *Life in Letters of William Dean Howells*, I, 243.
43. Diary entry, March 18, 1869, *Rossetti Papers, 1862 to 1870*, a compilation by William R. Rossetti (London, 1903), p. 386.
44. Letter to Miss E. P. Gould, quoted in Murdock, *A Leaf of Grass from Shady Hill*, p. 18.
45. Letter to Edward Lee-Childe, Aug. 18, 1874.
46. "The Life and Death of Jason," *Nation*, V (Aug. 22, 1867), 146.
47. "Feminine Poetry," *Nation, XXII* (Feb. 24, 1876), 132.
48. Letter to Ward, Feb. 24, 1900.
49. *Henry Wadsworth Longfellow; a Sketch of his Life, by Charles*

Eliot Norton, together with Longfellow's Chief Biographical Poems (Boston, 1907), p. 37.

50. Nov. 11, 1873.

51. Jan. 24, 1874.

52. Letter to Ward, Feb. 15, 1869.

53. Letter to Leslie Stephen, Oct. 4, 1885.

54. "Recollections of Carlyle, with Notes Concerning his Reminiscences," *New Princeton Review*, II (July, 1886), 16, 17–19. Ruskin liked Froude and was out of sympathy with Norton's attacks. His friendship with Norton was interrupted once again during this period. Recovering from a brief mental relapse, Ruskin wrote to Norton after this latest criticism of Froude, "You had better, by the way, have gone crazy for a month yourself than written that niggling and naggling article on Froude's misprints" (Letter to Norton, Aug. 28, 1886, *Letters of John Ruskin to Charles Eliot Norton*, II, 216).

55. Waldo H. Dunn, *Froude and Carlyle* (London, 1930), p. 85.

56. "James Russell Lowell," *Harper's Magazine*, LXXXVI (May, 1893), 847; *Letters of James Russell Lowell*, I, iii.

57. To S. C. Cockerell (Secretary of the Kelmscott Press), April 7, 1892.

58. Letter of Sept. 28, 1888.

59. March 5, 1878.

60. March 28, 1900.

61. Letter to Ward, Nov. 16, 1899.

62. Letter to Curtis, Sept. 6, 1864.

63. Miscellaneous manuscript undated and partly typed, with Norton's penciled insertions. Reference is made in the manuscript to a previous lecture, perhaps for a class at Harvard, or for the Trumbull Lectures which Norton delivered at Baltimore in 1894.

64. "The Text of Donne's Poems," *Studies and Notes in Philology and Literature*, V (1896, issued 1897), 6, 8, 18, 19.

65. *Nation*, XXII (Feb. 17, 1876), 114. Norton had not read Smollett when Carlyle praised him during a conversation which Norton entered in his Journal of 1873: "There's a vast gift of observation in the man, and great humanity, and verra little untruth or affectation" (Jan. 17). The words had an effect. On March 20, 1873, Norton recorded, "I have read Smollett's novels and letters."

66. "Gosse's Life of Donne," *Nation*, LXX (Feb. 8, 1900), 113.

67. Letter to Carlyle, May 17, 1874.

68. Manuscript copy, Norton Papers.

69. "Lectures on the History of Ancient Art," taken and compiled by Harry F. Brown, Lecture IV, Oct. 6, 1888, p. 16 (Archives, Harvard University Library).

70. Manuscript copy, Norwich Museum Address, 1888.

71. Letter to Leslie Stephen, Aug. 2, 1887.
72. Letter to Woodberry, Dec. 15, 1892.
73. Letter to Simon, Feb. 6, 1882.
74. Sara Norton and M. A. Howe, *Letters*, II, 226.
75. June 14, 1889.
76. April 21, 1901.
77. Letter to Ward, July 6, 1899.
78. "More Poetry of the War," *Nation*, III (Sept. 6, 1866), 187. This review of Melville's Civil War *Battle-Pieces* is assigned to Norton, but not with certainty, by Jay Leyda, *The Melville Log* (New York, 1951), II, 683. Internal evidence, while it is not conclusive, points to Norton's authorship. The review contrasts Melville's war verses unfavorably with Lowell's "Commemoration Ode," which Norton warmly admired. The criteria by which Melville is judged, especially the demand for clear expression, are Norton's. Some of the phrases carry a familiar sentiment and cadence ("the grandeur of the war — alike in its principles and its events —"), and the concept of the poet as an "imaginative realist'" appears in Norton's lecture notebooks and his later reviews of poetry.
79. Letter to Weir Mitchell, Dec. 22, 1905.
80. Letter to his mother, June, 1857.
81. Letter to Curtis, Nov. 17, 1871.
82. "Harvard University in 1890," *Harper's New Monthly Magazine*, LXXXI (Sept., 1890), 590.
83. Letter to Godkin, Dec. 31, 1901.
84. Letter of Nov. 27, 1905.

Chapter VII. The Intellectual as Citizen

1. Lecture on "American Culture," Oct. 29, 1867, Norton Papers.
2. Quotations from an Albion, Michigan, news clipping (undated) and New York *Evening Post*, Oct. 14, 1863, Norton Papers.
3. "The Church and Religion," *NAR*, CVI (April, 1868), 396.
4. Letter of June 7, 1870.
5. April 9, 1874, *Letters of John Ruskin to Charles Eliot Norton*, II, 72.
6. Norton made two references to Thoreau in later years. He wrote to F. B. Sanborn (Oct. 4, 1883), asking for information on Thoreau's "first experiment in camping out," but gave no reason for making the request. In 1898, he declined a gift of Thoreau's works in a new edition: "I do not hanker for more of Thoreau . . . We have got from him about all he can give us" (Letter to DeWitt Miller, Nov. 11, 1898).
7. Quoted in *Letters*, II, 95n.
8. Letter to Harrison, June 7, 1882.
9. Letter of July 23, 1882.

10. Letter to Sara Norton, July 20, 1883.

11. Letter to Sara Norton, Aug. 11, 1883.

12. Letter to Simon, Aug. 13, 1883.

13. Letter to Edward Lee-Childe, Sept. 29, 1883.

14. *Ibid.*

15. March 5, 1885.

16. March 25, 1885.

17. Letters of June 23, 1885, and Jan. 29, 1890.

18. Letter of June 23, 1885.

19. L. E. Chittenden, *Personal Reminiscences* (New York, 1893), p. 165.

20. July 14, 1864.

21. May 26, 1866.

22. Letter to Ruskin, July 17, 1873.

23. Letter to Lowell, Sept. 20, 1875.

24. *Letters,* II, 87.

25. From a circular in the Norton Papers. The nature studies, which included the best record of the weather, the names of flowers and their date of bloom, the names of birds and date of their arrival and departure, etcetera, paralleled the studies of the poet Gray so closely that the similarity cannot be accidental. After Ruskin's death, Norton had received Ruskin's copy of Linnaeus which formerly had belonged to Gray and contained the latter's marginal comments. Norton wrote in 1903 regarding Gray's interest in nature: "He kept minute diaries, in which he entered daily notes on the weather, and recorded the opening of the flowers, the ripening of the harvest, . . . the coming and departure of the birds, together with many miscellaneous remarks on the objects and aspects of nature" (*The Poet Gray as a Naturalist,* Boston, 1903).

26. *Memories and Milestones,* pp. 134–135.

27. Aug. 13, 1895.

28. Letter to Kate Stephens, July 16, 1892, in her *Curious History of Book Editing* (New York, 1927), p. 45.

29. Letter to DeWitt Miller, July 6, 1894.

30. Aug. 29, 1877.

31. Woodberry to Norton, Oct. 2, 1877; Norton to Woodberry, Oct. 11, 1877. In spite of Norton's encouragement, Woodberry presently returned to the East. But Willa Cather would have known what Norton meant.

32. The Address is preserved in the Norton Papers.

33. "The Intellectual Life of America," *New Princeton Review,* VI (Nov., 1888), 322.

34. Thomas E. Tallmadge, *The Story of American Architecture* (New York, 1927), p. 207.

35. *Education,* pp. 339–340.

36. Oct. 13, 1893.
37. Oct. 30, 1893.
38. From an address, "Art in America," delivered at Springfield, 1898; Somerville, 1898; Providence, 1899; and Worcester, 1900. Manuscript in the Norton Papers.
39. *Education,* p. 343.
40. From "Art in America," manuscript in Norton Papers.
41. "The Architecture at Harvard," *Nation,* LI (Sept. 18, 1890), 226.
42. "American Culture," manuscript in Norton Papers.
43. "Address at the Celebration of the Two-Hundredth Anniversary of . . . the Old Meeting-House at Hingham," manuscript in Norton Papers.
44. "The Intellectual Life of America," p. 313.
45. *Ibid.,* pp. 313, 314, 316, 319, 320, 321, 324.
46. *Scribner's Magazine,* V (May, 1888), 638, 639–640. In 1866, Norton had warned Americans, in slightly milder tones, of their wastefulness and included a note on the spiritual suicide committed in destroying the old home of one's childhood: "For the mere material waste implied in this destruction and rebuilding is not all. We fling away the inheritance of memories and associations which dignify and exalt life, which connect it by visible monuments with the past and the future. Both the imagination and the affections suffer where there is nothing venerable for them to cling to, where there is no hope of permanence for their highest achievements. We make our lives barren by this waste" ("Waste," *Nation,* March, 1866, p. 302).
47. *Technology Architectural Review,* II (Aug. 3, 1889), 19.
48. *Forum,* XX (Feb., 1896), 643, 644, 647, 649.
49. Letter to Ward, Feb. 11, 1896.
50. Dec. 22, 1895.
51. Jan. 8, 1896.
52. March 20, 1896.
53. Letter to Grant-Duff, April 19, 1896.
54. Letter to Mrs. Hart Davis, April 21, 1896.
55. Letter to Ward, April 26, 1896.
56. Nov. 27, 1896.
57. June 14, 1897.
58. Letter to Ward, July 14, 1897.
59. These letters, together with various newspaper clippings from which I have taken the succeeding quotations, are in the Norton Papers. Explanatory comments accompanying the materials are signed by Norton's daughter Sara.
60. July 13, 1898, *Letters,* Appendix D, II, 458.
61. July 15, 1898.
62. July 18, 1898.

Chapter VIII. Retirement

1. Oct. 10, 1898.
2. Feb. 20, 1900.
3. Letter to J. B. Harrison, May 17, 1902.
4. Dec. 15, 1904.
5. "The Poetry of Rudyard Kipling," *At. Mo.*, LXXIX (Jan., 1897), 113.
6. "Reminiscences of Old Cambridge," *Cambridge Historical Society Publications*, I (Oct., 1905), 15.
7. Nov. 5, 1901.
8. Sept. 8, 1889.
9. Aug. 2, 1899.
10. Manuscript in Norton Papers.
11. Letters to Ward, Sept. 19, 1900, and Feb. 4, 1904.
12. Letter to Ward, April 14, 1901.
13. Letter to Ward, June 24, 1905.
14. Jan. 26, 1903.
15. Aug. 30, 1905.
16. "For Professor Norton's Eightieth Birthday," *The Harvard Graduates Magazine*, XVI (Dec., 1907), 222–229.
17. Dec. 12, 1907.
18. July 14, 1908.

Conclusion: Norton's Reputation in the Twentieth Century

1. "An American Art-Scholar: Charles Eliot Norton," *Notes on Novelists* (New York, 1914), p. 415.
2. *Memories and Milestones*, pp. 131, 132, 140, 142.
3. *Character & Opinion in the United States* (New York, 1920), pp. 140–142. But in *The Genteel Tradition at Bay* (New York, 1931), Santayana reinforced the older stereotype. He described Norton as the Harvard professor with an old mentality, shaking his head as he told his classes "with a slight sigh, that the Greeks did not play football" (pp. 3–4).
4. *American Renaissance* (London, 1941), p. 183.
5. James Russell Lowell," *Harper's* LXXXVI (May, 1893), 846.
6. "The Public Life and Services of William Eustis Russell," *Harvard Graduates Magazine*, V (Dec., 1896), 194.
7. Four of More's letters to Norton are extant in the Norton Papers: May 6, 1898; Dec. 21, 1906; May 2, 1907; and Aug. 9, 1907.
8. "Charles Eliot Norton," *Nation*, XCVII (Dec. 4, 1913), 532.
9. In *Irving Babbitt: Man and Teacher*, ed. by Frederick Manchester and Odell Shepard (New York, 1941), p. 48.
10. Nov. 19, 1907.

11. Boston, 1908, p. viii.

12. *The Use of Poetry and the Use of Criticism* (London, 1933), pp. 13–14.

13. In *The Centenary of the Birth of Ralph Waldo Emerson* (Concord, 1903), pp. 55, 57–58.

14. *Ibid.,* p. 58.

INDEX

228; friendship with N., 89, 173; on *North American Review*, 101, 120–121; N. and his career, 150–158, 163; compared to Fuller, 160; on Twain's speech, 163–164; N. on, 180; on N., 223

Hugo, Victor, 35–36, 107

Humanism, function in America, 146; German influence, 182; N.'s influence on modern, 184, 228, 231, 232; T. S. Eliot on N.'s, 230. *See also* Art

Humanitarianism, development of N.'s, 33–35, 37, 60, 65, 89, 186; N.'s concern for labor, 37–46; seen as profitable, 42, 43; and slavery, 77; of N. in old age, 221–222

Hunt, Leigh, 178

Hunt, Richard Morris, 135, 202, 204

Hymns, N. edited, 47

Idealism, and Unitarians, 15; German, 17; in American literature, 153, 161; and life in America, 192

Imagination, N. defines, 127

Immigrants, N. distrusted, 42–43, 122, 194, 219, 233; Godkin on, 109; at Harvard, 139; in fiction, 155; assimilation, 207

India, 50, 65; N.'s visit, *1849*, 33–35; effects of visit, 37, 39, 48, 60

Industrialism, and art, 127–128; and natural resources, 189, 190, 194; in Italy, 191; effect on villages, 195, 197, 199; N.'s failure to comprehend, 233

Irving, Washington, 29

Italy, N. on Renaissance, 61–62, 71–72, 78, 187; on opera, 70; compared to U.S. South, 76; as art leader, 129–132; compared to Germany, 181; commercialization of, 191; N. visits, *1850*, 35, 37; *1855*, 53–58; *1856*, 60–61, 63; *1869–70*, 107–111, 126; *1883*, 191

Jackson, Andrew, 7, 115

James, Henry, 89, 101, 105, 113, 155, 177; N. on, 153, 180; essay on N., 225–226

James, William, 123, 196

Jarves, James Jackson, 53, 154, 155

Jefferson, Thomas, 39, 199

Jenckes Bill, 107

Johnson, Andrew, 95

Jones, John Ernest, 60

Jonson, Ben, 175

Journalism, N.'s contribution, 68; N. on, 86. *See also* Newspapers; specific periodicals

Kant, Immanuel, 2, 17

Kazin, Alfred, 228

Keats, John, 178

Kenyon, John, 36, 37, 63

King, Mackenzie, 221

Kipling, Rudyard, 178, 179–180, 219

Kirk, Russell, 231

Kirkup, Seymour, 144

Kittredge, George Lyman, 123, 183

Know-Nothing Party, 42–43, 56, 65

Kossuth, Lajos, 44

Laborers, N.'s sympathy with, 51, 93; English, 60, 104–106; N.'s program for, 39–46; N. on strikes, 198, 233

Lamartine, Alphonse de, 32, 35–36

Landor, Walter Savage, 178

Lane, George Martin, 26

Lea, H. C., 89

Leadership, by elite, 1–3, 44–46, 208; in South, 48, 76; N. on American, 95, 229

Lectures, at Lowell Institute, 83; N.'s at Harvard, 125–126, 133–134, 136–137; N. on archeology, 148–149; N. on industry, 198; N. on the future, 204

Lee, Robert E., 35

Lee-Childe, Mrs., 35

Leroux, Pierre, 44

Lewes, G. H., 103

Libraries, N. aids, 143–145, 197; Harvard, 144, 145–146, 174

Lincoln, Abraham, 3, 84, 94, 115, 211, 229, 233; N. on, 92–93, 95, 100, 192

Literary Miscellany, 15

Literature, under conditions of democracy, 2–3; Unitarians and, 18–19; N. on authors, 75, 165–167, 169,

MAY 2 5 2000 DATE DUE